WITHDRAWN

D0882678

HARVARD SEMITIC MUSEUM
HARVARD SEMITIC MONOGRAPHS

edited by

Frank Moore Cross, Jr.

Number 16

THE APOCALYPTIC VISION
OF THE BOOK OF DANIEL

by

John J. Collins

SCHOLARS PRESS
Missoula, Montana

THE APOCALYPTIC VISION
OF THE BOOK OF DANIEL

THE APOCALYPTIC VISION OF THE BOOK OF DANIEL

by

John J. Collins

Published by
SCHOLARS PRESS
for
Harvard Semitic Museum

Distributed By

SCHOLARS PRESS
University of Montana
Missoula, Montana 59812

THE APOCALYPTIC VISION
OF THE BOOK OF DANIEL

by
John J. Collins

Copyright © 1977

by

The President and Fellows of Harvard College

Library of Congress Cataloging in Publication Data
Collins, John Joseph, 1946-
   The apocalyptic vision of the book of Daniel.

   (Harvard semitic monographs ; no. 16)
   Includes bibliographical references.
   1. Bible. O. T. Daniel—Criticism, interpretation,
etc. I. Harvard University. Semitic Museum.
II. Title. III. Series.
BS1555.2.C64   224'.5'06   77-23124
ISBN 0-89130-133-X

Printed in the United States of America
1   2   3   4   5

Edwards Brothers, Inc.
Ann Arbor, Michigan 48104

To Dermot Ryan, Archbishop of Dublin,

who introduced me to the Hebrew Scriptures.

TABLE OF CONTENTS

ABBREVIATIONS

AB	Anchor Bible
AGSU	Arbeiten zur Geschichte des Spätjudentums und Urchristentums
AHR	*American Historical Review*
ANEP	J. B. Pritchard (ed.), *Ancient Near East in Pictures*
ANET	J. B. Pritchard (ed.), *Ancient Near Eastern Texts*
APOT	R. H. Charles (ed.), *Apocrypha and Pseudepigrapha of the Old Testament*
BASOR	*Bulletin of the American Schools of Oriental Research*
BHT	Beiträge zur historischen Theologie
Bib	*Biblica*
BJRL	*Bulletin of the John Rylands Library*
BKAT	Biblischer Kommentar: Altes Testament
BR	*Biblical Research*
BZAW	Beihefte zur *Zeitschrift für die alttestamentliche Wissenschaft*
CAT	Commentaire de l'Ancien Testament
CBQ	*Catholic Biblical Quarterly*
CTCA	A. Herdner (ed.), *Corpus des tablettes en cunéiformes alphabétiques*
DJD	Discoveries in the Judaean Desert
ETL	*Ephemerides theologicae lovanienses*
HAT	Handbuch zum Alten Testament
HDR	Harvard Dissertation Series in Religion
HR	*History of Religions*
HSM	Harvard Semitic Monographs
HTR	*Harvard Theological Review*
HTS	Harvard Theological Studies
ICC	International Critical Commentary
ITQ	*Irish Theological Quarterly*
JAOS	*Journal of the American Oriental Society*
JBL	*Journal of Biblical Literature*
JCS	*Journal of Cuneiform Studies*
JJS	*Journal of Jewish Studies*
JQR	*Jewish Quarterly Review*

JSJ	*Journal for the Study of Judaism*
JSS	*Journal of Semitic Studies*
JTC	*Journal for Theology and the Church*
JTS	*Journal of Theological Studies*
KAT	E. Sellin (ed.), Kommentar zum A. T.
LCL	Loeb Classical Library
NorTT	*Norsk Teologisk Tidsskrift*
NovT	*Novum Testamentum*
NovTSup	Novum Testamentum, Supplements
NTS	*New Testament Studies*
OTS	*Oudtestamentische Studiën*
PCB	M. Black and H. H. Rowley (eds.), *Peake's Commentary on the Bible*
PW	Pauly-Wissowa, *Real-Encyclopädie der classischen Altertumswissenschaft*
RB	*Revue biblique*
REG	*Revue des études Grecques*
RHR	*Revue de l'histoire des religions*
RevQ	*Revue de Qumrân*
RSV	*Revised Standard Version*
RTL	*Revue théologique de Louvain*
SB	Sources bibliques
SBL	Society of Biblical Literature
SBLDS	SBL Dissertation Series
SBM	Stuttgarter biblische Monographien
SBT	Studies in Biblical Theology
ST	*Studia theologica*
SUNT	Studien zur Umwelt des Neuen Testaments
TDNT	G. Kittel and G. Friedrich (eds.), *Theological Dictionary of the New Testament*
TLZ	*Theologische Literaturzeitung*
TRu	*Theologische Rundschau*
UF	*Ugaritische Forschungen*
VD	*Verbum domini*
VT	*Vetus Testamentum*
VTSup	Vetus Testamentum, Supplements
WMANT	Wissenschaftliche Monographien zum Alten und Neuen Testament

WUNT	Wissenschaftliche Untersuchungen zum Neuen Testament
ZAW	*Zeitschrift für die alttestamentliche Wissenschaft*
ZST	*Zeitschrift für systematische Theologie*

BREAKING THE SEAL

> But you, Daniel, shut up the words, and
> seal the book, until the time of the end.
> Many shall run to and fro and knowledge
> shall increase.
>
> Dan 12:4

This enigmatic sentence from the last chapter of Daniel is
peculiarly apt for the status of the book in modern scholarship. On the one hand there has been no lack of scholarly
interest in Daniel and the list of books and articles devoted
to it is vast. On the other hand, the nature of the book and
the type of literature to which it belongs have remained sealed
for many. Daniel is, with the Apocalypse of John, one of the
two universally accepted specimens of apocalyptic in the biblical canon, and consequently one of the two most extensively
studied apocalypses. Therefore the accusation of Klaus Koch
falls heavily on Danielic scholarship:

> even the critical historical methods which have been
> familiar for decades are only inadequately applied
> to this field. Instead, particular stereotypes and
> prejudices are carried over from decade to decade.
> ...In spite of remarkable individual achievements,
> scholars are still far from an adequate overall
> historical grasp of their subject.
>
> *The Rediscovery of Apocalyptic*
> (SBT 2/22; Naperville: Allenson,
> 1972) 11-12

In reviewing the scholarly literature on Daniel, perhaps
the most surprising observation is that very few scholars have
even attempted an "overall grasp" of their subject. Most have
been content to illuminate particular problems. Specifically,
two types of problem dominate the literature. First, there are
the standard "introductory" problems--the unity of the book,
its original language, the place and time of composition.
These questions are of fundamental importance, and can never be
ignored, but they stop well short of an overall grasp of the
message of the book. H. L. Ginsberg's *Studies in Daniel* remains a provocative and interesting work, but we can appreciate

it properly only when we realize that Ginsberg did not even
begin to look for the meaning or message of the book. His
studies, like so many others, dealt with preliminary matters,
the foundations on which an understanding of the book could be
built. Ginsberg, however, never completed the edifice, and
too many subsequent scholars and students have been content to
take the foundations for a finished structure.

The second major area of research in Daniel has been the
origins of its imagery. In particular, a disproportionate
amount of all studies on Daniel have been devoted to the figure
of the "Son of Man." Here again much important work has been
done to further our understanding of this imagery. Unfortunately, it has seldom been pursued to the point of illumi-
nating Daniel as a whole. Most often, this type of research
has been inspired by interest in the ancient myths and their
survival, or in the 'backgrounds' of the New Testament. Few
scholars have shown interest in the way in which this imagery
contributes to the meaning of Daniel.

The question of the origin of the imagery in Daniel is
part of a broader inquiry into the origins of apocalyptic.
There is a vast literature on the latter topic, and little
consensus. Important light has been cast on the meaning of
particular motifs, but too often scholars have confused the
question of meaning with the question of origins. Consequently, we are given the impression that apocalyptic is a form of
Iranian dualism or a revival of Canaanite or Mesopotamian myth.
Neither, of course, is the case. Whatever apocalyptic may have
derived from Iranian or Canaanite mythology is incorporated in
a new phenomenon which is quite different from any of its
sources. We should beware of thinking of apocalyptic as a
monolithic unit, which derived all its imagery from one source.
Even an individual book such as Daniel can use motifs from many
different sources to present its message. While we can often
speak of one predominant source, and say that a book stands in
a particular tradition, we must still beware of the genetic
fallacy. We will argue that Daniel draws most heavily on traditions which ultimately derive from Canaanite sources, but the

book is in no sense a Canaanite myth. The meaning of a book is
ultimately decided not by the sources of the traditions it
uses, but by the manner in which these traditions are structured and combined within the book.

The object of this study is to examine the meaning of the
book of Daniel as found in the Hebrew bible. As such, it is a
literary rather than a historical study. We are concerned with
the classical questions of the historical-critical method--when,
where and why,--but only as a means to an end. These questions
are only of interest insofar as they help us grasp the overall
message of Daniel, its world-view, its vision of life and
reality. This study is directed to elucidating *what* the book
is saying, rather than the historical question of its provenance.

This objective is not conceived as an alternative to the
goals of historical critical scholarship. Rather it is intended to complement them. The validity and value of the
classical introductory questions, and of the religio-historical
tracing of motifs, is not disputed. We will draw on such
studies throughout. We merely wish to carry the inquiry a
stage further, to examine the overall message of the book.
This we will do by considering the manner in which the various
parts of the book are interrelated, and by contrasting Daniel's
solution of the problems it discusses with other possible solutions.

Historical questions will play a significant role throughout the inquiry. The fact is that we cannot hope to read and
understand Daniel as we might a modern novel. Daniel was written long ago in a language (rather languages!) we no longer
speak, and in an environment very different from ours. The
more remote the world-view of a literary work is from our own,
the more important the role of historical questions in literary
criticism. Just as the meanings of the Hebrew and Aramaic
words, and the associations they carry with them, must be
learnt, so must the traditional symbolism and the historical
allusions, which are equally part of the language of the book.

We will begin, then, with the first and most basic question, the classical question of the unity of the book. We do not read an anthology or a book of short stories with the same expectation of coherence as we read a novel. It is universally recognized that some books in the bible, such as Isaiah, are collections of different works, where we cannot expect consistency of viewpoint throughout. We cannot simply assume that Daniel is a coherent unit. Further, traditional material can be used by an author for reasons quite unrelated to its original meaning. We can quote another author at length even if we disagree with him. We can also quote a passage because it makes a point we endorse, even though we do not agree with the main point of the passage. Similarly, it is possible that traditional material be included in a book like Daniel because of a partial or incidental relevance to the rest of the book. By redaction criticism we can detect passages which are not fully integrated into their new context, but which are nevertheless included for a purpose. The original purpose for which these passages were composed, or the meaning of these passages taken in isolation, may be quite insignificant for their secondary use. Much more important are the purpose for which they were incorporated and the particular points at which they are relevant to the rest of the book. In the first chapter we will argue that Daniel 1-6 consists of traditional material which is only partially relevant for the rest of the book. The second chapter will examine the points at which it is relevant, and therefore most significant for the meaning of the whole.

The second basic question which determines our approach to the book is the question of literary form. Our expectations and our perception are obviously determined by the form in which a message is presented. The court-tales of Daniel 1-6 include several incidents where Daniel interprets mysterious signs. The interpretation of mysterious signs, in the form of visions and scriptures, then becomes the mould in which the second half of the book is cast. In the third chapter we will consider the significance of that mould, and the way in which it influences the perception of reality.

In the fourth and fifth chapters we will discuss the imagery and symbolism of the visions. The connotations and associations of much of this imagery are not immediately accessible to us in the way that some universal symbolism, such as light and darkness, might be. Rather, it is traditional imagery which must be understood in the light of its literary and historical associations. Even natural symbolism, such as light and darkness, is enriched by its traditional use, and we lose some of its significance if we neglect the traditional dimension. Of course a symbol cannot be understood purely from its historical origin any more than a word can be understood from its etymology. In both cases the meaning is ultimately decided by the way it is used in a context. However, just as the meaning of a word is determined, within a certain range, by its traditional use, so also the meaning of a symbol or image is largely (though not completely) determined by tradition.

The most obvious characteristic which the visions of Daniel 7-12 share is their interest in historical events and expectation of a decisive event in the future. Accordingly, history and eschatology provide a framework which enables us to assess the interrelation of the various parts of Daniel. In the sixth chapter we will use this framework to examine the overall message of the book. The range of modern interpretations of the idea of history in apocalyptic provides a convenient foil to highlight the distinctive character of Daniel over against other possible ways in which history and eschatology could be viewed.

Finally in the last chapter we consider the function of the visions and their relation to their historical context. We are fortunately well informed about the historical setting in which Daniel was written. However, we can establish the relation of Daniel to other viewpoints and ideologies of the period only after we have analyzed its internal coherence and message. The historical and social setting is a highly important final stage in the inquiry as it enables us to see the function of this type of literature and the effect it is designed to achieve.

The goal of this study is to appreciate the particular perspective on life expressed in the book of Daniel. It must, of course, be clear that the most adequate formulation of that perspective is the book of Daniel itself. The task of the critic or exegete is not to improve the formulation found in the text, but to explain it by clarifying its motifs and the relationships between its various parts. An exegetical study is a companion piece or guide. In no sense can it replace the text, by distilling from it a philosophical or theological meaning. The impact of the book of Daniel remains intimately bound up with the rich symbols and patterns with which it is formulated. Our task, then, is to appreciate the language of Daniel and discover through it a vision of life and reality which can be compared with, though not reduced to, any other vision, whether philosophical, theological or poetic, which seeks to apprehend ultimate truths.

This manuscript was essentially completed in August, 1975. In the interval between completion and publication a number of studies on Daniel have appeared, but no significant new issues have been raised or new approaches advocated. The essay of A. A. di Lella, "The One in Human Likeness and the Holy Ones of the Most High in Daniel 7," (*CBQ* 39 [1977] 1-19), which is presumably representative of his forthcoming Anchor Bible Commentary, follows the all too familiar tendency of Anglo-Saxon scholarship to ignore the mythic and symbolic dimensions of apocalyptic language. So he argues that if the "holy ones of the Most High" were angelic beings, "Dan 7 would then have virtually no meaning or relevance for the addressees of the book" (p. 7). Now, irrespective of how one interprets the "holy ones of the Most High," angelic beings play a very prominent part throughout the book of Daniel. If, as di Lella argues, angelic beings could have little or no relevance in ch. 7, then we would have to conclude that the battle between Michael and Gabriel and the angelic "princes" of Greece and Persia in ch. 10 could have "virtually no meaning or relevance" for a human audience. In fact, on this approach, the greater part of apocalyptic literature which is dominanted by heavenly beings is meaningless. (Think, for examine, of the Qumran War

Scroll!) However, there is no doubt that this literature was meaningful for its authors and original audience. The modern commentator who finds it meaningless has simply failed to understand. In a similar vein, di Lella insists that the symbols of Daniel should be interpreted as "unireferential" and that to interpret them as ambiguous or multireferential implies "a deplorable use of symbolism" (p. 8). However, as Paul Ricoeur, among many others, has argued, it is of the essence of a symbol that it have more than one level reference. It is extremely doubtful whether a symbol can ever be simply unireferential, at least in literature or in religious language. Even the beasts from the sea in ch. 7, which are explicitly identified as kingdoms in the text, obviously contain a wealth of meaning over and above this identification. They give expression to primordial mythological powers of chaos and evil (see below, Chapter IV). This depth of allusion is lost if we say that they "symbolize only the four pagan empires." Rather we should heed the warning issued by Ricoeur (in his preface to the commentary on Daniel by André Lacocque, p. 9) against any rigidly univocal interpretation of apocalyptic symbols. The very fact that Daniel uses figurative language which admits of various interpretations should alert us that a "marge de jeu" is essential to its nature and that Ricoeur's advice "de laisser jouer plusieurs identifications concurrentes" is the better part of exegetical wisdom.

The commentaries of André Lacocque (CAT 15b) and Raymond Hammer (The Cambridge Bible Commentary) both of which appeared in 1976 provide more satisfactory lines of approach to the understanding of Daniel. Both the detailed exegesis of Lacocque and the more popular work of Hammer show a good grasp of what Hammer calls the "atmosphere" of the book. It is neither possible nor necessary here to debate the numerous points at which my interpretation differs from both these commentaries. It is sufficient to point out certain basic assumptions which we share. First, any interpretation must reckon both with the presence of traditional material and the coherence of the book in its present form. Second, the symbolic and mythological

character of the visions must be recognized, especially the
importance of the angelic world for human destiny. (Lacocque
fully appreciates the transcendent dimension represented by the
angelic world, despite the fact that he speaks, paradoxically,
of the author's use of such language as the "procédé de dé-
mythologisation de l'Auteur" [p. 121]). Third, the visions
serve the purpose of exhortation in a concrete historical situation. This monograph affirms the work of Lacocque and Hammer
at these basic points, although it differs significantly from
them in the details of interpretation.

My thanks are due to several people who read this manu-
script and contributed helpful suggestions. I am indebted to
Adela Yarbro Collins both for her detailed comments on this
volume and for the inspiration of her own ideas, developed in
The Combat Myth in the Book of Revelation (HDR 9; Missoula,
Scholars Press, 1976). Harold W. Attridge also read the entire
manuscript and helped to improve it in innumerable ways.
Others who read all or part of the book and made valuable sug-
gestions are John Strugnell, James Barr, Michael Stone, Bernard
McGinn and John Dominic Crossan. Finally my thanks are due to
Professor Frank Moore Cross for accepting this volume for the
Harvard Semitic Monographs.

CHAPTER I

COMPOSITION AND EDITORIAL DEVICES

The figure of Daniel appears on the biblical scene in the book that bears his name without father, mother or genealogy--like Melchizedek in the Epistle to the Hebrews. While other apocalyptic writings are attributed to prominent figures in the biblical tradition--Moses, Enoch, Elijah, Ezra--there is no certain reference to this Daniel elsewhere in the Hebrew bible. Further, the account given of the hero in the book of Daniel itself does not inspire much confidence in his historicity. He is introduced as a young man who was among the prisoners taken from Jerusalem by Nebuchadnezzar and remained active until the time of Cyrus the Persian, nearly seventy years later. The wonderful exploits of this Jewish youth and his companions, including their miraculous deliverance from the fiery furnace and the lions' den, are recounted against a framework that bristles with historical difficulties at every point.[1] We are clearly dealing with legendary tales, covered only with a light veneer of history. This material may indeed contain historical reminiscences, but the tales of Daniel are far from being historical reports. While we cannot exclude the possibility that there may have been a Jewish youth named Daniel during the exile, whose career gave rise to certain stories, no critical scholar could entertain much hope for the success of a quest for the historical Daniel.

The Figure of Daniel

While there are no clear references to Daniel in the other biblical books, there are a few possible allusions. Scholars who wish to secure for Daniel a foothold in history, however tenuous, relate him to the priest Daniel, of the sons of Ithamar, who is mentioned in Ezra 8:2 as one of those who went up from Babylonia to Jerusalem in the reign of Artaxerxes the king, or the Daniel who is mentioned in Neh 10:6 (possibly the same person).[2] It is further noted that the names of Daniel's companions, Azariah, Hananiah and Mishael, are also attested in

the book of Nehemiah. Neh 8:7 mentions a Levite named Azariah
and the name is also listed in Neh 10:2. One of the people who
stood with Ezra for the reading of the law in Neh 8:4 was named
Mishael. The name Hananiah is listed in Neh 10:23. These references prove that the names of Daniel and his companions were
names which were used by the Jews in the fifth century, but
nothing more. Nothing is said of these individuals which might
suggest affinity with the heroes of the book of Daniel, and in
any case the court-tales claim to be set in the exile, a century before the time of Nehemiah.

The other possible allusions to Daniel in the bible are
more promising. These are two references in Ezekiel.[3] In Ezek
14:14 we read that not even Noah, Daniel and Job could save a
city by their righteousness. Ezek 28:3 tauntingly asks the
king of Tyre "are you wiser than Daniel?"[4] Three things may be
noted about the Daniel of Ezekiel. He was a legendary gentile,
like Noah and Job, he was a righteous man and he was famous for
his wisdom. Daniel, the apocalyptic visionary, shares the latter two characteristics. The two figures are not identical,
but, unlike the references in Nehemiah, there is some reason to
associate them.

The references in Ezekiel are important for the book of
Daniel because they show that at the time of the exile the name
Daniel was associated with a legendary wise and righteous man.
Further attestation of this legendary figure can be found in
the Aqhat legend from Ugarit,[5] and, at the other end of the
biblical period, in the book of Jubilees. At Ugarit, Daniel
(or *Dnil*) is, among other things, a judge who defends the widow
and the fatherless. The function of judge is, of course, suggested by the name Daniel ("my judge is God," or possibly,
"judge of God")[6] and appears again in the story of Susanna,
where the wisdom of his judgment is emphasized. In Jub 4:20 we
are told that Enoch married "Edni, the daughter of Dânêl, the
daughter of his father's brother." We are given no further
information about this Dânêl, but it is fascinating that a name
so closely similar to Daniel, and possibly identical with it,
is associated with Enoch, the legendary wise man, who also gave
his name to an apocalyptic tradition. It is surely probable

that the righteous judge of Ugarit, the righteous wise man of
Ezekiel, and the pre-diluvian Dânêl of Jubilees are related.
Unfortunately, the evidence is too scant to permit any clear
view of their relationship or of the tradition history of this
legendary figure.[7] What is important for our purpose is the
fact that the name Daniel was associated with a legendary wise
man. The hero of the book of Daniel must have inherited some
of the associations of this figure. At least the authority and
prestige of the name Daniel was increased by the tradition that
he was a man of the same status as Noah and Job. Only in view
of the reputation of Daniel as a legendary wise man can we understand why a cycle of tales and visions should be attached to
the name of Daniel in the post-exilic period.

The Danielic Corpus

The literature attached to the name of Daniel is considerably more extensive than what we find in the Hebrew bible.
Some of this material has long been known, as it is included in
the Septuagint as part of the book of Daniel.[8]

The "Prayer of Azariah" and the "Song of the Three Young
Men" are inserted in Daniel 3 in the Greek translations. These
appear to be traditional prayers which have no intrinsic relation either to the figure of Daniel or to the context in which
they are inserted. They attest a tendency of Jewish scribes to
add hymns and prayers to religious stories, to make them more
edifying. The prayers which are added to the book of Esther in
the Greek translation provide a parallel example.

The other additions in the Septuagint are more specifically
Danielic. The story of Susanna is found after Daniel 12 in the
Septuagint, before Daniel 1 in the translation of "Theodotion."
It is often printed as Daniel 13. The story tells how the wise
intervention of Daniel saved the innocent Susanna from her de-
tractors. It has little in common with the tales of Daniel 1-6.
It is an independent story which illustrates the legendary wis-
dom of Daniel and the skill in judgment suggested by his name.

The stories of Bel and the Dragon show more similarity to
the tales of Daniel 1-6. They appear after Susanna in the

Septuagint, and after Daniel 12 in the translation of "Theodotion." Daniel acts more aggressively against the idolatrous
worship of Bel and the Dragon than he does against the idols in
Daniel 1-6. He is again thrown into the lions' den and miraculously preserved. The author of Bel and the Dragon obviously
knew the legend of Daniel in the lions' den, but it is unlikely
that he derived it from Daniel 6, as he gives quite a different
account of it. There is no clear evidence to indicate whether
Susanna or Bel and the Dragon should be dated before or after
the tales in Daniel 1-6.

The literature associated with the name of Daniel has now
been increased by two compositions found at Qumran. These are
the Prayer of Nabonidus and the apocalypse of Pseudo-Daniel.[9]
The Prayer of Nabonidus (4QPrNab) is strikingly similar to
Daniel 4. Nabonidus, king of Babylon and Assyria, recounts how
he was stricken with illness in the city of Teima. One of the
Jewish exiles "gave an interpretation" (presumably of the cause
of illness) and instructed that the king give praise to the
Most High God and reject idolatry. Another small fragment
tells how the narrator had a dream, but the contents and the
outcome are not preserved. The name of the interpreter is also
lost.

The relevance of this text for the book of Daniel is obvious. Scholars have long known that the sojourn of Nebuchadnezzar in the wilderness is a fiction prompted by the mysterious but historical sojourn of Nabonidus at Teima.[10] The biblical story substitutes the familiar, notorious, Nebuchadnezzar
for his lesser known successor. The Qumran fragments show that
there was another form of the story which preserved the names
of Nabonidus and Teima. Since the interpreter in the Qumran
document is Jewish, and he vigorously attacks idolatry, this
form of the story is evidently Jewish too.

The precise relationship between 4QPrNab and Daniel 4 is
difficult to establish. The prayer is almost certainly the
older of the two. Daniel 4 draws on the basic story but does
so very freely. The differences between the two tales are too
extensive to allow for direct literary influence. Rather, we
have two variants of a tradition based on the sojourn of

Nabonidus in Teima. 4QPrNab retains more accurate historical
reminiscences, but there is no evidence that either tale depends on the other.

The second "Danielic" writing from Qumran is the apocalypse of Pseudo-Daniel (4QpsDan). This consists of fragments
of three Aramaic manuscripts, two of which are copies of the
same work. It is not certain that the third manuscript belongs
to the same composition, but it can plausibly be integrated
with the other fragments. These fragments present a summary of
world history which Daniel recites "before the ministers of the
king." Milik argues that history after the Babylonian exile is
divided into four kingdoms.[11] The evidence for this, however,
consists of a fragmentary reference to "the first kingdom" in
vs. 20. There is no reference to any further numbered kingdom.
In view of the highly fragmentary nature of the text, Milik's
suggestion is possible, but only hypothetical. Finally, if we
accept the third manuscript as part of the same work, the
apocalypse contains a statement that certain people will "rise
up" (*yqwmwn*) in the eschatological period. This should probably be interpreted as a reference to resurrection.

In view of the fragmentary nature of 4QpsDan, little can
be said of it with any confidence. Milik has suggested a date
about 100 B.C. on the basis of a possible reference to Alexander Balas, but this is far from certain. The Qumran document
shares a number of basic points with the canonical book.
Daniel speaks in a royal court, he prophesies the course of
history and (probably) his review of history concludes with a
reference to resurrection. Apart from these points there is
considerable divergence in detail. The review of history in
4QpsDan begins with the flood, and so is much more extensive
than anything found in Daniel. The prediction of resurrection
is not given in a courtly context in Daniel 12, but we do find
a review of history in Daniel 2 which is given in the presence
of the king.

There is little likelihood that Daniel depends on 4QpsDan.
The court-setting is elaborated in the canonical book, but
merely referred to in the Qumran work, which presupposes a more
complete account of the setting. The exclusion of pre-exilic

history also suggests that Daniel was not modelled on 4QpsDan.
If Milik's dating is correct, this possibility would in any
case be excluded. It is quite possible that Daniel served as a
source for the Qumran work, suggesting the court-setting, review of history (especially if the four kingdom schema is found
in both) and resurrection. On this hypothesis, 4QpsDan would
have used its source with considerable freedom and produced a
largely independent review of history. We must, however, also
reckon with the possibility that the two works are independent
of each other. 4QpsDan may be based on a tradition of a courtier named Daniel who prophesied the course of history. Such a
tradition would be similar to Daniel 2, though not necessarily
identical with it. The reference to resurrection could be
added independently as part of the eschatological tableau.

    In all, then, we have a corpus of four works--Susanna, Bel
and the Dragon, 4QPrNab and 4QpsDan--which are closely related
to the book of Daniel, and also two passages, the Prayer of
Azariah and the Song of the Three Young Men, which were inserted into the book though not intrinsically related to it.
What, if any, is the significance of this material for a study
of the book of Daniel?

    The significance of the additions in Daniel 3 is clear
enough. If prayers and hymns could be added to the book after
it had taken the form now found in the Hebrew bible, then we
must ask whether any similar insertions are found already in
the Masoretic text. We will pursue this question later especially with reference to the prayer in Daniel 9.

    The significance of the other material is more complex.
The tales, especially 4QPrNab and Bel and the Dragon, contain
important parallels to Daniel 1-6, but there is no evidence of
direct literary influence between any of these works. Since
tales such as 4QPrNab and Bel and the Dragon seem to have circulated independently, we must allow for the possibility that
some of the tales in Daniel 1-6 were also originally independent. Therefore we may expect to find traditional material in
Daniel 1-6 which was not originally composed for its present
context.

In view of its fragmentary nature, the significance of 4QpsDan is limited. It may show merely that, after the composition of the canonical book, Daniel was recognized as an apocalyptic visionary, to whom further visions could be ascribed. There is in fact a long tradition of later Danielic apocalypses which continues down to the Middle Ages.[13] At most 4QpsDan would show that the name of Daniel was used in apocalyptic writings independently of the canonical book, but the evidence is too ambiguous to permit any inferences from this possibility.

The Unity of the Book of Daniel

The main conclusion drawn from our review of the Danielic writings is that we must reckon with the possibility that the book of Daniel is in some part a collection of traditional writings. In fact there are already ample indications within the book itself that it was not simply composed out of whole cloth as a literary unit.

Two factors in particular complicate the question of the unity of Daniel. First, two languages are used in the book: Hebrew in 1:1-2:4 and chs. 8-12, Aramaic in 2:4-7:28. Second, Daniel 1-6 consists of tales about Daniel and his associates which are told in the third person, while Daniel 7-12 recounts the visions of Daniel in the first person. The central introductory problem of the book of Daniel is that the natural division between the tales and the visions does not coincide with the division between the two languages.

Despite the fact that several fragments of the book of Daniel have been found at Qumran no new light has been shed on this central problem.[14] Apart from a few rare variants which support the Septuagint reading, these fragments closely support the Masoretic text. The transition from Hebrew to Aramaic in Dan 2:4 is preserved in 1QDan[a]. The transition from Aramaic to Hebrew in Dan 7:28-8:1 is preserved in both 4QDan[a] and 4QDan[b]. Other fragments from Cave 1 preserve Dan 3:22-28 and 3:27-30, but contain no trace of the Septuagint addition in that chapter. The dates of these fragments vary. One is said to be closer to

the autograph than any other biblical manuscript we have, but
unfortunately it does not touch on any crucial point.[15]   The
problem of the unity of Daniel is left at the mercy of scholarly ingenuity.

Not surprisingly, scholarly ingenuity has "resolved" the
problem with a bewildering variety of contradictory solutions.[16]
However, general agreement has been reached on one important
point, which may serve as the starting point for our inquiry.
The visions of Daniel 7-12 were composed between the return of
Antiochus IV Epiphanes from his second campaign against Egypt
in 167 B.C. and his death late in 164.[17]   These limits are derived from Daniel 11.   In Dan 11:29-39, Antiochus' second campaign is described with such precision that it is clearly a
vaticinium *ex eventu*, but the prophecy of the king's death
(beginning in 11:40) is no longer in accord with historical
fact.   It is, of course, possible that different parts of Daniel 7-12 were written at slightly different times.   At least
there were occasional adjustments of the length of time the
persecution was to last--in Dan 8:14 we find 1,150 days; in Dan
12:11, 1,290 days; in Dan 12:12, 1,335 days.   At least the figure in Dan 12:12 must have been added slightly later than that
in Dan 12:11.   However, it is quite clear that all of Daniel
7-12 is set in the persecution of Antiochus IV Epiphanes
(therefore no earlier than 169 B.C.) and at least Daniel 8-12
was written after the profanation of the temple (167).[18]   The
only possible exception is the prayer in Daniel 9 which we will
discuss below.

The dating of Daniel 7-12 to the time of Antiochus Epiphanes is of basic importance for the analysis of the composition of the book, since the tales in Daniel 1-6 do not reflect
the same historical situation and must have originally been
independent of the later chapters.

The Tales in Daniel 1-6 Are Not From Maccabean Times

There is wide, though not universal, agreement that the
tales in Daniel 1-6 did not originate in the time of Antiochus
IV Epiphanes.   This position rests mainly on the argument that

chs. 1-6 contain no clear reference to Antiochus Epiphanes or his times. Two other considerations support the view that chs. 1-6 form a distinct, older, body of material. One is formal: these chapters consist of tales about Daniel and his companions, told in the third person, while the visions in chs. 7-12 are narrated by Daniel in the first person. This formal difference is not in itself incompatible with a unified composition, but it reinforces the transition in the subject matter. Second, the events related in chs. 7-12 either take place in or vitally concern Palestine. The tales in chs. 1-6 are set in the Diaspora. There is no obvious reference to events in the land of Judah. Again, this argument is not decisive in itself. The question of the unity of the book ultimately depends on whether the tales in chs. 1-6 reflect the persecution of Antiochus Epiphanes.

The most eloquent dissenter from the majority opinion is the prolific British scholar, H. H. Rowley.[19] Rowley concedes that the tales contain traditional material "probably taken from various sources oral and written," but insists that the tales as they now stand are documents of the persecution of Antiochus.

Rowley asserts that "point can be found for every story of the first half of the book in the setting of the Maccabean age."[20] For instance, the statue erected by Nebuchadnezzar in ch. 3 may correspond to the "abomination of desolation" set up in the temple by Antiochus. Again, ch. 4 tells how Nebuchadnezzar is punished with madness. Polybius tells us that Antiochus was sometimes called Epimanes (mad) instead of Epiphanes (manifest god).[21] In ch. 5, the king (Belshazzar) profanes the temple vessels. Antiochus is said to have removed the vessels from the temple with his own hands.[22]

Rowley has well demonstrated how someone who read these tales in the time of Antiochus could apply them to his own situation. This, however, does not prove that the tales were written with that situation in mind. In fact, if we consider the tales as wholes and do not simply isolate scattered elements from them, we find that they are quite inappropriate for the Maccabean period. The treatment of the kings in Daniel 2-6

contrasts sharply with what we find in the visions of chs. 7-
12. In Daniel 2, Nebuchadnezzar is flattered as the "head of
gold"--hardly the image of Antiochus suggested by ch. 7. In
Daniel 6, Darius is a benevolent king who is sympathetic to
Daniel. Even the arrogant Nebuchadnezzar of Daniel 3 and 4
repents and converts to the Most High God, and at the end of
ch. 4 is raised to new heights of greatness. Daniel 7-12 never
envisages the possibility of such reconciliation with Antiochus
Epiphanes. Again, Daniel 2, which is allegedly similar to
Daniel 7, passes over the fourth, Greek, kingdom without any
real condemnation. While that kingdom is said to be strong as
iron, and to crush the other kingdoms (2:40), its fall is not
brought about by any offence against God but by the relatively
innocuous cause of intermarriage, by which it is weakened.
Obviously this portrayal of the Greek kingdom is far removed
from the "little horn" which blasphemes against God in Dan 7:8.
Finally we may note that neither Daniel nor his friends actually undergoes martyrdom. If these stories had been composed
to console the faithful during the persecution of Antiochus, we
should expect that they be modelled more closely on the Maccabean martyrs. Significantly, the righteous in Daniel 11 are
not preserved from death but are restored to life by resurrection. The court-tales, however, show no belief in resurrection,
and no experience of the problem of martyrdom which gave rise
to that belief. In short, the differences between Daniel 1-6
and the visions of the rest of the book far outweigh the points
at which the tales might seem appropriate for Maccabean times.

Not only were the tales not written by the author of the
visions, they were not even edited to show any clear references
to the persecution of Antiochus or to express the same theology
as the rest of the book. None of the points listed by Rowley
was peculiarly characteristic of Maccabean times. The temple
vessels were profaned in the Babylonian exile. The madness
with which the king is punished in Daniel 4 has no real ana-
logue in the career of Antiochus, and Antiochus was not the
first king who might have merited such a fate. The madness of
Nebuchadnezzar can be explained more satisfactorily by analogy
with the sickness of Nabonidus in 4QPrNab. Again, there are

abundant examples of colossal statues in the ancient Near East, and there is nothing in the text to suggest that the statue in Daniel 3 should be identified with the "abomination of desolation." In any case, Antiochus aroused the horror of the Jews more by the violation of the temple than by the actual statue. Worship of idols was, of course, a problem for Jews long before the second century B.C.

Despite Rowley's lengthy arguments, it is clear that the court-tales in Daniel 1-6 were not written in Maccabean times. It is not even possible to isolate a single verse which betrays an editorial insertion from that period. We will speculate in a later chapter on the actual provenance of these tales. For the present it is sufficient to note that they do not come from the same setting as the visions.

This conclusion is very important for understanding the composition of Daniel. Chapters 1-6 are certainly included for a purpose, and are important for the meaning of the whole book, but their significance here is not necessarily identical with the purpose for which they were composed. To appreciate the role these tales play in the book of Daniel, we must not only examine them in themselves, but especially look for those points at which they have influenced and are related to the rest of the book.

We have argued, then, that the court-tales were not originally composed as part of a unit with the visions. Further, they betray no signs of editorial insertions. Yet they are not simply juxtaposed with the rest of the book. They are integrated with it by means of two editorial devices, the symmetrical arrangement of chs. 2-7 and the use of both Hebrew and Aramaic in both halves of the book. We now turn to examine these devices.

The Symmetrical Arrangement of Daniel 2-7

The symmetrical arrangement of chs. 2-7 has been demonstrated most clearly by A. Lenglet.[23] Lenglet has argued that the Aramaic chapters show a concentric structure--ch. 7 corresponds to ch. 2, ch. 3 to ch. 6 and chs. 4 and 5 really form

one story which contrasts two gentile kings. This observation
has obvious merit. Chapters 2 and 7 share the sequence of four
kingdoms followed by an intervention of God. Chapters 3 and 6
share at least the miraculous rescue of people whose lives were
endangered for religious reasons. Chapters 4 and 5 are both
concerned with the punishment of a gentile king for the sin of
hybris, or pride. We must assume that the final editor of
Daniel was aware of this symmetry. This fact may explain to
some extent why these chapters were allowed to stand in Aramaic
while the rest of the book was in Hebrew.

Lenglet has proceeded from this observation to the conclusion that Daniel 2-7 was originally a separate unit, and that
the individual elements were designed with this symmetry in
mind. However, this conclusion does not follow. The fact that
the chapters are arranged symmetrically does not at all influence the argument which we have outlined above. Daniel 7 is
clearly an interpretation of the persecution of Antiochus Epiphanes, whereas the tales in chs. 2-6 show no clear references
to that situation and appear inappropriate for it at several
points.

Lenglet's argument that Daniel 2-7 was composed as an
original unit rests ultimately on his analysis of the parallelism between ch. 2 and ch. 7. He argues that these two chapters not only share certain motifs, but that ch. 7 repeats ch.
2 in an expanded form, and carries the same message. Here he
overlooks some crucial differences between the two chapters.

We have already noted the major features which distinguish
Daniel 7 from Daniel 2. Whereas ch. 7 is dominated by the figure of Antiochus Epiphanes, ch. 2 does not refer to him at all.
In ch. 2 we find no passionate condemnation of any of the kingdoms. Nebuchadnezzar is even addressed as the "head of gold,"
scarcely a derogatory title. In ch. 7, by contrast, each of
the kingdoms is a monster of chaos, a beast rising out of the
sea. The fact that Nebuchadnezzar is transformed temporarily
into a beast in ch. 4 does not lessen the contrast between
Daniel 2 and Daniel 7 on this point. Again, the dissolution of
the fourth kingdom in ch. 2 is primarily due to internal weak-
ening by intermarriage. The fourth beast in ch. 7 is destroyed

because of the blasphemous revolt of the little horn. Finally
Lenglet makes an elaborate comparison between the "rock hewn
from the mountain" in ch. 2 and the "one like a son of man" in
ch. 7. The interpretation of each of these expressions is, of
course, highly disputed. We will see later that they refer to
two quite different conceptions of the eschatological kingdom.

Lenglet concerns himself only with the dream and its interpretation in ch. 2--vss. 31-45. By leaving aside the context in which that dream is set, he seriously distorts the
meaning of Daniel 2. The effect of that chapter is not primarily to present an eschatological vision but to demonstrate
the superiority of Daniel over the pagan wise men. The king
reacts by praising Daniel's god for his power to reveal secrets
--not for his power to control history. The dream in Daniel 2
is an element in a court-tale, which builds a contrast between
Daniel and other wise men, and by implication between their
gods. Daniel is similarly contrasted with the pagan wise men
in chs. 4 and 5, and their hostility in ch. 6 is plainly due to
envy. Daniel 2 very definitely belongs to the category of
court-tale. There is no trace of such a setting in ch. 7.

From the preceding arguments it should be clear that ch. 7
is not simply a repetition and expansion of ch. 2. It is still
true that the two chapters share important motifs. In view of
this, and in view of the fact that they mark the beginning and
end of the Aramaic section of the book, we must ask whether the
editor of Daniel wished to group ch. 7 with chs. 2-6 rather
than with chs. 8-12.

At this point we must consider a very important indication
of the structuring of the book which Lenglet has overlooked.
This is the fictional chronology in which the book is set.

In the opening chapter we are told that Daniel was carried
off to Babylon by Nebuchadnezzar and that he was there until
the time of Cyrus the Persian. Chapters 2, 3 and 4 are set in
the time of Nebuchadnezzar. Chapter 5 refers to the transition
from Belshazzar the Babylonian to Darius the Mede. Chapter 6
is set in the reign of Darius but ends with a reference to
Cyrus. The sequence of Nebuchadnezzar, Belshazzar, Darius and
Cyrus is not, of course, historical, but it corresponds to the

traditional sequence in the schema of the four kingdoms, in
which the Persians are always preceded by the Medes.[24] So the
kings in question represent a sequence of Babylon (chs. 2-5),
Media (chs. 5-6) and Persia (end of ch. 6). It is unlikely
that the tales in chs. 1-6 were originally composed to fit this
sequence. If they were we would scarcely find two Babylonian
kings and no tale set in the time of Cyrus.

The same chronology runs through chs. 7-12. Daniel 7 and
8 are set in the reign of Belshazzar, Daniel 9 in the reign of
Darius, chs. 10-12 in the reign of Cyrus. The fictional chronology of chs. 7-12 does not continue that of 1-6 but rather repeats it. Daniel 7 reverts to the reign of Belshazzar although
Daniel 6 was already set in the time of Darius and ended with a
reference to Cyrus. This cannot be explained as a return to
the beginning, since the reference is to Belshazzar, not to
Nebuchadnezzar. The book of Daniel then clearly presents two
cycles of dates and Daniel 7 is grouped with chs. 8-12, not
with chs. 2-6.[25]

An analysis of the composition of Daniel must take account
of all the factors which we have discussed--the symmetry in the
Aramaic chapters noted by Lenglet, the fact that chs. 2-6 do
not reflect the same situation as ch. 7, and the fictional
chronology which groups ch. 7 with chs. 8-12. The lack of any
reference to the Antiochan persecution in the court-tales shows
that chs. 2-6 were originally distinct from the visions of chs.
7-12. However, the two blocs of material are interlocked by
the way in which ch. 7 is related both to what goes before and
to what comes after. On the one hand, Daniel 7 is grouped with
chs. 2-6 by the symmetry of chs. 2-7, which has been demonstrated by Lenglet. On the other hand, ch. 7 is grouped with
chs. 8-12 by its place in the sequence of the four kingdoms.
It does not continue the sequence of Daniel 2-6 but begins that
of chs. 7-12. Therefore, Daniel 7 serves as a linking chapter
by which the two halves of the book are interlocked.

The interlocking of the two halves of the book is also
achieved by the use of both Hebrew and Aramaic in each half.
Some light can therefore be thrown on the vexed problem of the
two languages of Daniel.

The Problem of the Two Languages

Students of the book of Daniel have always been perplexed by the fact that the transition from Hebrew to Aramaic, and again from Aramaic to Hebrew, does not coincide with the formal distinction between tales and visions. Three main solutions to the problem raised by the two languages have been proposed:

(a) The Aramaic chapters, 2-7, were originally a distinct corpus.

(b) The entire book was originally written in Aramaic and the Hebrew chapters are a translation.

(c) The tales in chs. 1-6 were originally written in Aramaic. Then ch. 7 was composed in Aramaic, perhaps because it was modelled to some extent on Daniel 2. The other apocalyptic visions, which were less closely related to Daniel 2, were written in Hebrew. Finally the opening chapter was translated into Hebrew to provide symmetry between the beginning and the end.

The first of these theories (a) is most extensively argued by Lenglet. We have already seen why it cannot be maintained. The other two theories require some discussion.

(b) The theory that the Hebrew of Daniel is a translation from Aramaic has been advanced in greatest detail by H. L. Ginsberg.[26] Some of Ginsberg's examples of translation Hebrew rest on a tendentious view of what the text should mean. So he assumes that the word "host" in Dan 8:10-11 cannot have the same reference as it has in Dan 8:12-13, that in the first case it must refer to the pagan gods and in the second to the faithful Israelites. He then notes that "host" is not a natural term for pious Israelites, and hypothesizes an original Aramaic *ḥsyn*, pious, *misread* or *corrupted* to *ḥyl'* (Aramaic for host).[27] This highly arbitrary procedure is quite unnecessary. The host in each case is Yahweh's heavenly army, as we shall later demonstrate. This type of tendentious reasoning unfortunately mars much of Ginsberg's work.

Some of his examples are intriguing. In Dan 11:35 the expression that some of the wise "will stumble, to purify them" is very odd. Ginsberg's suggestion, that we have here a

mistranslation of the Aramaic *tql*, which can mean either to
stumble or to test, would give the reading "some of the wise
will be tested, to purify them" which makes far better sense.[28]
Again, in 11:17, the phrase "she will not stand (*'md*) and will
not be (to him)" sounds suspiciously like the phrase of Isa
7:7: "it will not succeed (*qwm*, which also means to stand) and
will not be." If a translator saw the word *qwm* (stand or succeed) in Aramaic, he might well translate it by *'md* (stand,
only).[29] However, even in these cases the Hebrew reading is
not entirely impossible, and so the Aramaic version remains
hypothetical, however intriguing. The plausibility of Ginsberg's suggestions diminishes when he has to accompany them
with radical textual surgery. For example, Dan 11:38 reads "he
will honour the god of fortresses," which is a quite intelligible reading. Ginsberg, however, would read "he will insult the
god of the pious"--by assuming that "fortresses" is a mistranslation of the Aramaic for pious, *ḥsyn* (the Aramaic for fortress
is *ḥsn*) and that the word for "honour" is either a euphemism or
a textual corruption.[30] Here the Aramaic retroversion is again
highly ingenious but the textual emendation is without founda-
tion.

There is no denying that the Hebrew of Daniel, especially
ch. 11, is of poor quality and does not read at all smoothly.
Perhaps the author's primary tongue was Aramaic, a factor which
could explain some of the cases listed by Ginsberg. Despite
Ginsberg's twenty page discussion, he has not amassed enough
persuasive evidence to establish the existence of a written
Aramaic original.

Ginsberg's hypothesis has been further weakened by the
finds at Qumran. The fragments discovered show that the two-
language text of Daniel was current from an early stage. While
Aramaic fragments of books such as Enoch and Tobit have been
found, and 4QpsDan is written in Aramaic, no evidence for an
Aramaic original of Dan 8-12 has been discovered. Further dis-
coveries may yet justify Ginsberg, but for the present the
weight of the evidence is heavily against him.

Even if Ginsberg's theory, that the Hebrew of Daniel is a
translation, were to be proved right, this would still not

solve the problem of the two languages. Why, after all, was part of the book translated into Hebrew and the other part not? Some scholars have suggested that part of the Hebrew text was lost and the Aramaic version was substituted, or vice versa. Such a mechanical explanation has rightly been rejected as un-convincing by the majority of scholars.[31] We must conclude that the book of Daniel was neither originally entirely in He-brew nor entirely in Aramaic, but was composed as a bi-lingual work.

(c) The third theory advanced to explain the use of two languages in Daniel presumes a gradual evolution of the book. First, the tales were written in Aramaic, next ch. 7 was added in the same language, then chs. 8-12 were written in Hebrew and finally ch. 1 was either translated from Aramaic or composed as an introduction to the whole book. This theory admits of sev-eral variants. It may require only two stages of composition, if the same person was responsible for chs. 7-12 and the Hebrew translation of ch. 1. On the other hand, some scholars argue for a much more complicated development through four or more stages.[32]

This third approach to the problem seems to be correct at two basic points. First, the use of two languages is due to the fact that the book was not originally composed as a unit. The final author/redactor incorporated a group of Aramaic tales, but he himself preferred to write in Hebrew. Second, Daniel 7 was not part of the complex of Aramaic stories of chs. 2-6. Any explanation of the problem of the two languages must start from those two points. However, none of the scholars who have espoused this third approach has advanced a satisfactory ex-planation as to why ch. 7 is found in Aramaic and ch. 1 in Hebrew.

Some light can be thrown on the alternation between the two languages by the principle of interlocking which we have already found to be operative in the book. The final author/editor of Daniel integrated the court-tales with the visions, not by making insertions in the tales but by creating an over-lap between the two halves of the book in ch. 7. Daniel 7 is

linked to chs. 8-12 by its place in the sequence of the four
kingdoms. Like these chapters it is a vision, not a court-
tale, and reflects the persecution of Antiochus Epiphanes.
However, it is also linked to the preceding chapters by the
symmetrical arrangement of Daniel 2-7. It is further related
to these chapters by the fact that it is written in Aramaic.
The use of Aramaic in Daniel 7 is then a further device to bind
together the two halves of the book.

The final author/redactor of Daniel was obviously bi-
lingual, and wrote for a bi-lingual public. He did not feel
obliged to reduce his book to one language. Precedent for a
bi-lingual work could be found in the book of Ezra, where not
only the official documents are presented in Aramaic but also
the short narrative passages which connect them, as in Ezra 5:
1-5. The poor quality of the Hebrew in Daniel 8-12 suggests
that the author may have been more comfortable with Aramaic.
He preferred to write his apocalyptic visions in Hebrew, perhaps because of nationalistic fervour in the face of the Antiochan persecution. However, he wrote Daniel 7 in Aramaic to
provide an overlap with the tales of chs. 2-6, and so interlock
the two halves of the book.

The editorial unification of the book of Daniel was completed by the translation of ch. 1 into Hebrew. It is possible
that this chapter was composed, in Hebrew, as an introduction
to the entire book. However, since it is very closely related
thematically to chs. 2-6 but shows no trace of theconcerns
which dominate chs. 7-12, it is more probable that it was
originally part of the corpus of Aramaic tales. By translating
this chapter into Hebrew, the final editor enclosed the Aramaic
material within a Hebrew framework and so further bound his
book into a unity.

There is no decisive evidence whether the tales of Daniel
1-6 were already combined before they were incorporated into
the book of Daniel as we now have it. A few considerations
suggest that they were already combined. Daniel 7 does not
continue the chronological sequence of tales. Whereas Daniel 6
had already reached the time of Cyrus the Persian, Daniel 7 reverts to the reign of Belshazzar. This break in the sequence

might indicate that the tales had already been organized in chronological order before they were taken over. The editor then incorporated them *en bloc* rather than interweave them with the visions to form a continuous story. The lack of reference to the Antiochan persecution in Daniel 1-6 might also indicate that the tales were already combined. If the editor had selected each tale individually we might expect more explicit indication of the relevance of each tale to the overall work.

The Editorial Unity of the Book

The preceding analysis of the composition and unity of Daniel has certain consequences for the way we read the book. If the tales of chs. 1-6 were originally independent of the rest of the book, then their significance in their present context is not necessarily identical with their meaning in their original setting, or taken in isolation. Instead we must look for those aspects of the tales which are picked up and emphasized in the visions of chs. 7-12. On the other hand, the tales cannot be dismissed as irrelevant material which is merely juxtaposed with the visions. As we have seen, they are integrated in the book by a careful editorial process of interlocking, which is attained by the symmetry of ch. 7 with chs. 2-6 and by the use of both Hebrew and Aramaic in both halves of the book. It is evident therefore that the tales are important for the overall message of the book. In the following chapter, we will inquire wherein that importance lies.

Our main conclusion, then, on the unity and composition of Daniel is that the book is made up of a collection of traditional court-tales and a group of apocalyptic visions which were composed in the time of Antiochus Epiphanes. These two blocs of material are combined by the process of interlocking which we have described.

Later Additions to the Book

While traditional material is constantly used within the individual chapters, it is nearly always well integrated in its new context so that nothing is gained by distinguishing further sources at this point. Only in one case (in the Masoretic text) can we point to a significant passage which diverges in style and theology from the rest of the book, and must therefore be bracketed off as a later addition. This passage is the prayer in Daniel 9. It is regarded as secondary by a wide range of scholars, though not by all.[33]

The arguments that the prayer in Daniel 9 is a secondary addition are both literary and theological. Whereas the remainder of Daniel 8-12 is written in very clumsy Hebrew, which often shows Aramaic influence, the prayer in ch. 9 reads like a patchwork of phrases from the OT and is written in perfectly good Hebrew. Apart from a single reference in Dan 1:2, all the occurrences of the name Yahweh or Adonai in Daniel are in the prayer or its immediate framework, and here it recurs repeatedly. The introduction and conclusion to the prayer are marked by clumsy doublettes in vss. 3-4a and 20-21. The prayer itself is a *communal* confession of sin, although Daniel is an individual, praying for his own enlightenment. The theological perspective of the prayer, dominated by the confession of sin and the recollection of the saving deeds of Yahweh in the past is not paralleled elsewhere in the book. The sense of ch. 9 as a whole is not disrupted if we omit the prayer and pass from vs. 3 to vs. 21.

We know from the prayer of Azariah and the Canticle of the Three Young Men that prayers were sometimes added to the book of Daniel. We may easily assume that the prayer of Daniel in ch. 9 was added too. The point is not that the prayer should be deleted from the text. Even if it were placed here by the original author, its formulaic language makes clear that it is a traditional piece, not something composed especially for the context. Dan 9:4-20 is included here not for its content, or theology, but simply because it is a prayer. It is not legitimate to use the content of the prayer as a source for the theology of the book. We will discuss the theology of the prayer and its relation to the rest of the book in an appendix to Chapter VI below, in the context of history and eschatology in Daniel.

No good purpose would be served at this point by discussing every verse in Daniel which has ever been regarded as secondary. Such a discussion would require a verse-by-verse commentary on the entire book. Some of the more important disputed verses will be discussed incidentally in other chapters. Apart from the prayer in ch. 9, there are no significant later additions to the Hebrew or Aramaic text, after the composition of the book in the time of Antiochus Epiphanes.

We proceed then on the assumption that chs. 7-12 constitute a literary unity and that the various parts can be used to clarify each other. As we have indicated, the relation of the court-tales in chs. 1-6 to the visions in chs. 7-12 is more complex, but the tales can still throw significant light on the visions. We examine the court-tales and their role in the book in the following chapter.

NOTES

CHAPTER I

[1]See the classic treatment of these problems by H. H. Rowley, *Darius the Mede and the Four World Empires* (Cardiff: University of Wales Press Board, 1935).

[2]So H. Schmid, "Daniel, der Menschensohn," *Judaica* 27 (1971) 203.

[3]See M. Noth, "Noah, Daniel und Hiob in Ez 14," *VT* 1 (1951) 251-60.

[4]The name Daniel in Ezekiel is spelled with the consonants *Dn'l* and vocalized Daniel. In the book of Daniel, the *i* is represented by a *mater lectionis*--so *Dny'l*, also vocalized Daniel. The identity of the two names could be disputed, but is accepted by most scholars.

[5]*CTCA*, 17-20; *ANET*, 149-55.

[6]See O. Eissfeldt, *The Old Testament: An Introduction* (New York: Harper and Row, 1965) 590.

[7]H.-P. Müller, "Magisch-mantische Weisheit und die Gestalt Daniels," *UF* 1 (Neukirchen-Vluyn: Butzon & Bercker Kevelaer, 1969) 79-94, has tried to elaborate this material further. Müller considers the Daniel of Ugarit to have been a "wise man" by virtue of his power to utter magic formulae. However, the relevance of this type of "wisdom" to the Daniel of the biblical books is open to question. Müller also adduces the Dânêl of 1 Enoch 6:7 and 69:2. This Dânêl is an angelic figure, so again, his relevance must be disputed.

[8]For a recent commentary on the Septuagint additions to Daniel, see M. Delcor, *Le Livre de Daniel* (SB; Paris: Gabalda, 1971) 100-05, 260-92.

[9]See J.-T. Milik, "'Prière de Nabonide' et autres écrits d'un cycle de Daniel," *RB* 63 (1956) 407-15; Alfred Mertens, *Das Buch Daniel im Lichte der Texte vom Toten Meer* (SBM 12; Würzburg: Echter, 1971) 34-50. The most complete discussion of 4QPrNab is by R. Meyer, *Das Gebet des Nabonid* (Sitzungsberichte der sächsischen Akademie der Wissenschaften zu Leipzig, Phil.-hist. Kl. Bd. 107, Heft 3; Berlin: Akademie Verlag, 1962).

[10]So already W. von Soden, "Eine babylonische Volksüberlieferung vom Nabonid in der Danielerzählungen," *ZAW* 53 (1935) 81-89.

[11]Milik, "Prière," 413.

[12]Ibid., 415.

24

[13] See especially F. Macler, "Les Apocalypses Apocryphes de Daniel," *RHR* 33 (1896) 37-53, 163-76, 288-319. Also P. J. Alexander, "Medieval Apocalypses as Historical Sources," *AHR* 73 (1968) 997-1018; Albert-Marie Denis, *Introduction aux Pseudépigraphes Grecs d'Ancien Testament* (Leiden: Brill, 1970) 309-14.

[14] The Daniel fragments from Cave 1 were published by D. Barthélemy, DJD 1. 150-52. See also J. C. Trever, "Completion of the Publication of some Fragments from Qumran Cave I," *RevQ* 5 (1964/65) 323-44. On the fragments from Cave 4 see F. M. Cross, "Le travail d'édition des fragments manuscrits de Qumrân," *RB* 63 (1956) 56-58. The fragments from Cave 6 are published by M. Baillet, DJD 3. 114-16.

[15] F. M. Cross, Jr., *The Ancient Library of Qumran* (Garden City: Doubleday, 1961) 43. For the other end of the spectrum, see J. C. Trever, "1QDan[a], the latest of the Qumran Manuscripts," *RevQ* 7 (1969/70) 277-86.

[16] The extensive scholarship on the composition of Daniel is summarized by Eissfeldt, *The Old Testament*, 512-29, updated now by J. C. H. Lebram, "Perspektiven der gegenwärtigen Danielforschung," *JSJ* 5 (1974) 5-11.

[17] For the date of Antiochus' death, see A. J. Sachs and D. J. Wiseman, "A Babylonian King List of the Hellenistic Period," *Iraq* 16 (1954) 209. Eissfeldt, *The Old Testament*, 520, mistakenly gives the date as April 163. This point was brought to my attention by Professor John Strugnell.

[18] Even this point of consensus is still rejected by a small group of conservative scholars who insist that the entire book of Daniel is a genuine prophecy, written during the exile. The most prominent exponent of this viewpoint is E. J. Young, *The Prophecy of Daniel* (Grand Rapids: Eerdmans, 1953). See also D. J. Wiseman et al., *Notes on some Problems in the Book of Daniel* (London: Tyndale Fellowship, 1965).

[19] H. H. Rowley, "The Unity of the Book of Daniel," *The Servant of the Lord and Other Essays on the Old Testament* (London: Lutterworth, 1952) 237-68. Rowley engaged in a lively debate with the arch-fragmenter of the book, H. L. Ginsberg. For references, see Eissfeldt, *The Old Testament*, 518-19.

[20] Rowley, "Unity," 264-67.

[21] Polybius, *Histories*, 26.10.

[22] 1 Macc 1:21-24.

[23] A. Lenglet, "La structure littéraire de Daniel 2-7," *Bib* 53 (1972) 169-90.

[24] The schema of the four kingdoms will be discussed in detail in the following chapter. The usual sequence was Assyria, Media, Persia and Macedonia. Daniel substitutes Babylonia for Assyria.

[25]So also O. Eissfeldt, "Daniels und seiner 3 Gefährten Laufbahn im babylonischen und persischen Dienst," *ZAW* 72 (1960) 134-48.

[26]H. L. Ginsberg, *Studies in Daniel* (New York: The Jewish Theological Seminary of America, 1948) 41-61. Also R. H. Charles, *The Book of Daniel* (Oxford: Clarendon, 1929) xlvi-xlviii; F. Zimmermann, "Hebrew Translation in Daniel," *JQR* 51 (1960/61) 198-208.

[27]Ginsberg, *Studies*, 52-54.

[28]Ibid., 41.

[29]Ibid., 57.

[30]Ibid., 42-46.

[31]Eissfeldt, *The Old Testament*, 516.

[32]For variants of this theory, see J. A. Montgomery, *The Book of Daniel* (ICC 19; New York: Scribners, 1927) 91; O. Plöger, *Das Buch Daniel* (KAT 18; Gütersloh: Mohn, 1965) 27; Delcor, *Daniel*, 10-11.

[33]For a recent summary of arguments and bibliography, see C. A. Moore, "Toward the Dating of the Book of Baruch," *CBQ* 36 (1974) 314-16. Scholars who regard the prayer as secondary include Charles (*Daniel*, 226) and A. Bentzen (*Daniel* [HAT 19; Tübingen: Mohr, 1952] 75). The most elaborate defence of the authenticity of the prayer is that of M. Gilbert, "La prière de Daniel," *RTL* 3 (1972) 284-310.

CHAPTER II

THE COURT-TALES

We have seen in the preceding chapter that the court-tales in Daniel 1-6 were not written in the same situation, or for the same purpose, as chapters 7-12. Further, we argued that the tales do not even show redactional elements which unambiguously reflect the Maccabean setting of the visions. However, the two halves of the book are interlocked by a careful editorial process. The court-tales are evidently included for a purpose. Moreover, since the tales now constitute half the entire book, their importance for the overall impact of Daniel is considerable.

The Function of the Court-Tales

The most obvious function of the court-tales is to introduce the figure of Daniel. The visions in chs. 7-12 are written in the first person and attributed to Daniel. The tales in chs. 1-6 are written in the third person and provide information about this figure and his companions. The visionary in chs. 7-12 is therefore identified with the hero of the tales.

This fact is significant for the self-understanding of the author (or authors) of the visions, who wrote in the name of Daniel. He must have felt that the descriptions of Daniel in the tales adequately represented his own ideals, and that his visions would be enhanced by association with this figure. The practice of pseudepigraphy automatically assumes a measure of identification of the real author with his pseudonymous hero. We will return in the following chapter to discuss the nature of this "identification" insofar as we can discover it. For the present, we wish to note that the choice of Daniel as a pseudonym involves the affirmation of the lifestyle of Daniel and the values with which he is associated. By incorporating an extensive body of tales about Daniel in his book, the Maccabean visionary held up the hero of these tales as a model to his readers, but also expressed his own affirmation of this ideal figure.

There are two apparent reasons why these tales might be
chosen to establish the identity of the visionary, and simultaneously provide an example for the readers. First, the
visionary may have seen an analogy between the situations described in the court-tales, and the crises in which he and his
contemporaries found themselves. Specifically, he may have
incorporated the court-tales because they provided examples
of persecution, and the response of an ideal Jew. Second, the
visionary may have included the tales about Daniel the courtier
because he attached importance to his character and way of life.
He may have wished to present Daniel as an ideal wise man, even
apart from situations of persecution.

We are fortunate to have some evidence both of the situation in which the visions were written and the type of character to which their author laid claim. We read in Dan 11:33-35
that during the persecution of Antiochus Epiphanes:

> those among the people who are wise shall make many
> understand, though they shall fall by sword and
> flame, by captivity and plunder, for some days...
> and some of those who are wise shall fall, to refine
> and to cleanse them...

In Dan 12:3, we find that after the resurrection:

> those who are wise shall shine like the brightness
> of the firmament; and those who turn many to righ-
> teousness, like the stars for ever and ever.

The Hebrew term for "those who are wise" in these passages is
maskîlîm, literally "those who cause to understand," or wise
teachers. There is no serious doubt among scholars that the
author of Daniel 7-12 understood himself as one of these
maskîlîm, or wise teachers. From these passages it is apparent
that the visionary could be attracted to the figure of Daniel
both because of the elements of persecution in the tales and
because of Daniel's character as a wise man.

Scholars have tended to assume that the relevance of the
tales for the Maccabean visionary lay chiefly in the stories of
persecution, in Daniel 3 and 6. H. H. Rowley, as we have seen,
even claimed that these chapters were composed with reference
to the persecution of Antiochus Epiphanes. However, it is

noteworthy that the account of the persecution in ch. 11 contains no allusion to the miraculous rescue of the three young men from the furnace or of Daniel from the lions' den. On the contrary, the wise leaders did not expect a miraculous deliverance from death. At least some of them actually died. Both Daniel and his friends and the wise leaders (by the resurrection) are ultimately delivered from an apparently hopeless situation, but the manner of deliverance is strikingly different in each case. Undoubtedly the rescue of Daniel and of his friends was a relevant lesson in hope for the Jews of Maccabean times, but its relevance is not noted in Daniel 7-12. Accordingly, there is nothing to indicate that this was the primary reason why the visionary incorporated the court-tales in his book.

On the other hand, the designation *maskîlîm* (wise leaders), in chs. 11-12, points explicitly to Daniel and his companions, who are described in 1:4 as *maskîlîm* in all wisdom. Even as the visionary took over the name of Daniel, so he adopted one of the terms applied to the wise men of the exile as the primary designation for the group to which he belonged. His primary interest in the court-tales would therefore appear to derive from the fact that he saw himself and his companions as wise men after the model of Daniel and his companions. The court-tales, then, are important primarily because of the model of the wise man which they present.

The major characteristics of the wise man, as presented in Daniel 1-6, are already present in chapter 1, which serves as an introductory chapter.

Daniel 1: An Introductory Chapter

The opening chapter of Daniel sets the scene for the other tales, by explaining how Daniel and his friends came to be present at the royal court, their official role and the problems to which it gave rise. It is especially important for the information it gives about the model of a wise man which is presented in the tales.

Some of the Jewish youths "both of the royal family and of the nobility" are set aside by the king to be specially trained as wise men. They must be "skilful in all wisdom," (*maskîlîm bᵉkol ḥokmāh*), "understanding learning," (*mᵉbînê maddā'*) and "competent to serve in the king's palace" (Dan 1:4). In preparation for the royal service they are instructed in "the letters and language of the Chaldeans," for three years (1:5). At the completion of their training the youths are endowed with learning and skill in all letters and wisdom, and Daniel has "understanding in all visions and dreams" (1:17). We are told that the king found them ten times better than all the "magicians and enchanters" of his kingdom, with whom they evidently competed in their function as counsellors.

Three features of this description are particularly important. First, Daniel and his companions become royal counsellors. We can get some idea of the role of a counsellor from the popular international tale of Aḥikar, which represents the ideal counsellor as a man of amazing versatility, whose competence ranged from the knowledge of proverbs to military strategy.[1] There is no doubt that such counsellors played an important role in all governments of the ancient world. We know that some Jews attained positions of prominence at foreign courts. The most important example is probably Nehemiah, who was a cupbearer to the Persian king, Artaxerxes I, and subsequently governor of the province of Judah. The case of Nehemiah shows that it was at least possible for Jews to function as royal courtiers while remaining loyal Yahwists. It is possible that the court-tales of Daniel originated in the circles of Jews who served, in any capacity, at a gentile court. This, of course, cannot be proved, and is not a necessary hypothesis. However, the identity of the first authors of these tales is relatively unimportant. Much more significant for our purpose is the fact that the tales endorse the life-style of such courtiers, and the type of wisdom they represent.

Second, royal counsellors were learned men. The "letters and language" of the Chaldeans refers not to Imperian Aramaic (which is called *'ărāmît* in 2:4) but to Akkadian, and perhaps even Sumerian.[2] We know that "Chaldean learning" continued to flourish into the Roman period. Pliny names three cities which were particularly famous for it, Babylon, Warka and Hipparene.[3]

We can get some idea of the range of learning of a Chaldean
sage in the Hellenistic age from the fragments of Berossus, a
Babylonian priest from the early third century B.C.[4] Berossus
is variously represented as an astronomer, astrologer, mythographer and historian. His major work, the *Babyloniaka*, was
composed in Greek and dedicated to Antiochus I. It was a comprehensive history of Babylonia, starting from the cosmogony,
and it displayed imposing learning in ancient myths and chron-
icles. Berossus was not a courtier, and we should not suppose
that everyone trained in Akkadian literature equalled the scope
of his learning. However, he clearly shows that the interests
of a Babylonian sage were not confined to proverbs or divination, but extended to a broad range of learned traditions. We
must assume that students who spent three years in the study of
Chaldean letters acquired some mastery of the rich traditions
preserved by the scribes.

Third, Daniel's skills included the interpretation of
dreams. This skill was especially associated with a Babylonian
priestly caste but was not confined to it. A. L. Oppenheim has
distinguished three methods of dream interpretation in the ancient Near East:[5]

(a) Interpretation by intuition. In this case an interpreter
    might be qualified by age, social status or simply by
    personal charisma.

(b) Interpretation by precedent. In this case the interpreter
    must be a trained scholar learned in the collections of
    dream-omina.

(c) Interpretation by a further revelation. The interpreter
    could turn to the deity who was the source of the dream
    either for verification of a proposed interpretation or for
    an unequivocal message. This type of interpretation was
    done by priests, *šailu* or *bārū* (or their female equiva-
    lents). These were professionals who had special skills
    and rituals which could be applied to the situation.

At court, Daniel and his companions are compared to the
Babylonian "magicians and enchanters." The terms used for the
these professionals in Daniel 1 are *ḥartummîm* and *'aššāpîm*.
The word *ḥartum* is ultimately of Egyptian origin. It is used

in the Joseph story for Egyptian dream-interpreters. The term
'*assapîm* is derived from an Akkadian term for divination
priests.[6] Various other names are applied to these people in
Daniel, the most notable being perhaps "Chaldeans." This term
was used in a non-ethnic sense to denote "astrologers" as early
as Herodotus (1.187). Astrology was undoubtedly a major interest of the Chaldean caste, but they also engaged in other
divinatory activities. Diodorus Siculus 2.29-31 noted that
they also engaged in interpreting dreams and in making predictions, often of a political nature.[7] Prognostication was always a function of the Babylonian (and Near Eastern) wise man,
usually on the basis of omens, whether astrological, cosmological (such as earthquakes) or dream-omens.[8] The predictive
element in Babylonian wisdom is repeatedly emphasized in
Deutero-Isaiah's polemic against "those who divide the heavens,
those who gaze at stars, who at the new moon predict what shall
befall you."[9] Similarly in Esther 1:13 the Persian wise men
are those "who know the times." This predictive function of
the wise man is obviously relevant to Daniel.

The various terms for wise men in Daniel are not used in a
strictly defined technical sense. Montgomery is probably right
that "the writer has no special knowledge of the elaborate development of those castes."[10] All these terms apply to the
learned wise men, equipped with skills of divination and dream
interpretation, who acted as royal counsellors at the Babylonian, Persian and Seleucid courts. This type of royal counsellor was known throughout the Near East, from Egypt to Babylon.
Daniel and his friends are presented as trained wise men of
this international type.

However, the youths do not simply merge with the Chaldean
wise men. At one point they hold themselves apart. They
faithfully observe the Jewish food laws, even at the risk of
giving offence to the king. Precisely because of this, God
gives them wisdom far greater than their rivals. The point of
the story is clear. Jews who succeed at court do so because of
their wisdom. God gives wisdom to his servants who faithfully
obey his laws. The thrust of the argument is not that one can
have a successful career at a foreign court while remaining a

loyal Jew, but that strict obedience to the Jewish law, even in
its distinctive elements, is a necessary prerequisite of the
wisdom which brings success.[11] Fidelity to the God of the Jews
is an essential element of wisdom.

Daniel 1, then, gives us a basic outline of the ideal of
wisdom which is presented in the court-tales. The methods of
Chaldean wise-men, their learning and use of dreams are accepted. Now Chaldean wisdom was not conceived as a purely
human product. It ultimately drew on a divine source. The
Jewish courtiers also drew on a divine source, but a different
one. Accordingly, there could be no complete assimilation.
While the Jews engaged in the same activities as the Chaldeans,
they inevitably rejected their religious presuppositions. The
aspiration of Jews to become wise men after the manner of the
Chaldeans already contained the seeds of religious confrontation.

The Tales in Daniel 2-6

The wise men with whom Daniel and his companions are
grouped constitute a type which was widely known throughout the
Near East. There was also a widespread literature of typical,
even stereotypical, stories about such wise men and their for-
tunes at court. The best known examples are the biblical
stories of Joseph and Esther and the tale of Aḥikar.[12] There
are also numerous instances in Egyptian literature, most notably the "Instructions of Onksheshonqy."[13] It is not necessary
here to review all the variations of the tale of the wise
courtier.[14] The tales in Daniel fall into two categories, to
which we may refer as "tales of contest" and "tales of conflict."[15] In the "tales of contest," Daniel 2, 4 and 5, the
focus is on the wisdom of Daniel, and he is shown to be superior to the wise men of the kingdom. The "tales of conflict,"
Daniel 3 and 6 are essentially dramas of danger and deliverance.
Here the Jewish courtiers come into direct conflict with their
pagan rivals. In the tales of conflict found in Daniel, the
wisdom of the courtiers plays very little role. The heroes do
not escape danger by their own wisdom (as Aḥikar, for example,
does) but by the miraculous intervention of God.

The Tales of Contest

The three tales which we have classified as tales of contest share a common pattern which can be outlined as follows:
1. The king is confronted with dreams or signs which he cannot understand (Dan 2:1, 4:5, 5:5-7. Cf. Pharaoh's dream in Gen 41:7-8).
2. The Babylonian wise men fail to understand (Dan 2:10-11, 4:7-8, 5:8. Cf. Gen 41:8).
3. Daniel succeeds where the Babylonian wise men failed (Dan 2:25-45, 4:19-27, 5:25-29. Cf. Gen 41:25-36).
4. Daniel is then exalted to high position (Dan 2:46-49, 5:29. Cf. Gen 41:39-42). The exaltation is omitted in Daniel 4 since Daniel is already in a position of authority.

However, within this common pattern the emphasis may fall differently in the individual tales. In Daniel 2 the interest is focused on the wisdom of Daniel and his god, and the actual content of the dream interpretation is of lesser importance. In Daniel 4 and 5 greater emphasis is laid on the message communicated by Daniel, specifically on the critique of the gentile kings in these chapters.

Daniel 2: The Skill of the Wise Courtier

Chapter 2 is structured in such a way as to highlight the wisdom of Daniel. This is indicated by a number of factors. Since the king refuses even to disclose the dream, the achievement of the interpretation is heightened. The miracle in Daniel 2 is simply that a man can narrate and interpret a dream which he has not been told, irrespective of the content of the dream. Again, the king does not react to Daniel's interpretation. He is amazed at Daniel's wisdom, but he ignores the content of the prophecy. Unlike Daniel 4 and 5, no reference is made to the subsequent fulfillment of the prophecy. The point of Daniel 2 is summed up in the words of Nebuchadnezzar: "Truly your God is God of gods and Lord of kings, and a revealer of mysteries, for you have been able to reveal this mystery" (2:47).

The tale describes how Daniel and his friends rose to power in the Babylonian court. No claim can be made that this story is historical. However, the details of the story are drawn from life at a Near Eastern court, and it has enough verisimilitude to ensure that it could be told as an intelligible story, which was not inherently incredible. The key to the success of the Jewish courtiers is Daniel's skill as a wise interpreter of dreams. We have already seen that dream interpretation was an important element in the profession of a Chaldean wise man. There is abundant evidence of the importance attached to dreams throughout the ancient Near East. Within the supposed life-span of Daniel, Nabonidus (the probable prototype of Nebuchadnezzar in Daniel 4) was especially famous for his interest in dreams.[16] Herodotus reports dreams of Astyages (1.107-8), Cyrus (1.209) and Polycrates (3.124) among others. Other famous dreams are attributed to Alexander,[17] Nektanebo,[18] and to the legendary Persian king, Hystaspes.[19] Two instances are especially interesting. First, Cicero (De Divinatione 1.23.46) relates a dream of Cyrus which was interpreted for him by the Magi. The interpretation referred to the duration of his sovereignty. Second, in the Oracle of Hystaspes, the king's dream is interpreted by a prophetic youth (puer) and refers to the downfall of a world-empire. Each of these dreams bears obvious resemblance to Daniel 2, but in neither case is historical influence likely.[20]

It has been suggested that Nebuchadnezzar's threat to execute the wise men if they failed to interpret the dream may contain a reminiscence of the slaughter of the Magi by Darius I, recorded in Herodotus 3.79. This hypothesis is not necessary. The threat is simply a device to heighten the drama of the story. Various parallels have also been adduced for the statue. It is at least clear that the use of several metals in statues was a known phenomenon in the ancient Near East.[21]

Montgomery suggests that "Nebuchadnezzar's visions appear to belong to a cycle of legend on which our writer has drawn."[22] This may well be true, especially in view of the traditional material which we will find in Daniel 4. In any case, the picture of the wise man and his operations is one which would have been intelligible and credible in the Near East at any time in the Babylonian, Persian or Hellenistic periods. This, of course, is not to suggest that the story is historical.

We have already seen that Daniel's recourse to God falls within the range of methods of dream interpretation used in the ancient Near East. Daniel does not employ the ritualistic methods typical of Babylonian divination, but the Chaldeans would have shared his belief that such wisdom is revealed by a god. Accordingly, the key to Daniel's success is the fact that the god he worships is more powerful and omniscient than the god of the Chaldeans.

Daniel 2 pointedly contrasts the Chaldean wise men (and implicitly their gods) with Daniel and his god. Yet there is no real hostility toward the gentiles. On the contrary, Daniel is grouped with the Chaldean wise men and intervenes so that they will not be put to death. The king is in no way anti-Jewish. His kingdom is given by God and Daniel identifies him as the head of gold. Even the Chaldeans with whom Daniel is contrasted are not portrayed as hostile rivals. The superior wisdom of Daniel and his god are readily employed in the service of the king and for the benefit of the other wise men.

A Babylonian Political Oracle in Daniel 2

The attitude to the gentiles which we find in the story of Daniel 2 is, then, remarkably open and tolerant. Unlike the later chapters 4 and 5, it does not even suggest a criticism of the Babylonian king. In the context of this story, the actual content of the dream and interpretation may appear startling, since it contains the typical apocalyptic schematisation of history into four kingdoms, culminating in the destruction of all gentile dominion by the kingdom of God. It is particularly striking that this prophecy evokes no reaction from the king, other than amazement at the wisdom of Daniel. If we understand Daniel's interpretation in the usual way, as a Jewish prophecy of the decline of gentile power and the advent of a messianic Jewish kingdom, then the reaction of the king is scarcely explicable. We should at least expect him to repent of his ways, as he is said to do in Daniel 4. In Daniel 2 he does not even worship Daniel's god, but offers sacrifices to Daniel (!) and prostrates himself before him.

All scholars are agreed that neither Daniel 2 nor the
other tales were composed by their Jewish author out of whole
cloth. Rather they were developed from older traditions which
were largely legendary, but may have included historical elements. So, for example, it is well known that a tradition about
Nabonidus underlies the story of Nebuchadnezzar's madness in
Daniel 4. Again, all scholars agree that the pattern of four
kingdoms in Daniel 2 was derived from a non-Jewish tradition.
We wish to suggest that the extent of the borrowing has been
underestimated and that much light can be thrown on the problems of the chapter if we consider the prophecy as a Babylonian
political oracle rather than as a Jewish apocalypse.

The interpretation of the statue in Daniel 2 combines two
complexes of traditional ideas. These are:

(a) The sequence of four kingdoms, followed by a fifth of a
    more lasting nature, which was widely used in political
    propaganda in the Hellenistic Near East.

(b) The distinction of four world ages identified by metals.

The Schema of the Four Kingdoms

The sequence of four kingdoms, followed by some decisive
eschatological event, is found in three documents from the
Hellenistic age which were probably composed before the visions
of Daniel, and are roughly contemporary with Daniel 2.[23]

First, the schema is found in a fragment of the Roman
chronicler Aemilius Sura, which is preserved by Velleius Pater-
culus:

> Aemilius Sura in his book on the chronology of Rome:
> The Assyrians were the first of all races to hold
> power, then the Medes, after them the Persians and
> then the Macedonians. Then, when the two kings
> Philip and Antiochus, of Macedonian origin had been
> completely conquered, soon after the overthrow of
> Carthage, the supreme command passed to the Roman
> people.[24]

Since Aemilius considered the second Punic war (218-201 B.C.),
shortly before the defeat of Antiochus III, as the end of
Carthage, he must have written before the third Punic war (149-
146 B.C.). Since he considers that Philip, who died in 179 B.C.,

marked the end of Macedonia, he must have written before the third Macedonian war (171-168 B.C.). He has therefore been dated before 171 B.C. Aemilius evidently saw Rome as the definitive heir to world dominion.[25] Therefore, his use of the four-kingdom schema served as pro-Roman propaganda.

The sequence of the four kingdoms was not, however, peculiar to Roman propaganda. It is also found in the fourth Sibylline Oracle (*Sib. Or.* 4:49-101) in a passage which is probably pre-Maccabean and possibly non-Jewish.[26] Again, the kingdoms are identified as Assyria, Media, Persia and Macedonia. The schema of four kingdoms is superimposed on a division of world-history into ten generations. Six generations are allotted to the Assyrians, two to the Medes, one to the Persians and one to the Macedonians. The Macedonian kingdom is the last of the sequence and coincides with the last generation. In the present form of *Sib. Or.* 4, there follows a lengthy oracle on Rome (vss. 102-51), but this is not integrated to the numerical sequence, and Rome is not envisaged as a lasting definitive empire. Evidently the reference to Rome was a later addition, designed to update the oracle. The four-kingdoms passage, however, which concludes with the Macedonians, must have been written early in the Hellenistic period. It was almost certainly composed before the battle of Magnesia in 190 B.C., which marked the advent of Rome as a power in the Near East.

The sibylline passage on the four kingdoms is now embedded in a Jewish oracle from the late first century A.D., probably from Syria. The Hellenistic oracle may have been Jewish, but in fact contains nothing which could not have been written by a Gentile.

We cannot be sure how the original oracle concluded, but there is nothing to suggest Roman sympathies. Whatever followed the fourth kingdom, whether another kingdom (as in Aemilius Sura) or cosmic destruction (as in the present conclusion of *Sib. Or.* 4), it is clear that the fourth kingdom, the Greek, would be destroyed. Accordingly, the sibylline oracle reflects an anti-Macedonian ideology, and could represent the resistance of any Near Eastern people to Hellenistic rule.

A third example of the schema of four kingdoms, in a document from the Hellenistic period, is found in the Persian Zand-ī Vohūman Yasn, or Bahman Yasht.[27] This is a late "midrashic" elaboration of a lost text of the Avesta, the Vohūman Yasn. The original Yasn is certainly pre-Christian, but the Zand contains later material. However, the passage which refers to the four kingdoms (the first chapter of the Zand) dates from the Hellenistic period. The first three kingdoms in the Zand are Persian, but the fourth is that of the "divs with dishevelled hair." S. K. Eddy has argued that this expression refers to the Macedonians.[28] In the Persepolis reliefs, the Great King appears with neatly arranged hair and beard, surrounded by trim courtiers. By contrast, all the representations of Alexander on coins or statues show him with his hair wildly tousled. Even apart from this argument, it is most natural to suppose that the first non-Persian kingdom in the sequence refers to the first people who conquered the Persians --i.e., the Greeks. So, while the Zand-ī Vohūman Yasn contains materials from the Christian era in other chapters, the sequence of the four kingdoms can most plausibly be dated to the Hellenistic period in the aftermath of Alexander's conquests.[29]

We have, then, three documents which can plausibly be dated earlier than the book of Daniel in its final form. The diversity of the sources suggests that the schema was very widely known. Most scholars who have studied the schema associate it with Near Eastern resistance to Hellenistic rule.[30] In Aemilius Sura, *Sib. Or.* 4 and Daniel, the Medes figure as the second world empire. This may seem odd, since the Medes never ruled over Syria, Palestine or any western area of the Near East. The oddity is explained if we assume that the schema originated in Persia or Media, or in some place where Media had ruled.[31] The schema became popular in the west with the spread of revolts against the Seleucids. Eventually the Romans took it over and adapted it for their purposes.

Because of the manner in which the material has been transmitted, we get no clear picture of what would follow the fourth kingdom. For Aemilius Sura, the fourth kingdom was already overthrown and supreme power had passed to the Roman

people. The oracle in *Sib. Or.* 4 was updated to the first
century A.D., so its original ending was either lost or dis-
placed. In its present form, *Sib. Or.* 4 ends with a confla-
gration and a resurrection of the dead. In the Zand-ī Vohūman
Yasn, the fourth kingdom simply marks the end of a millenium.
In Daniel 7, the sequence concludes with the enigmatic kingdom
of the saints of the Most High. Despite this confusion, we
can be virtually certain that most natives of the Near East who
looked forward to the destruction of the fourth, Greek, kingdom expected that it would be replaced by the restoration of
their own native kingdom.

The schema of the four kingdoms, then, was widespread in
the Near East in the Hellenistic age. It cannot have been derived from Daniel, since neither Aemilius Sura nor the Sibyl
included Babylon in the sequence. The schema was essentially
designed for anti-Hellenistic propaganda, and implied a hope
for the restoration of native Near Eastern kingdoms.

The Four Metals

The second traditional complex involved in Daniel 2 is the
distinction of four world ages, identified by metals. This is
found in Hesiod's *Works and Days* 106-201, and also in the
Zand-ī Vohūman Yasn (which has steel instead of copper as the
third metal). The original purpose of this schema was to sig-
nify a gradual deterioration of the world. This is quite evident in Hesiod. It is not possible to demonstrate that Hesiod
derived his schema of metals from a Persian source, or vice
versa, although some historical connection is highly probable.
In any case, the schema did not originate with Daniel 2.

Daniel 2 applies the schema of the four metals to the four
kingdoms. The purpose of combining the two schemata can only
have been to suggest a gradual decline in the political situation. As Daniel 2 now stands, this decline is not emphasized.
Rather, all the metals are destroyed at once by the mysterious
stone in 2:34-35. It seems probable, therefore, that the combination of the metals and the kingdoms was not made specifically for Daniel 2 as it now stands. It is more likely that

the Jewish author took over an oracle which already described the political kingdoms in terms of the metals.

The combination of metals and kingdoms is also found in the Zand-ī Vohūman Yasn. This passage shows striking similarity to Daniel 2. Zarathustra sees in a dream a trunk of a tree with four branches, one of gold, one of silver, one of steel and one of mixed iron. In the interpretation each is equated with a reign or sovereignty. The similarity with Daniel is too close for mere coincidence. Yet neither dream simply repeats the other. In the one case we have a tree, in the other a statue. Daniel's third metal is bronze, in the Zand it is steel. Direct influence, in either direction, cannot be excluded, but, equally, cannot be proved. In view of the differences in detail it is more probable that both derived from a common prototype.

The original oracle in Daniel 2 was presumably written under the fourth kingdom and regarded it as the nadir of history. It looked back to the golden age as an ideal period. This is also the case in the Persian Zand, where the fourth period is an "evil sovereignty" but the first, golden, kingdom is "when I and thou will hold a conference of religion, king Vistâsp shall accept the religion, the figures of the divs shall totter." Now it is striking that Daniel, in his interpretation, addresses Nebuchadnezzar as the "head of gold" and thereby implies that his reign is the golden age. Such glorification of Nebuchadnezzar is scarcely in accordance with a Jewish viewpoint. Nebuchadnezzar was the king who captured Jerusalem and destroyed the temple. He was remembered in Jewish legend as an archetype of evil, as we can see from the book of Judith.[32] However, there is evidence that during the Hellenistic period the Babylonians recalled the reign of Nebuchadnezzar as a golden age. Berossus, writing about 275 B.C., exalted Nebuchadnezzar above all previous kings of Babylon. According to Megasthenes, he surpassed even Heracles. His exploits were developed to surpass those of Alexander the Great and Seleucus.[33] The identification of Nebuchadnezzar with the head of gold appears far more appropriate in the mouth of a hellenistic Babylonian than in that of a contemporary Jew.

In no case that we know is the sequence of the four kingdoms or of the four metals an end in itself. Even Hesiod, be-
moaning his birth in the evil fourth age, indicates that there
is a better age yet to come.[34] The schema always points beyond
the decline to a new beginning. In the political oracles, the
four kingdoms would be followed by a fifth, lasting kingdom.
Similarly in Dan 2:44 we are told that the god of heaven will
set up a kingdom which will never pass to another people.

If we can, for the moment, refrain from identifying this
kingdom with that received by "one like a son of man" in Daniel
7 and consider the passage in its own context as a dream interpretation at a Babylonian court, its implications may appear
quite different from what is usually assumed. The passage is
addressed to Nebuchadnezzar. The statement that the kingdom
will never pass to another people would most naturally be understood by Nebuchadnezzar to mean that this kingdom will belong to the Babylonian people. The fact that a kingdom is set
up by the god of heaven does not necessarily mean that it is a
Jewish kingdom. All the peoples of the ancient Near East believed that their kingdoms were set up by a god. The text nowhere suggests that this final kingdom is Jewish. If Nebuchadnezzar understood the final kingdom to be a reconstitution of
the Babylonian kingdom, his enthusiastic reaction to Daniel
becomes much more readily explicable.

Many of the problems which we noted in Daniel 2 can be
removed by supposing that the Jewish author of Daniel 2 took
over a Babylonian oracle which recalled Nebuchadnezzar as the
head of gold and looked to a future restoration of a Babylonian
kingdom by a god (presumably Marduk). The only element in the
vision and interpretation which seems inappropriate for a Babylonian is the stone which smashes not only the feet of the
statue (the Greek kingdom) but also the other metals, including
the golden Babylonian kingdom. To some extent the simultaneous
destruction of the metals is required by the imagery of the
statue--if the feet are crushed the whole statue falls. However, the fact that all the metals are destroyed is explicitly
emphasized in Daniel 2. It is surely easier to understand the
stone as the contribution of the Jewish redactor. We will discuss the significance of this redactional element below.

We can get an idea of the Babylonian oracle which is adapted in Daniel 2 by considering the first chapter of the Zand-ī Vohūman Yasn. There we read that Zarathustra in a dream saw a tree on which there were four branches, one of gold, one of silver, one of steel, and one of mixed iron. This dream is interpreted by Ahura Mazda. Each of the branches is identified with a kingdom. The fourth kingdom will coincide with the tenth generation and the end of a millenium. Then there will follow a new millenium, which is not symbolized in the dream. The statue which Nebuchadnezzar saw may originally have been analogous to the tree which Zarathustra saw. In both cases, the decline of history is visually represented but the future restoration is only implied.

The Jewish Redaction of Daniel 2

The original oracle underlying Daniel 2 could reasonably be described as a theology of history. It divided the course of the world into periods and looked for a final period of stability. This schematization of history is a prominent feature of Jewish apocalyptic but is not peculiar to it. Whether or not we posit a Babylonian oracle underlying Daniel 2, the same schematization can be found in the Zand-ī Vohūman Yasn and in the Roman authors. In all these passages we find a concern for the chronological development of history and the advent of a final kingdom.

The Jewish redactor of Daniel 2, however, was not primarily interested in the development of history or in predicting a messianic kingdom. The image of the stone which crushes the statue completely ignores the element of chronological sequence. H. L. Ginsberg has tried to reconcile Daniel 2 with historical chronology, but his effort is unconvincing. Ginsberg argues ingeniously that Daniel 2 was written at a time when Babylonian, Median, Persian and Greek kingdoms existed simultaneously.[35] The "residual" Median and Persian kingdoms consisted of the "more or less independent principalities" of Atropatene and Persis. The Babylonian kingdom was either that of Seleucus I between 307 and 301, or during the period 292-261, when

Seleucus I and Antiochus I in turn shared the royal title with
their sons and placed them in charge of their eastern dominions. Despite its ingenuity, Ginsberg's suggestion must be
considered unsuccessful. It is extremely doubtful that the
Seleucid regency of Babylon would be considered a Babylonian
kingdom by either Chaldean or Jew, and the "more or less independent principalities" similarly can not be realistically
equated with the world empires.

The destruction of the metals in Daniel 2 becomes more intelligible if we bear in mind the attitude of the Jewish redactor to statues and metals in the other tales. In Daniel 3,
Nebuchadnezzar sets up an "image of gold." The Jewish heroes
are prepared to die rather than worship it. In Daniel 5, Belshazzar comes to grief, because "you have praised the gods of
silver and gold, of bronze, iron, wood and stone" (5:23). It
is probable that the Jewish redactor in Dan 2:35 is thinking
not in terms of a series of kingdoms in chronological order,
but of a statue composed of the metals of idolatry. Therefore,
insofar as the redactor of Daniel 2 is interested in the content of the dream, he is concerned less with the future rule
of the world than with the transcendent power of God to destroy
all idols and the human kingdoms which worship them.

It is, of course, significant that the transcendent power
of God can be expressed in terms of a future kingdom. The
stone which becomes a mountain must have been understood by
Jews as a messianic kingdom.[36] However, no attempt is made to
describe this kingdom, beyond its sudden appearance and destruction of all other kingdoms. It is not the focus of interest.
The main emphasis of the dream and interpretation falls on the
destruction of idolatry. In the broader context of Daniel 2,
the dream and interpretation serve primarily to illustrate
Daniel's wisdom and the superior power of his God. Their content is of secondary importance.

In fact, the main emphasis of the dream, the transcendent
power of God to destroy all kingdoms, goes hand in hand with
his power to reveal all mysteries. Much light is cast on Daniel
2 by comparison with the oracles of Deutero-Isaiah, which also
have a Babylonian setting.[37] The astrologers and Chaldean wise

men are powerless. Specifically they are unable to foretell
the future, although that is their profession.[38] The reason is
that their idols have no power or wisdom, or (in Daniel) that
their gods live far away and are not accessible.[39] Yahweh is
able to reveal the future because he controls it. He "changes
times and seasons, he removes kings and sets up kings."[40] He
does not reveal mysteries to the Chaldean wise men, but only to
his servants. In Isa 44:25-26, it is Yahweh who "frustrates
the omens of liars, and makes fools of diviners; who turns wise
men back and makes their knowledge foolish; who confirms the
word of his servants." Dan 2:24-30 emphasizes that no Chaldean
wise man could tell the dream and that Daniel could not tell it
by his own power, but only by the revelation of his God. The
superiority of Daniel over the Babylonian wise men is the cor-
ollary of the superiority of his God, and consequently of the
transcendent power of his God over all kingdoms.

We have discussed Daniel 2 at some length because it is
the tale which has most obvious similarities to the apocalyptic
visions. It is also the only one of the tales which provides a
substantial clue to its date. Since the four kingdoms begin
with Babylon, the fourth must be the Greek. Therefore the
oracle cannot be earlier than Alexander. The mixture of iron
and clay in the feet of the statue is explained in 2:43: "so
they will mix with one another in marriage, but they will not
hold together." Now there were a number of occasions on which
members of the Seleucid and Ptolemaic houses intermarried. The
earliest of these was the marriage of Antiochus II and Berenice
in 252 B.C. This alliance did not last and Berenice's brother
Ptolemy III overran most of Syria and Babylonia in 246. Daniel
2 must be later than these events. There is nothing to indicate whether the allusion to intermarriage is redactional. If
we consider the reference to intermarriage to be part of the
oracle taken over by Daniel, then the Jewish redaction could
hardly be earlier than the last quarter of the third century.
As for the *terminus ante quem*, the chapter has no trace of an
allusion to Antiochus Epiphanes, who figures so prominently in
the adaptation of the four kingdoms schema in Daniel 7. Daniel
2 can be dated anywhere in the intervening period, say 240-170

B.C. The favourable picture of the king suggests that the tale
was written at a time when Jews enjoyed good relations with
their gentile rulers. Some of the other tales reflect rather
different situations but we can probably assume that all were
written within the same broad period of seventy years.

Daniel 2 is even more important for the picture it presents of Daniel as a wise man. First, he is explicitly associated with the Chaldean wise men. It is assumed that he performs the same type of services as the Chaldeans, specifically,
in this case, the interpretation of dreams. This role as wise
man could involve making prophecies about the course of history.
Second, and this is the point which is emphasized in Daniel 2,
Daniel's wisdom derives from the superiority of the god of the
Jews. Daniel may function as a Chaldean wise man, but his success ultimately rests on the rejection of the gods of his col-
leagues and his fidelity to his own. Naturally, this require-
ment could give rise to tension on occasion.

Daniel 4 and 5: The Critique of the Kings

Two other tales, Daniel 4 and 5, show us Daniel in the
role of a wise man at court.[41] Like Daniel 2, both these
stories use the form of a court contest. Daniel succeeds where
the Babylonian wise men have failed. In both these tales, the
emphasis falls on the content of Daniel's message rather than
on the demonstration of his wisdom. This is indicated in Daniel
4 by the fact that the narrative is told by the king. Consequently, interest centers on what happens to the king. The
tale ends with the restoration of Nebuchadnezzar, not with the
glorification of Daniel. In Daniel 5, the emphasis of the tale
is indicated by the manner in which Daniel recounts the story
of Nebuchadnezzar from ch. 4 before he interprets the writing
on the wall. Thereby he heightens suspense before giving his
interpretation. Again, the tale does not conclude with the exaltation of Daniel, but with the fulfillment of the prophecy--
the fall of Belshazzar to "Darius the Mede."

Despite this shift in emphasis, however, there is no essential difference between Daniel 2 and these chapters, either

in theology or in their presentation of the wise man. Both
tales illustrate the superior power of Daniel's God, and find
an example of that power in the superior wisdom of Daniel.
Daniel 4 and 5 differ from Daniel 2 primarily in their negative
appraisal of the gentile king. The different attitudes towards
the king may reflect different historical circumstances in
which the tales were composed.

Traditional Elements and Redaction in Daniel 4 and 5

　　Like Daniel 2, chs. 4 and 5 incorporate traditional material. As we have seen in our first chapter, the traditional
elements in Daniel 4 have now been illuminated by the Prayer of
Nabonidus (4QPrNab), from Qumran. While the differences between Daniel 4 and 4QPrNab are too great to allow for direct
literary influence, the two stories share a number of points:
(a) The king speaks in the first person.
(b) The king has a dream. Nabonidus was in fact noted for
　　 his interest in dreams.[42] The relevance, if any, of the
　　 dream in 4QPrNab to the rest of the story is not preserved.
(c) The king is afflicted for seven years (or, in Daniel 4,
　　 seven "times"). According to the Harran inscriptions,
　　 Nabonidus spent ten years in exile.[43]
(d) A Jewish interpreter plays a prominent role in both stor-
　　 ies. This element is found in 4QPrNab and is therefore not
　　 original in Daniel. It is not, of course, attested in the
　　 inscriptions of Nabonidus.
(e) The king's affliction is a punishment for idolatry. This
　　 again is a Jewish element. It should be noted, however,
　　 that the historical Nabonidus aroused the enmity of the
　　 priests of Marduk by his devotion to the moon-god Sin. The
　　 charge of idolatry may have developed from the king's un-
　　 orthodox piety.
　　Rudolf Meyer has argued convincingly that 4QPrNab and
Daniel 4 are mutually independent variants of a tradition which
originated with a confession of Nabonidus, similar to what we
find in the Harran inscriptions.[44] The use of the first person
in Daniel 4 and 4QPrNab would then derive from this original
confession.[45]

Neither 4QPrNab nor the inscriptions of Nabonidus make any contrast between successful and unsuccessful interpreters. Such a contrast is made in Daniel 4. Therefore some importance is attached to the superiority of Daniel's wisdom over that of his Chaldean rivals. As in Daniel 2, Daniel does not reject the practices of Chaldean wisdom. Like his rivals, he engages in dream interpretation, but he is more successful because of the greater power of his God.

The message of Daniel 4 is summarized neatly in Dan 4:34-35, where the king blesses the Most High God:

> for his dominion is an everlasting dominion, and his
> kingdom endures from generation to generation; all
> the inhabitants of the earth are accounted as nothing
> and he does according to his will in the host of
> heaven.

This message is essentially the same as what we find throughout Daniel 1-6, often expressed in poetic utterances of praise. We find similar hymnic passages in Dan 2:20-23, 4:3 and 6:26-27.[46] In each case, the omnipotence of the God of the Jews is proclaimed. The superior wisdom of Daniel is a manifestation of that omnipotence.

The difference between Daniel 4 and Daniel 2 lies neither in the portrayal of God nor in the role of the wise man, but in the presentation of the gentile king. Nebuchadnezzar in Daniel 2 was not subjected to criticism. In Daniel 4, however, Daniel confronts the king as Nathan confronted David in 2 Samuel 12, points out his sins and exhorts him to repent. The king is humiliated and reduced to a bestial state. The restoration of Nebuchadnezzar at the end of the chapter may be a traditional element, since the historical Nabonidus did in fact return to Babylon. The fact that such a conclusion is preserved, however, shows that the author of Daniel 4 had not despaired of good relations with his gentile rulers.

Daniel 4 makes explicit an aspect of Daniel's wisdom which was only potentially present in Daniel 2. The insistence of the Jews on the uniqueness and sovereignty of their God led inevitably to confrontation with gentile religion. This confrontation becomes more explicit in the tales of conflict.

Virtually the same remarks can be made about Daniel 5.
Here we cannot isolate a traditional story, although there may
well have been one. There is a tradition in the Greek histori-
ans that Cyrus entered Babylon during a festival "in which all
the Babylonians danced and revelled the whole night."[47] There
is no poetic praise of Yahweh to formulate the message of the
chapter, but the points at issue are clearly set out in Daniel's
denunciation of the king in vss. 17-23. Belshazzar is destroyed
because he failed to recognize the true God, practised idolatry
and violated the temple vessels. Again the tale insists on the
sovereignty of the God of the Jews.

Belshazzar is even more harshly treated than Nebuchadnezzar. He has no redeeming feature. He uses the holy vessels
blasphemously. He does not even acknowledge the god of Daniel
at the end. Rowley has interpreted this portrayal of Belshazzar as an allegory of Antiochus Epiphanes, noting especially
the profanation of the vessels.[48] While Belshazzar is a more
plausible allegory for Antiochus than either Nebuchadnezzar or
Darius, there is nothing in the text which requires this interpretation. The allusion to the vessels is natural in the context of the feast.

The negative appraisal of the kings in Daniel 4 and 5 reflects a situation of estrangement between Jews and their gentile rulers, though not necessarily persecution. The tensions
between Jewish and gentile religion have become more explicit
than they were in Daniel 2. However, there is no change in the
portrayal of the wise man in these chapters. Daniel performs
like any Chaldean wise man, only better. He engages in dream-
interpretation and deciphers mysterious writing. He differs
from his Chaldean rivals only in his fidelity to the God who is
the supreme source of wisdom. Daniel's wisdom goes hand in
hand with the superior power of that God.

Daniel 3 and 6: The Tales of Conflict

The tales in Daniel 3 and 6 belong to the second category,
the tales of conflict. They are less directly concerned with
the wisdom of the heroes, but present a drama of danger followed

by salvation.[49] They follow a pattern found in the Joseph story, Esther and Aḥikar:

1. The heroes are in a state of prosperity. Joseph is in charge of Pharaoh's household. Esther is queen and Mordecai is in attendance at court. Aḥikar is secretary to the king. Daniel's friends are in charge of the province of Babylon (3:12). Daniel is one of the three chief ministers and the king has it in mind to appoint him over the whole kingdom (6:1-3).

2. The heroes are endangered, usually because of a conspiracy. Joseph is falsely accused by Potiphar's wife. Mordecai and all the Jews are plotted against by Haman. Aḥikar is victim of a plot by Nadan, his nephew. In Dan 3:8-18 there is no conspiracy but the three youths are accused because they fail to worship the statue. In Dan 6:4-14 Daniel is victim of a conspiracy of the satraps.

3. The heroes are condemned to death or prison. Joseph is thrown into prison by Pharaoh. In Esth 3:13 an order is given to exterminate the Jews. In Aḥikar 4:4-6, Aḥikar is condemned to death. In Dan 3:19-23, the three friends are thrown into the fiery furnace. In Dan 6:16 Daniel is thrown into the lions' den.

4. The heroes are released, for various reasons. Joseph is released to interpret a dream. Aḥikar is spared by the executioner and then recalled to solve a problem at court. In Esther the Jews are saved by the intervention of the queen. Both the three young men in the furnace and Daniel in the lions' den are miraculously preserved.

5. Finally the wisdom/merit of the heroes is recognized and they are exalted to positions of honour. Joseph is appointed viceroy. Mordecai is put in charge of Haman's house. Aḥikar conducts a brilliantly successful mission to Egypt and is honoured in turn by Pharaoh and Sennacherib. In Daniel 3 the king promotes the three youths to positions of authority. In Daniel 6 the king issues a decree in honour of the God of Daniel and Daniel himself prospers.

By contrast with Aḥikar, Mordecai and Joseph, Daniel and his companions do not bring about their release and exaltation

by any action or skill of their own. They are rescued by a
purely miraculous intervention of God. Unlike Daniel 2, these
tales in no way display the wisdom or skill of the protagonist.
A further difference between Daniel and the tales of Joseph,
Esther and Aḥikar is that both Daniel and his friends are endangered for specifically religious causes.

In this respect, a contrast with Esther is instructive.
Like Daniel 1-6, Esther is set at a royal court in the eastern
Diaspora. Mordecai and Esther are ambitious and successful
Jews who rise to prominence in the court. We have seen already
that such success was possible for Jews on occasion. The story
of Esther and Mordecai is in many respects a fantasy of wish-
fulfillment, but it does not exceed the bounds of conceivable
possibility.

The aspirations of a Jew such as Mordecai conflicted
directly with those of professional courtiers such as Haman.
The crisis which develops is primarily a power-struggle. Mordecai refuses to bow to Haman. His motive can scarcely have
been religious. Elsewhere in the story Esther has no hesita-
tion about prostrating herself before the king, and feels no
religious scruples about being a member of the king's harem
or later his wife. Religious scruples could be suspended if
the occasion demanded. The confrontation between Mordecai and
Haman is a matter of professional rivalry. Mordecai's behav-
ior endangers all the Jews, not for theological or religious
reasons but because the Jews are a tightly-knit powerbloc who
hold themselves distinct from every other people. This was a
common charge against Jews in the Diaspora, and recurs later in
Alexandrian polemics.[50] The fact that the Jews were also a
distinct religion no doubt aggravated the problem, but it was
not the primary factor. Again, the solution in Esther does not
require an act of God, but simply political intrigue.

Daniel 6 is closer to Esther than is Daniel 3.[51] Daniel's
troubles are brought about by the envy of his professional rivals. The point at issue is Daniel's position of authority.
However, because Daniel is a pious wise man, and not a rather
unscrupulous politician like Mordecai, the trap which is laid
for him is of a religious nature. Therefore a conflict

develops between Daniel's religious duty and the royal decree.
It should be emphasized that in Daniel 6 the king is completely
sympathetic to Daniel. There can be no question of a religious
persecution, and no real analogy to Antiochus Epiphanes. The
question of religion only arises because this is the area in
which Daniel appears most vulnerable to his enemies.

The conflict of duties which Daniel now encounters could
be resolved in any of a number of ways. Daniel might have attempted some sort of compromise, or he might have at least
pleaded with the officials, as he does in Daniel 2, or as
Esther does. Daniel 6, however, definitely rules out any human
solution to the problem. The impossibility of compromise is
underlined by making the decree of the king irrevocable.

The conflict between royal decree and Jewish religion is
ultimately resolved. After the miraculous escape of Daniel and
his companions, the king acknowledges the God of the Jews and
decrees that he be revered. However, this resolution requires
a miracle, even though the king is well disposed throughout.

The tale reflects the problems which confronted the ambi-
tions of Jews at the royal court. The hopes of the Jews rested
on their God and so on their religious observance. Since their
religious observance differed from that of the king and other
officials, they could be vulnerable to their professional rivals on this point. There is no historical record that religious issues were used to block the success of Jews in the
Diaspora, but a tale such as Daniel 3 shows that the Jews were
keenly aware that the tension was always potentially there.

Daniel 3 is very similar to Daniel 6.[52] The main difference lies in the character of the king. Unlike Darius, who is
sympathetic to Daniel and his god throughout, Nebuchadnezzar
emerges as arrogant and hostile. He sets up an idol by his own
decision. When the youths refuse to worship it, he flies into
a rage. The hybris of the king is made explicit in his question "who is the god that will deliver you out of my hands?"[53]

H. H. Rowley has seen in the statue a reference to the
self-divinization of Antiochus Epiphanes.[54] However, the
statue should not be identified with the king. This is clear
from Dan 3:12, 14--"These men...do not serve your gods or

worship the golden image which you have set up." There are
plentiful examples of such statues in the ancient world. We
can compare the "great, golden statue of Zeus" which Herodotus
(1.183) saw in Babylon and three golden images which stood on
top of the Belus temple, one of which was forty feet high.[55]
Again, the ordeal of the three young men recalls the fate of
"Zedekiah and Ahab, whom the king of Babylon roasted in the
fire" (Jer 29:22). These parallels do not argue that Daniel 3
is historical, but they show that the elements of the story
need not have been invented as allegories for Antiochus Epiphanes and his times.

Montgomery is very probably right that Daniel 3 and 6,
like the other chapters, drew materials from old legends.
There is an interesting parallel between Daniel 3 and a passage
in the Hellenistic Jewish historian Eupolemus: "Then Jonachim
(Jehoiakim); in his time prophesied Jeremiah the prophet. He
was sent by God and found the Jews sacrificing to a golden
image, the name of which was Bel. And he showed to them the
calamity which was to come. Jonachim then attempted to burn
him alive."[56] The worship of the golden idol, linked to the
attempted burning of the dissenter, recurs in Daniel 3, but
with reference to a Babylonian king and different dissenters.
There is no need to posit direct influence between the tales.
Each picked up popular motifs. We should therefore reckon with
the presence of traditional elements in Daniel 3.

We have noted in our first chapter above that the story of
Daniel in the lions' den, which we find in *Bel and the Dragon*,
may be an independent variant of Daniel 6. If so, we should
probably take Daniel 6 as a redaction of a traditional story.
The favourable portrayal of Darius may reflect a recollection
of the generally good relations between Jews and Persians in
the time of Cyrus. The message of the final editor of the tale
is clearly set out in the poetic exclamation of Darius, which
proclaims that Daniel's God is "the living god," a savior, a
deliverer, and a worker of signs and wonders."

It is possible that the difference between Nebuchadnezzar
in Daniel 3 and Darius in Daniel 6 is due to the traditional
material underlying those chapters. Undoubtedly Nebuchadnezzar

had a much worse reputation in Jewish history than Darius.
However, it is also possible that the two stories reflect different stages in the relationship between Jews and gentiles,
and that Daniel 3 reflects the time of a hostile ruler. In any
case, the main point of both tales is to stress the transcendent power of the God of the Jews--whether the gentile king was
favorable or not. This transcendent power is exercised on behalf of the wise men who are faithful to God. Even though
these sages are aspiring to the role of Chaldean courtiers,
their wisdom is derived directly from God and depends on religious fidelity.

The Provenance of the Tales

　　Two features emerge clearly from the tales in Daniel 1-6.
Daniel is a wise man who engages in the same types of activity
as the Chaldeans--study of Chaldean letters, interpretation of
dreams, political prophecy, etc. Because of the strong elements of prediction and divination in this profession, we may
characterize Daniel as a practitioner of "mantic" wisdom. On
the other hand, he accepts no compromise with Babylonian or
other gentile religion. His very success as wise man depends
on his rigorous loyalty to his own God.

　　As the tales stand, they are woven together into a coherent unit. Daniel 2 presupposes the introduction of Daniel in
ch. 1, Daniel 5 presupposes the story of Nebuchadnezzar in ch.
4, and so forth. Since there are no redactional elements which
clearly refer to the persecution of Antiochus Epiphanes, it is
probable that the tales were already collected before they were
combined with Daniel 7-12. We must inquire, then, into the
provenance of this collection of tales.

　　While such tales could obviously be told for entertain-
ment, they are also clearly intended to edify and to provide
models of a Jewish lifestyle. The terms of the edification,
the characteristics presented as models, are significant for
the question of provenance. The tales not only assert the
superiority of Judaism over gentile religions, they also endorse in large part the function and interests of the Chaldean

wise man. Daniel and his companions must be understood to embody the values of the authors of the tales.

There is wide agreement among scholars that the tales originated in the Eastern Diaspora.[57] While this thesis cannot be conclusively proved, it carries a strong weight of probability. There is no apparent reason why a Jew in Palestine should either compose or collect a set of tales all of which are set in Babylon, and whose hero functions like a Chaldean wise man. Such tales would be much more clearly relevant to Jews in the Diaspora, especially to those who functioned or aspired to function in any capacity at a gentile court.[58] This holds not only for the individual tales but also for the collection. The idealization of Chaldean wisdom (subject to the God of the Jews) reflects a strong interest in this way of life.

The interest in Chaldean wisdom must have been shared by the final Maccabean editor of the book, since he uses the tales to establish the identity of the visionary, and since the martyrs in ch. 11 are described, like Daniel and his friends, as *maskîlîm*. Now it is widely agreed that the apocalyptic visions of Daniel originated in the circles of these *maskîlîm*. These in turn are usually identified with the *Ḥasîdîm*, a rather nebulous group, of which we have little clear knowledge.[59] The most detailed attempt to describe this group is that of Viktor Tcherikover.[60] According to Tcherikover, the *Ḥasîdîm* were the "chief scribes and authoritative interpreters of the regulations and commandments of the Torah."[61] The best example we have of this scribal class in the early second century B.C. is Ben Sira. Tcherikover does not say that Ben Sira was one of the *Ḥasîdîm*, but he does treat him as the main representative of a scribal class sympathetic to Simon the Just, and he associates Simon with the origins of the *Ḥasîdîm*.[62] Tcherikover's attribution of Daniel to this scribal class might seem to support the broader thesis of Gerhard von Rad, that apocalyptic was an outgrowth of wisdom. Von Rad particularly emphasizes affinities between apocalyptic writings and Ben Sira.[63]

Yet it is impossible to associate Daniel with wisdom circles of the type represented by Ben Sira. The incongruity of such a pairing is obvious if we consider that sage's attitude

to divination and dream-interpretation--the "mantic" wisdom
practiced by Daniel:

> As one who catches at a shadow and pursues the wind,
> so is he who gives heed to dreams.
> The vision of dreams is this against that,
> the likeness of a face confronting a face....
> Divinations and omens and dreams are folly,
> and like a woman in travail the mind has fancies.
> Unless they are sent from the Most High as a visita-
> tion
> do not give your mind to them.
> For dreams have deceived many
> and those who put their hope in them have failed.
> Without such deceptions the law is fulfilled.[64]

Despite Ben Sira's allowance that dreams can be sent "as a
visitation from the Most High," he evidently does not think
that they usually are. There is a huge gulf between this attitude to divination and what we find in Daniel 1-6. Yet the
mantic, Chaldean wisdom of Daniel is one of the major elements
in the tales.

The nature of the *maskîlîm* in Daniel has been clouded by
the ambiguity of the category wisdom, and in particular by the
failure of von Rad to make two basic distinctions:

(a) The distinction between proverbial wisdom and mantic
wisdom: Proverbial wisdom, which constitutes most of the books
of Proverbs and Ben Sira leaves very little trace in the
apocalyptic writings, especially in Daniel.[65] Mantic wisdom
on the other hand is the wisdom practiced by Daniel which enables him to interpret dreams and read the writing on the wall.
This type of revelatory wisdom is clearly of the utmost importance for apocalyptic. We should note that the word used for
dream interpretation in Daniel is *pesher*. The same word is
used for the interpretation of scripture at Qumran.[66] If we
understand the domain of mantic wisdom to extend to the interpretation of scripture, then it includes, in effect, all the
major media of revelation in apocalyptic. However, mantic wisdom is in many respects closer to OT prophecy than to proverbial wisdom. A political oracle such as we find in Daniel 2,
or a critique of kings such as Daniel 4 or 5, has closer affinities with the prophetic books than with Proverbs or Ben
Sira.

(b) A distinction must also be made between the traditions
which provide the content of apocalyptic and the function or
profession of the carriers of apocalyptic. The traditions
found in apocalyptic passages such as Daniel 7-12 are drawn
from many sources, but predominantly from OT prophecy and
Canaanite myth, and scarcely at all from OT wisdom.[67] On the
other hand, at least in the circles which produced Daniel, the
carriers of the tradition saw themselves as "wise men" rather
than as prophets. We should emphasize that the learning of
wise men, both in Palestine and in the Diaspora, was far more
extensive than what appears in the collections of proverbs.
Daniel and his companions were educated in "the letters and
language of the Chaldeans" (1:4), including, presumably, the
ancient myths. Berossus was certainly well versed in mythology.
Even Ben Sira's ideal scribe was broadly interested in "the
wisdom of all the ancients" and "concerned with prophecies"
(Sir 39:1). Accordingly, even if the visions of Daniel were
written by "wise men" it does not follow that the material in
those visions is related to the contents of the OT wisdom books.

The *maskîlîm* of Daniel have little in common with the
scribes of Ben Sira's type. It is reasonable to assume that
Daniel originated in the circles of *maskîlîm*, but this group
cannot be identified with the chief scribes and authoritative
interpreters of the Torah.[68]

Where, then, in Palestine, at the time of Antiochus Epiphanes, might we locate a group of *maskîlîm* whose ideal of
wisdom was mantic rather than proverbial and legal? Obviously,
any answer to this question must be hypothetical. Such a group
may simply have emerged in response to the situation and otherwise not be identifiable.

It is, however, striking that the *maskîlîm* formulated
their ideal of mantic wisdom by using a collection of tales set
in the Diaspora. If we are correct that the tales originated
in the eastern Diaspora, they must at some point have been
brought back to Palestine. It seems reasonable to hypothesize
that the people who brought back the tales from Babylon were
related to the *maskîlîm* of ch. 11--perhaps their immediate ancestors, perhaps even identical with them. The Maccabean

visionaries would then have used the court-tales because they were traditional material cherished by their group, giving expression to their self-identity or aspirations. Various scholars have, for various reasons, posited a migration of Jews from the eastern Diaspora to Palestine in the early second century B.C.[69] The *maskîlîm* of Daniel (or their immediate ancestors) may well have been part of such a migration.

This is not to suggest that apocalyptic as found in Daniel 7-12 was an import foreign to Judaism.[70] The identity of the group which produced Daniel does not necessarily tell us anything about the religio-historical origins of the material found in the visions. There is no reason to doubt that the authors of Daniel 1-6 were learned in Israelite as well as Babylonian traditions. The model of the wise man used in the tales was international and had a biblical precedent in Joseph. The fact that the stories of Daniel and his friends were brought back from the Diaspora in no way diminishes their relevance for the Jewish tradition.

No suggestion on the historical or geographical provenance of Daniel 1-6 can ultimately be more than hypothetical. Fortunately, the provenance of the tales is not of great importance for the book of Daniel. Of far greater significance is the model of wisdom presented in these chapters, which has a profound influence on the apocalyptic visions of Daniel 7-12. This wisdom was based on a resolute adherence to Jewish religion and rejection of other gods. However, it endorsed the mantic character of Chaldean wisdom, with its interest in the interpretation of mysterious dreams and signs. The model of wisdom found in the tales is adapted in certain respects in Daniel 7-12, as we shall see. Yet the main characteristics of the wise man formulated in chs. 1-6 will throw much light on the apocalyptic visions. These visions are products of a learned wisdom which is especially interested in the interpretation of mysteries, while uncompromising in its affirmation of the sovereignty of the God of the Jews. The interest in the interpretation of mysteries is related to the particular form in which the visions are presented. The affirmation of the sovereignty of God leads to confrontation with the Seleucid

king Antiochus Epiphanes, and gives the book of Daniel its
strongly political character.

NOTES

CHAPTER II

[1]An Aramaic version of the tale of Aḥikar from Elephantine is available in A. E. Cowley, *Aramaic Papyri from the Fifth Century B.C.*(Oxford: Clarendon, 1923) 204-50. English translations in *APOT*, 2.715-84 and *ANET*, 427-30.

[2]See G. R. Driver, *Semitic Writing* (London: British Academy, 1948) 66.

[3]Pliny, *Natural History*, 6.30; cf. Strabo 16.1; Montgomery, *Daniel*, 120.

[4]P. Schnabel, *Berossos und die babylonisch-hellenistische Literatur* (Leipzig: Teubner, 1923); F. Jacoby, *Die Fragmente der Griechischen Historiker*, 3.C (Leiden: Brill, 1958) 364-97.

[5]A. Leo Oppenheim, "The Interpretation of Dreams in the Ancient Near East," *Transactions of the American Philosophical Society* 46 (1956) 221.

[6]Cf. Delcor, *Daniel*, 109.

[7]On the Chaldeans, see further, H. Ludin Jansen, *Die Henochgestalt* (Skrifter utgitt av Det Norske Videnskaps-Akademi i Oslo II. Hist.-Filos. Klasse. 1; Oslo: Dybwad, 1939) 13-21.

[8]Cf. Oppenheim, "Dreams," 237-44. Also S. K. Eddy, *The King is Dead* (Lincoln: University of Nebraska, 1961) 65-71 (on the Magi). For examples of Mesopotamian prophecies, see A. Grayson and W. G. Lambert, "Akkadian Prophecies," *JCS* 18 (1964) 7-30.

[9]Isa 47:13. Cf. 44:25-26.

[10]Montgomery, *Daniel*, 137.

[11]Contrast the thesis of W. Lee Humphreys, "A Life-Style for the Diaspora: A Study of the Tales of Esther and Daniel," *JBL* 92 (1973) 211-23: "One could, as a Jew, overcome adversity and find a life both rewarding and creative within the pagan setting." See further J. J. Collins, "The Court-Tales in Daniel and the Development of Apocalyptic," *JBL* 94 (1975) 218-34.

[12]See L. A. Rosenthal, "Die Josephgeschichte mit den Büchern Ester und Daniel verglichen," *ZAW* 15 (1895) 278-85; S. Talmon, "'Wisdom' in the Book of Esther," *VT* 13 (1963) 419-55; Humphreys, "Life-Style," 217.

[13] S. R. K. Glanville, *The Instructions of 'Onksheshonqy* (Catalogue of Demotic Papyri in the British Museum 2; London: British Museum, 1955).

[14] For such a review, see D. B. Redford, *A Study of the Biblical Story of Joseph* (VTSup 20; Leiden: Brill, 1970) 94-97.

[15] Following Humphreys, "Life-Style," 217-20.

[16] See Oppenheim, "Dreams," 202-5.

[17] Josephus, *Ant.*, 11.8, 5(333-35).

[18] Eddy, *The King is Dead*, 288-89.

[19] H. Windisch, *Die Orakel des Hystaspes* (Verhandelingen der Koninklijke Akademie van Wetenschappen te Amsterdam, Afdeeling Letterkunde, Nieuwe Reeks, Deel 28/3; Amsterdam: Koninklijke Akademie van Wetenschappen, 1929) 46-49.

[20] Ibid., 46.

[21] See *ANEP*, 166. Delcor (*Daniel*, 79) notes an Orphic poem which uses the parts of a statue as allegories for parts of the world. Cf. also Marneptah's dream of a statue of Ptah (Montgomery, *Daniel*, 140).

[22] Montgomery, *Daniel*, 140.

[23] The most thorough discussion of the four kingdoms is that of D. Flusser, "The four empires in the Fourth Sibyl and in the Book of Daniel," *Israel Oriental Studies* 2 (1972) 148-75. See also M. Hengel, *Judaism and Hellenism* 1 (Philadelphia: Fortress, 1974) 181-83.

[24] See J. W. Swain, "The Theory of the Four Monarchies: Opposition History under the Roman Empire," *Classical Philology* 35 (1940) 1-21. Swain's translation is followed here.

[25] The pattern recurs frequently in later historiography. See Tacitus, *Histories*, 5.8-9; Dionysius of Halicarnassus 1.2.1-4; Appianus, *Roman History*, introduction; Polybius, *Histories*, 38.22.1-3. Not all Romans who used the schema thought of Rome as an eternal eschatological kingdom. Polybius reports that Scipio, reflecting on the fall of Carthage, said that Rome too would one day pass like the other kingdoms.

[26] See J. J. Collins, "The Place of the Fourth Sibyl in the Development of the Jewish Sibyllina," *JJS* 25 (1974) 365-80.

[27] See idem, *The Sibylline Oracles of Egyptian Judaism* (SBLDS 13; Missoula: Scholars' Press, 1974) 9-12. The translation followed is that of B. T. Anklesaria, *Zand-ī Vohūman Yasn and Two Pahlevi Fragments* (Bombay: published privately, 1957).

[28] Eddy, *The King is Dead*, 19.

[29]The antiquity of the Zand-Ī Vohūman Yasn is further defended by Eddy (ibid., 17-19) on the basis of parallels with the Oracle of Hystaspes, and by Flusser ("The four empires," 166-67) who reconstructs the Avestan text by comparing the Zand with Denkard 9. 8.

[30]See especially Swain, "Four Monarchies," 1-21.

[31]The sequence of Assyria, Media and Persia is attested already by Herodotus (1.95,30) and Ctesias (Diodorus Siculus, 2.1-34). However, the adaptation of this sequence for political oracles is most likely to have taken place in a land which had been ruled by the Medes, but not by the Babylonians.

[32]Cf. E. Haag, *Studien zum Buche Iudith* (Trier: Paulinus, 1963) 9-10.

[33]Josephus, *AgAp* 1.19(132-44). See Eddy, *The King is Dead*, 125-27. On the recollection of Babylonian and Egyptian monarchs in Hellenistic times, see M. Braun, *History and Romance* (Oxford: Blackwell, 1938) passim.

[34]Hesiod, *Works and Days*, 175-77: "Would that I were not among the men of the fifth generation, but had either died or been born afterward."

[35]Ginsberg, *Studies in Daniel*, 6-7.

[36]For the stone or rock as a motif in the OT, see E. F. Siegman, "The Stone Hewn from the Mountain (Daniel 2)," *CBQ* 18 (1956) 364-79.

[37]See P. von der Osten-Sacken, *Die Apokalyptik in ihrem Verhältnis zu Prophetie und Weisheit* (Theologische Existenz Heute, 157; Munich: Kaiser, 1969) 18-27.

[38]Isa 47:13, 44:25; Dan 2:27.

[39]Isa 44:8-20, Dan 2:11.

[40]Dan 2:20-21, Isa 40:23-24. In Isa 40:24, the kings are blown away like chaff. The metals suffer the same fate in Dan 2:35.

[41]The first of these tales extends from Dan 3:31 to 4:34 in the Masoretic text, but in the *RSV* it is given as 4:1-37-- i.e., it coincides with ch. 4. For convenience, the *RSV* numbering is followed here.

[42]Oppenheim, "Dreams," 202-5.

[43]C. J. Gadd, "The Harran Inscriptions of Nabonidus," *Anatolian Studies* 8 (1958) 88.

[44]Meyer, *Gebet*, 53-67. On the relevance of Nabonidus for Daniel 4, see further, W. Dommershausen, *Nabonid im Buche Daniel* (Mainz: Grünewald, 1964).

64

[45]Daniel 4 may, of course, contain traditional imagery
which is unrelated to Nabonidus. So, for example, the great
tree in the dream is a traditional motif. For Babylonian parallels to the tree, see Meyer, *Gebet*, 42-51. For OT parallels,
see L. F. Hartman, "The Great Tree and Nebuchodonosor's Madness," *The Bible in Current Catholic Thought* (ed. J. L.
McKenzie; New York: Herder, 1962) 75-82.

[46]See W. S. Towner, "The Poetic Passages of Daniel 1-6,"
CBQ 31 (1969) 317-26.

[47]Xenophon, *Cyropaedia*, 7.5. Also Herodotus, 1.191. On
the historical Belshazzar, see R. P. Dougherty, *Nabonidus and
Belshazzar* (Yale Oriental Series 15; New Haven: Yale, 1929);
Dommershausen, *Nabonid*, 31-36.

[48]Rowley, "Unity," 265. Cf. 1 Macc 1:21-23, where Antiochus removes the vessels from the temple.

[49]This type of court-tale is analyzed by G. W. E. Nickelsburg, *Resurrection, Immortality and Eternal Life* (HTS 26; Cambridge: Harvard, 1972) 48-58.

[50]Esth 3:8. Cf. Josephus, *AgAp* 2.6(66), 2.10(121-22).

[51]On Daniel 6, see A. Bentzen, "Daniel 6: Ein Versuch zur
Vorgeschichte der Märtyrerlegende," *Festschrift Alfred Bertholet*
(Tübingen: Mohr, 1950) 58-64.

[52]On Daniel 3, see C. Kuhl, *Die Drei Männer im Feuer*
(BZAW 55; Giessen: Töpelmann, 1930).

[53]Dan 3:15. Cf. the king of Assyria in Isa 36:15-17; 2
Kgs 19:21-23.

[54]Rowley, "Unity," 265.

[55]Diodorus Siculus, 2.9. See further, Montgomery, *Daniel*,
194.

[56]Eusebius, *Praeparatio Evangelica* 9.39. Trans. Montgomery, *Daniel*, 194.

[57]See most recently, Humphreys, "Life-Style," 221-22.

[58]Such a court is not necessarily located in Babylon.
Both the Persian and Seleucid empires administered their territories through satraps who seem to have functioned like kings
in their own territories. There were, then, a number of such
court settings. See F. E. Peters, *The Harvest of Hellenism*
(New York: Simon and Schuster, 1970) 227-28.

[59]See the discussion of Hengel, *Judaism and Hellenism* 1.
175-80.

[60] V. Tcherikover, *Hellenistic Civilization and the Jews* (New York: Atheneum, 1970) 125-26, 196-98 (reprint of 1st ed. by the Jewish Publication Society, 1959).

[61] Ibid., 197. Few scholars venture such a specific definition of the Ḥasîdîm, but most agree that they were a scribal group.

[62] Ibid., 125.

[63] G. von Rad, *Theologie des Alten Testaments* (4th ed.; Munich: Kaiser, 1965) 2. 315-37. See the important critique by H.-P. Müller, "Mantische Weisheit und Apokalyptik," VTSup 22 (Leiden: Brill, 1972) 268-93; Collins, "Court-tales," 232.

[64] Sir 31:1-8 (34:1-8). Also 40:5-7. See E. L. Ehrlich, *Der Traum im Alten Testament* (BZAW 73; Berlin: de Gruyter, 1953) 164-67.

[65] See von der Osten-Sacken, *Die Apokalyptik*, passim.

[66] See A. Szörenyi, "Das Buch Daniel, ein kanonisierter *pescher?*" VTSup 15 (Leiden: Brill, 1966) 278-94; A. Finkel, "The pesher of dreams and scriptures," *RevQ* 4 (1963) 357-70.

[67] See especially the programmatic essay of F. M. Cross, "New Directions in the Study of Apocalyptic," *Apocalypticism* (R. W. Funk, ed.; *JTC* 6 [1969]) 157-65, and in greater detail P. D. Hanson, *The Dawn of Apocalyptic* (Philadelphia: Fortress, 1975) passim. The continuity with prophecy is also stressed by H. H. Rowley, *The Relevance of Apocalyptic* (New York: Association, 1964) 13-53 and O. Plöger, *Theocracy and Eschatology* (Richmond, VA: John Knox, 1968).

[68] The relation between the *maskîlîm* of Daniel and the Ḥasîdîm will be discussed below in Chapter VII.

[69] D. N. Freedman, "The Prayer of Nabonidus," *BASOR* 145 (1957) 31-32, argued that the presence of 4QPrNab at Qumran, with its echoes of Babylonian traditions, supported such a migration.

[70] So, for example, M. Buber, *Kampf um Israel: Reden und Schriften* (Berlin: Schocken, 1933) 59-60. See the critique of P. D. Hanson, "Jewish Apocalyptic against its Near Eastern Environment," *RB* 78 (1971) 31-58.

CHAPTER III

THE MEDIA OF REVELATION

The court-tales of chs. 1-6 present Daniel and his companions as wise men after the manner of the Chaldeans, who are
successful because of their fidelity to their God. These chapters are anonymous tales which refer to Daniel in the third
person. In chs. 7-12 Daniel presents his visions in the first
person. In these later chapters, emphasis is transferred from
the example of Daniel to the content of the revelation. At the
same time, the visions are put in a context by which they are
related to the wisdom of Daniel presented in the tales.

The Phenomenon of Pseudepigraphy

The pseudonymous attribution of writings to ancient figures is a standard feature of Jewish apocalyptic. It was not,
however, peculiar to apocalyptic, nor even to Judaism, but was
found all over the Hellenistic-Roman world, in poetry, epis-
tolography, testaments, philosophy and oracles.[1] Quite a
variety of motives may have given rise to it in its various
settings. The fact that the phenomenon was so widespread
should warn us that it cannot be fully explained within the
context of Judaism alone.

A number of explanations for the use of pseudepigraphy in
apocalyptic writings have been proposed, with varying degrees
of plausibility. Occasionally scholars have suggested that
pseudonymity was merely a device to conceal the identity of the
true author and avoid retaliation by the authorities.[2] Such an
explanation does not attempt to account for the general popularity of pseudepigraphy in the Hellenistic age, but only for
its use in writings which have political import. However, even
within the range of political prophecy, and within Judaism, we
find pseudepigraphic writings where fear of retaliation can not
have been a factor. The third Sibylline Oracle, which was composed by an Egyptian Jew in the mid-second century B.C., expected a messianic king from the Ptolemaic line.[3] Its author
had scarcely any reason to fear retaliation from the Ptolemies

67

for such a prediction. Yet he attributed his oracle to the
ancient Sibyl. Pseudepigraphy in political oracles can not,
then, be adequately explained as a disguise motivated by fear.
Further, many Jewish apocalyptic writings, notably Daniel (chs.
11-12) and the Testament of Moses (chs. 9-10) place a very high
value on martyrdom. It would be strangely inappropriate if an
author who explicitly advocated martyrdom had recourse to
pseudonymity lest he become a martyr himself.[4]

A more widely accepted scholarly theory relates the phenomenon of pseudonymity to the decline of prophecy. There are
a number of indications that prophecy declined in prestige
after the Persian period. The classical Hebrew term for prophet, $n\bar{a}b\hat{\imath}$', is not used for any figure after Malachi. The
changing attitude towards prophecy is shown clearly in an oracle of the Persian period, Zech 13:2-6:

> I will remove from the land the prophets and the
> unclean spirit. And if anyone again appears as a
> prophet, his father and mother who bore him will
> say to him, "you shall not live, for you speak
> lies in the name of the Lord"....On that day every
> prophet will be ashamed of his vision when he
> prophesies.

The situation envisaged in the oracle is not the absolute ces-
sation of prophecy, but its rejection as a medium of revelation.
Later Judaism would close the canon with the Persian period.[5]
So Josephus wrote:

> From the death of Moses, until Artaxerxes who suc-
> ceeded Xerxes as king of Persia, the prophets subse-
> quent to Moses wrote the history of the events of
> their own times in thirteen books. (*AgAp* 1.8[41])

A number of passages in 1 Maccabees reflect the belief that
prophecy had ceased. In 1 Macc 9:27 we read that "there was
great distress in Israel such as had not been since the time
the prophets ceased to appear among them."[6] Evidently, then,
authoritative prophecy was widely thought to belong to a bygone age. There might yet be seers and visionaries who uttered
oracles, but they were not accorded the same status as the
classical prophets. Accordingly, these later visionaries might
hesitate to speak out in their own name because prophecy was no
longer accepted as an authoritative medium.

The force of this deterrent is not diminished by the fact that we actually know of some people who behaved as prophets during this period.[7] These included the Essene seers, Judas, Menahem and Simon, whose prophecy consisted of making specific predictions.[8] There were also others of a more classical mould. We read in Josephus of a group of Pharisees who opposed king Herod. They claimed to have knowledge of future events and they foretold that Herod's throne would be taken away. Their leaders were put to death for their opposition to the king.[9] It is striking that Josephus never uses the term *prophētēs* for these individuals, but reserves it for the canonical prophets. The seers and prophets of the Hellenistic period are *manteis*, a term never applied to the canonical prophets.[10] Even Josephus' own prophecy to Vespasian is described as *manteia* in *JW* 4.10.7(625).[11] The distinction in terminology reflects a difference in prestige and authority. Most of the seers reported by Josephus appear to have been less concerned with ethical preaching than the classical prophets, but there is none the less considerable similarity between them. The similarity is particularly striking in the case of an eschatological prophet such as John the Baptist.[12] However, the decline in the authority of prophecy was probably sufficient to have some deterring effect on aspiring prophets.

Some scholars, notably R. H. Charles, have seen in the decline of prophecy the main reason for the popularity of pseudepigraphy. Charles believed that not only was prophecy dead in the Hellenistic period, but the law was so supreme that new revelation was impossible. So "all Jewish apocalypses, therefore, from 200 BC onwards, were of necessity pseudonymous if they sought to exercise any real influence on the nation."[13]

The fact that prophecy was so widely associated with a bygone age may well have been a factor in the popularity of pseudonymous writings. However, the decline of prophecy alone is not an adequate explanation. Other examples of pseudonymous oracles, which have much in common with Jewish apocalyptic, are found outside Judaism. Notable examples are the Egyptian Demotic Chronicle, which was composed in the Ptolemaic period, but claimed to be written in the time of the Pharaoh Tachos

(362-361 B.C.), and the Persian Oracle of Hystaspes.[14] Gentiles, Jews and Christians alike attributed oracles pseudonymously to the sibyl over a span of several centuries.[15] The gentile oracles were not influenced by any ideas of a canon of revelation, or by the decline of Hebrew prophecy! Further, if Charles were right that Judaism was so utterly dominated by the Law that no other means of revelation was recognized, we should expect that apocalyptic would explicitly claim to be an exegesis or midrash on the canonical scripture as there would be no other source of valid inspiration. This, however, is not the case. Interpretation of the law and the prophets was certainly important in the intertestamental period, but it was never the sole means of revelation. Visionaries such as Daniel could also lay claim to revelations which were not in any sense contained in the Torah or earlier prophets. The use of pseudepigraphy in Jewish apocalyptic can not be explained as a necessity imposed on the author by external circumstances, either the political danger of repression or the supposed theological monopoly of the law. It must have been more directly related to the purpose and nature of this type of writing.

The most obvious reason why any writing should be attributed to a famous or legendary ancient figure is that the name of that figure would enhance the prestige of the work. A book which bore the name of Moses or Daniel would carry more authority than the undisguised composition of some unknown Jew. The decline of prophecy was one factor which would cause a writer of the Hellenistic age to use such an authoritative pseudonym. However, as we have seen, pseudepigraphy was also practiced outside of Judaism, so the decline of prophecy can not have been the only factor.

In the case of writings which are concerned with politics or historical events, the use of pseudepigraphy is also bound up with a certain view of history. It provides an occasion for a *vaticinium ex eventu*, or a prophecy after the fact. If a prophecy written in the second century B.C. is attributed to Daniel, who lived during the Babylonian exile, then the events "foretold" by Daniel can include the history of the post-exilic period, prior to the second century. Such a *vaticinium ex eventu* could serve two purposes for the author:

(a) It served to guarantee the accuracy of the predictions. If all the events down to the time of the reader were
accurately predicted, there was reason to believe that the eschatological prophecy was reliable too.

(b) It conveyed a sense of determinism. If the subsequent
course of history could be predicted by Daniel, during the
exile, or by Enoch, before the flood, then these historical
events must have been already determined in the time of these
seers. Also, the eschatological prophecy is reliable because
those events are pre-determined too. The sense of determinism
is often accentuated by dividing history into a set number of
periods--4, 7, 10 or 12. If a given number of these periods
has already elapsed, we can easily locate ourselves in the
march of world history. Such periodization is illustrated by
the seventy weeks of years in Daniel 9. We will return in
Chapter VI below to examine the view of history in Daniel in
greater detail. For the present, we note that one of the purposes of pseudepigraphy in a writing such as Daniel is to convey a sense of determinism.

Pseudepigraphy, then, is a device to augment the prestige
of a work by relating it to a famous name. It also provides
the occasion for a *vaticinium ex eventu* which confirms the
reliability of the prophecy, and implies a deterministic view
of history.

The Psychology of Pseudepigraphy

A number of scholars have attempted to explain the use of
pseudepigraphy by the supposed psychology of the visionary.[16]
The apocalyptic author is assumed to have felt a sense of psychological identification with his pseudonymous hero. Such an
approach might explain not only why an author used pseudepigraphy at all, but why he selected a particular pseudonym.

Since we have really no evidence about the visionary's
state of mind, it is quite impossible to verify this theory.
Yet it should not be excluded from consideration. The visionary lays claim to revelations which are not necessarily derived
from scriptures or earlier traditions. Presumably, then, he is

conscious of being the immediate recipient of revelation. Yet
he attributes it to a legendary or traditional hero. It is at
least possible that the experience of receiving revelation involved simultaneously a sense of identity with a prophet, seer
or wise man of the past.

The precise nature of this "sense of identity" is difficult to establish. D. S. Russell apparently thinks of a
quasi-mystical feeling of union, and appeals to the alleged
Hebrew ideas of "corporate personality" (expounded by H.
Wheeler Robinson) and "contemporaneity" (proposed by Thorlief
Boman).[17] By "corporate personality," the apocalyptic writers
could "rightly regard themselves as not original writers at
all, but simply as inheritors and interpreters of what, under
divine inspiration, they had already received."[18] By "contemporaneity," two events could be so alike in their "psychological contents" that they could be readily equated in the writer's mind.[19] Both the ideas of corporate personality and of
contemporaneity, however, have been sharply and effectively
criticized.[20] Insofar as these theories try to reconstruct the
state of mind of the ancient authors, they go beyond the available evidence. We simply do not know whether the Jewish visionary of Maccabean times really believed he was mystically
identical with the wise man of the exile.

We can, however, speak of identification in a less psychological sense. It seems clear that the apocalyptic writers
felt they could validly attribute their visions to their
pseudonymous authors, and that the attribution was appropriate
and justified. They must also have accepted their pseudonymous
authors as models who adequately represented their own values
and ideas. They "identified" with these ancient figures insofar as they claimed that there was a basic similarity between
them. We must assume that the pseudonymous author was deliberately chosen because he was particularly appropriate for the
real author's purpose. His name must have added to the effec-
tiveness of the work, not only because of his authority, but
also because of the values and ideas associated with it.
Whether "identification" in this sense carried any emotional
sense of mystic union or not we cannot say.

Such an identification of the visionary with his pseudonymous hero appears particularly plausible in the case of Daniel.
As we have seen, the tales, narrated in the third person, establish the identity of Daniel, who is then presented as the
visionary of chs. 7-12. The identification is based in part
on the similarity of the author's situation to that of Daniel,
more directly on their common role as wise men, practitioners
of mantic wisdom and recipients of revelation. The visionary
thus recalled and endorsed the example of Daniel and presented
him as a model both in his conduct and in his wisdom.

One other consideration mentioned by Russell can help to
throw light on the problem.[21] Pseudepigraphy may have served
to indicate continuity with a tradition. Already in the Pentateuch we find the book of Deuteronomy ascribed, pseudonymously,
to Moses. Since the contents of Deuteronomy had been handed on
in a tradition, probably oral, for a long time, people may well
have believed that the tradition went back to Moses, and so he
could realistically be said to be the author of the book. Additions could be made to the tradition if they were faithful to
the spirit of Moses. Similarly people continued to write
Psalms of David, and ascribe wisdom books to Solomon, and some
post-exilic prophecies could be attributed to Isaiah. Now the
visions of Daniel were not traditional material in the sense
that their ultimate origin might be in doubt, as was the case
with some Pentateuchal laws. However, if we are right that the
court-tales of Daniel were traditional material cherished by a
particular group, then the author of the visions may well have
felt that he was validly continuing the Danielic tradition.
Such a sense of continuity with tradition is highly compatible
with the suggestion that the visionary endorsed the example of
Daniel as a wise man.

It appears, then, that various factors influenced the use
of pseudepigraphy in Daniel. The recourse to pseudepigraphy
was due in some part to the desire to enhance the visions with
the reputation of a famous name, and to provide an occasion for
ex eventu prophecy with the view of history which it implied.
The choice of Daniel in particular was motivated by the author's

sense of affinity with Daniel as a wise man, and by the sense
that he was continuing a Danielic tradition.

The question remains whether pseudepigraphy was a conscious
convention or whether the readers, or even the authors, believed
that the book was written by Daniel during the exile. We have
no hard evidence which would permit a definitive answer to this
question. On the one hand, since the phenomenon was so widespread, in both Jewish and gentile circles, it must have been
recognized as a convention, at least by some people. On the
other hand, it is hard to see how pseudepigraphy could have
served any purpose if everyone knew that it was a fiction.

We should probably distinguish between the attitude of the
authors and their readers. In Daniel 11, a clear distinction
is made between the wise $mask\hat{\imath}l\hat{\imath}m$ and the common people, the
$rabb\hat{\imath}m$. We have seen that the author of Daniel was almost certainly one of the $mask\hat{\imath}l\hat{\imath}m$. The members of that enlightened
group can hardly have been unaware of the real authorship of
the visions. The $rabb\hat{\imath}m$, however, may well have been credu-
lous. People are found to this day who accept the authorship
of the book of Daniel by a prophet during the exile. The popularity of pseudepigraphic writing in antiquity suggests that
there were many people then, too, who accepted the antiquity of
such works.

We need not conclude that the visions of Daniel were written with intent to deceive. Evidently the ancient world was
much less concerned with the issue of individual authorship
than we are.[22] The author may have felt that the use of the
pseudonym was justified by his affinities with Daniel, or his
continuity with a Danielic tradition.

Pseudepigraphy, then, is best understood as a literary
device. By it the author indicated his sense of continuity
with the Daniel of the tales. The use of pseudonymity also
served to communicate a sense of determinism, through its association with $ex\ eventu$ prophecy. We will find that a similar
impression is conveyed by other literary devices in the book.

Revelation as Interpretation

In the tales, Daniel appears as a wise interpreter, endowed with "knowledge and understanding of books and learning

of every kind" and he has a particular gift for "interpreting
visions and dreams of every kind" (1:17). His skills are
illustrated by interpretations of dreams in chs. 2 and 4 and
by reading the writing on the wall in ch. 5. In chs. 7-12,
Daniel is no longer the interpreter, but the recipient of
revelation. However, this revelation is not communicated
directly, but through the mediation of an angel who explains
Daniel's visions in chs. 7 and 8, and interprets the prophecy
of Jeremiah in ch. 9. Again, in ch. 11, while the angel is
speaking directly to Daniel, he is only communicating to him
"what is written in the book of Truth" (10:21).

There is an obvious similarity between the role of Daniel
as interpreter of dreams and signs in chs. 2 and 5 and that of
the interpreting angel in chs. 7-12. In ch. 2, Daniel's prayer
is answered in a vision of the night, without reference to an
angel. The angel might then appear superfluous in the second
half of the book. The fact that he is introduced there serves
to emphasize that revelation is a mystery in the visions of
Daniel, just as it is in the dreams of Nebuchadnezzar. In
neither half of the book is the word of the Lord given directly
to men as it was to the classical Hebrew prophets. Instead,
revelation is given first in a cryptic form, whether in dreams
or visions, mysterious writing or biblical prophecy. The re-
ception of revelation calls not for the obedience of the prophet, but for the wisdom of an interpreter, and this wisdom itself derives from a heavenly source. The function of Daniel in
the tales is taken over by the angel in the visions. In both
cases interpreters are necessary. The revelation is mysterious
and not amenable to direct understanding.

The indirect nature of revelation, the fact that it must
be filtered through an interpreter, reinforces an impression
made by the use of pseudonymity. God is distant. He does not
reveal himself directly even to the prophets. Revelation was
allegedly given long ago, to Daniel, and even then it required
interpretation. In the present, God is hidden and we can learn
of his ways only by deciphering mysterious signs.

We touch here on a fundamental distinction between prophecy and apocalyptic. The prophetic oracle is addressed directly

to the people, calling for decision and repentance. The visions of destruction which they see could conceivably be averted. In Amos 7:4 the prophet sees a typically apocalyptic vision: "The Lord God was calling for a judgment by fire, and it devoured the great deep and was eating up the land." But then "the Lord repented concerning this: 'This also shall not be' saith the Lord." Such a reprieve is no longer possible in apocalyptic, no matter how the people repent. An apocalyptic writing such as Daniel is not communicating a conditional threat. It is interpreting what has already been revealed in cryptic form. Its future predictions have the character of *information* rather than threats or promises.[23] The mysteries contained in either visions, dreams or writings are already set. Nothing the audience can do will change the course of events. All they can do is understand and adapt to the inevitable.

The indirect mode of revelation, which emphasizes understanding and interpretation, implies a deterministic view of the world. This is clearly evident in Daniel 9. If the mysteries of the future are contained in the prophecies of Jeremiah, then the future must be already decided. Similarly, dreams and visions which require interpretation have a certain degree of autonomy. They could conceivably remain for an indefinite length of time before they are interpreted. In this they differ sharply from the prophetic oracles which are urgent messages directed to a specific situation. There is no explicit urgency in Daniel. The visionary is not told to "get you to the house of Israel and speak with my words to them" (Ezek 3:4) but to "shut up the words, and seal the book, until the time of the end."[24]

Consequently, the impression is given that we are dealing with an esoteric writing, which is hidden from the multitude and only revealed to a chosen few. Now apocalyptic writings were sometimes really guarded and preserved as esoteric lore in the intertestamental period.[25] This attitude is clearly expressed in 4 Ezra 14:45-46, where Ezra is told:

> The twenty four books that thou hast written, publish,
> that the worthy and unworthy may read therein; but
> the seventy last thou shalt keep, to deliver them to
> the wise among the people.

Josephus tells us that the members of the Essene sect swore
never to divulge the contents of their secret books, the names
of the angels or any of their secret doctrines.[26] The people
of Qumran used cryptic alphabets in copying some of their
sacred books. J.-T. Milik refers to the use of two such alphabets with arbitrarily chosen signs, and to one particular manuscript where Greek and Phoenician letters are sometimes substituted for the Hebrew.[27]

Despite such efforts to preserve secrecy in sectarian con-
texts, the esotericism of Daniel must be regarded as a literary
fiction. The book is sealed until the time of the end. It is
however presumed that the end is now at hand and the time has
come to publish the secrets. The secrecy of Daniel only refers
to the manner in which the material was transmitted, and explains why material allegedly written during the exile was not
hitherto known. It is therefore a consequence of the pseudonymity of the visions. At the end, however, the *maskîlîm* will
give instruction to the common people (*yabînu lārabbîm*, 11:33)
and the mysteries will not longer be hidden.

The command to "seal the book" in Daniel 12 does not,
then, imply that the visions were to become the exclusive prop-
erty of a select conventicle. Rather, it must be seen as a
literary device which is related to pseudepigraphy. Similarly,
the distinction between cryptic visions and subsequent interpretations in chs. 7 and 8 must also be regarded as literary
fictions. There is no reason to doubt that both visions and
interpretations were written by the same person.[28] As we shall
see, it is not even possible to read the interpretation as
point by point explanations of the visions. They only indicate
the referents of the visions in a minimal way.[29] In short, the
interpretations are not real attempts to de-code the visions.
It is, however, significant that the author chose to present
his material in this form. The literary distinction of vision
and interpretation in chs. 7 and 8 is parallel to the real
distinction between prophecy and interpretation in ch. 9. In
each case, revelation is given, as vision or as prophecy, independently of the recipient. The role of Daniel is to understand and to interpret. There is a clear analogy here with the

role of the wise man in the tales of chs. 2-6. The literary
format of the visions minimizes the author's claim to creativ-
ity and suggests that he is interpreting the manifestation of
pre-determined events.

Pesharim

The essential connection between the media of revelation
in chs. 1-6 and those in 7-12 is confirmed by the use of the
word *pesher*.[30] This term occurs in Daniel 2 for the interpretation of a dream, in Daniel 5 with reference to the writing on
the wall, and in Daniel 7 for the interpretation of a night-
vision. In each case it refers to the deciphering of a mystery,
whether dream, writing or eschatological vision. At Qumran,
the word *pesher* refers to the interpretation of scripture, almost invariably in the sense of eschatological prophecy.[31] The
relevance of this usage to Daniel 7-12 is immediately obvious.[32]
The visions in Daniel 7 and 8 are followed by interpretation
which relate them explicitly to eschatological events, and in
Daniel 9 a scriptural passage is similarly interpreted. The
interpretations in Daniel are neither as arbitrary nor as
atomistic as the Qumran *pesharim*, but they presuppose a common
idea of revelation. God's messages are concealed in codes,
whether visions, dreams or scriptures. There is need of a wise
interpreter to understand the mysteries.

The existence of the Qumran community was to a large extent based on the premise that they had found such a wise interpreter in the "Teacher of Righteousness to whom God made
known all the mysteries of the words of his servants the prophets" (1QpHab 7:4).[33] He was the "Searcher of the Torah."[34]
When sectarians were fully initiated, they were entrusted with
the secret lore of the community, "that which was hidden from
Israel, but found by the Man who sought" (1QS 8:11-12). While
the doctrines of the Teacher were basically the interpretation
of scripture, the "mysteries of the prophets," this interpretation was itself the object of special revelation:

> These things I have known because of Thine understand-
> ing, for Thou hast uncovered my ear to marvellous
> Mysteries. (1QH 1:21)

or again:

> And I, gifted with understanding, have known thee O
> my God, because of the Spirit which Thou hast put in
> me; and I have heard what is certain according to Thy
>   marvellous secret
> because of Thy holy Spirit.
> Thou hast opened Knowledge in the midst of me
> concerning the Mystery of Thine understanding.
>   (1QH 12:11-13)

The process of revelation is similar to what we find in Daniel.
The Teacher is given understanding, and insight into mysteries
which were always there. However, this insight is itself a
gift from God and a revelation, just as it is for Daniel.

The "mysteries" of Qumran relate to all God's workings
with the universe, both historical and cosmological.[35] They
involve both men and angels:

> for great is your majestic plan and your marvelous
> mysteries (*rzy npl'wtykh*) on high with you for
> raising up to you from the dust and casting down
> angels. (1QM 14:14)

Very often they relate to the future of Israel. All things are
to come in due time as he has ordained for them in the mysteries of his wisdom (*brzy 'rmtw*, 1QpHab 7:13-14), and we read of
the "mystery to be" (*rz nhyh*, 1QS 11:3-4). But the mysteries
can also refer to the workings of the cosmos:

> (Hast Thou entrusted) the heavenly lights according
> to their mysterious (laws), the stars according to
> the paths (which they follow)...the providential
> reservoirs according to their functions (and snow
> and hailstones) according to their mysterious (laws).
>   (1QH 1:11-12)

The mysteries of Qumran are set forth more comprehensively than
is the case in Daniel, but we shall see that Daniel, too, is
interested in more than the prediction of future events.

The predominant medium of revelation at Qumran is undoubtedly the interpretation of scripture. That is why there must
not "lack a man who studies the Law night and day" (1QS 6:6).
But other media are also recognized. There is a remarkable
lack of emphasis on visions and dreams, but horoscopes and astrological texts have been found.[36] Scripture was not the only
medium through which mysteries were revealed.

All these mysteries which are the object of revelation at Qumran are already in existence. Consequently the wisdom and understanding of the Teacher of Righteousness presumes a pre-determined universe:

> What can I say that is not already known
> and what can I utter that has not already been told?
> The world is graven before Thee
> with the graving tool of the reminder
> for all the unending seasons
> together with the cycles of the number of everlasting
>   years
> with all their times;
> they have not been hidden nor concealed from before
>   Thee. (1QH 1:21-25)

We may compare the importance of the "heavenly tablets" else-where in Jewish apocalyptic.[37] Such tablets were allegedly the source of the wisdom of Enoch.[38] We find a kindred idea in the "Book of Truth" in Dan 10:21, which is the alleged source from which the angel reveals the history of the Hellenistic age and the eschatological events. Again in Dan 12:1, the people who will be saved are "every one who is written in the book."[39] Ultimately the concept of a heavenly writing or a book from primordial times which contains all the secrets of the universe is related to the Babylonian "tablets of destiny."[40] The Qumran passage could mean that the nature or history of the universe is graven on heavenly tablets, but it might also mean that the world itself is a book--i.e., that its secrets and future can be read in its cosmology, in the movements of the stars and other omens.[41]

Indirect Revelation in the Hellenistic World

The idea of revelation which we find at Qumran, which its implications of determinism, was directly influenced by the terminology of Daniel.[42] However, we should not think of this as a development confined to Jewish apocalyptic circles. Ra-ther, it was a characteristic of the Hellenistic age.[43] A. M. J. Festugière lists four types of revelation which were recog-nized and respected in the Hellenistic world.[44] The first two of these were "direct" revelations, either visual, by dreams and ecstatic visions, or audial by conversation with a

supernatural being. The other two were indirect, by the interpretation of sacred writings or of heavenly signs.

A particularly interesting example of the interpretation
of sacred writing is the Demotic Chronicle from early Ptolemaic
Egypt. This consists of a commentary on an ancient text,
strikingly similar to the Qumran *pesharim*.[45] It is particularly concerned with political events and the succession of rulers:

> 'Moon, bewitch the stream (the Nile?)--when the
> prince travels around in the whole land.' That means:
> The ruler who will succeed them will forsake (or,
> plunder) Egypt.

The Chronicle looks forward to the restoration of a native
monarchy:

> It is a man of Heracleopolis who will rule after the
> Ionians. 'Rejoice, O prophet of Harsaphes.' That
> means: The prophet of Harsaphes rejoices after the
> Ionians. For a ruler has arisen in Heracleopolis.[46]

It is particularly important to note that the interpretation of
sacred writings was not a uniquely Jewish phenomenon and that
even within Judaism it was only one medium of revelation among
others. At least since the time of Wellhausen, many scholars
have tended to regard the interpretation of prophecy, or of
scripture, as the key to apocalyptic and to intertestamental
Judaism.[47] There is no doubt that interpretation of scripture
played an extremely important part in this period, but it was
never the exclusive medium of revelation.

We find a similarly indirect type of revelation in the interpretation of heavenly signs. Heavenly phenomena were also
thought to reflect political events. We find a good example in
the astrological writing of Nechepso and Petosiris, written in
Egypt in the second century B.C. The following is a typical
oracle:

> Kometes....When this comet is turned away it brings
> misfortune on those from whom it turns away. If it
> looks to the south, the Nile will give abundantly,
> there will be peace and prosperity in Egypt, harmony
> and true tranquility for all. But if it turns away,
> and with the east behind it looks to the west, there
> will be unlimited prosperity for the Romans. For
> they will defeat the Persians in war...[48]

Here, as in the interpretation of prophecy, cryptic signs are
interpreted to refer to the political situation.

The importance attached to heavenly signs, and especially
to astrology, was particularly characteristic of the Hellenistic age.[49] Astrology was especially associated with the Chaldeans in antiquity, but was known in Greece by the time of
Plato. Babylonian astrology was expounded to the Greeks by
Berossus in the early third century B.C. Its popularity in
Egypt is attested by the oracles of Nechepso and Petosiris.
Astrology implied a deterministic universe. The fates of nations and individuals could be read from the stars because they
were decided in advance. The movements of the stars became
very important for intertestamental Judaism, despite an occasional polemic.[50] We find horoscopes and astrological texts at
Qumran, and some Jewish writings, such as the Book of the Heavenly Luminaries in 1 Enoch 72-82 are dominated by interest in
the stars. We will find that some of the imagery in Daniel 8
is drawn from the associations of specific signs of the zodiac
with different countries in the Hellenistic age.[51] More important is the similarity in the understanding of revelation. In
astrology, the meaning of the universe was written in the
heavens and so was available to the wise interpreter. We find
a similar interpretation of mysterious signs, though not particularly astrological ones, in Daniel.

Astrology in the Hellenistic world was especially associated with the Babylonians. The most evident source for the
understanding of revelation in Daniel 7-12 is the Chaldean wisdom which Daniel is said to practice in chs. 1-6. Astrology
was only one aspect of that wisdom. The Chaldeans were concerned with all kinds of mantic and divination, including omens
and dream-interpretation.[52] All these forms of divination
shared with astrology the belief that the future is already
determined and can be learned by one who is skilled in interpreting signs and omens.

Dreams and Visions in the OT

In the court-tales, Daniel's expertise is concentrated on
dream-interpretation, although he can also decipher the writing

on the wall. In Daniel 7-12, we read of 'visions of the night' rather than dreams. There can scarcely be any phenomenological difference between dreams and visions of the night, and in Dan 7:1 dreams and visions appear to be virtually synonymous. Yet the terminological preference for 'visions' is significant. Dreams were a valid and important medium of revelation in the patriarchal stories but had been the object of bitter attacks on the part of the prophets and Deuteronomy.[53] Most frequently dreams were associated with false prophets:

> I have heard what the prophets have said who prophesy
> lies in my name saying, 'I have dreamed, I have
> dreamed.' How long shall there be lies in the heart
> of the prophets who prophesy lies, and who prophesy
> the deceit of their own heart....Let the prophet
> who has a dream tell the dream, but let him who has
> my word speak my word faithfully....I am against
> those who prophesy lying dreams, says the Lord,
> and who tell them, and lead my people astray by their
> lies and their recklessness. (Jer 23:25-32)

Among the canonical prophets, only Joel speaks positively about dreams, and that is in the context of the messianic age.

Accordingly, dreams were suspect as a mode of revelation in Israel, although they were quite acceptable for a foreign king. Even in Daniel 2, while Nebuchadnezzar has a dream, Daniel receives the interpretation in a vision of the night. The shift in terminology is significant. What we find both in Daniel 2 and in 7-12 is an attempt to Judaize this medium of revelation and exempt it from the polemic of the prophets against dreams. However, the essential characteristic of symbolic dream interpretation is retained in Daniel 7 and 8. The vision, like the dream, is mysterious. Its message is hidden and can be found only by a wise interpreter.

Indirect Revelation in the OT

For much of its history, Israel had been content with the advice of Deut 29:29: "The secret things belong to the Lord our God, but the things that are revealed belong to us and to our children." This principle did not, of course, completely exclude the possibility of further revelation. The sage in Prov 30:3-4 emphasized the limits of human knowledge by the

question "who has ascended to heaven and come down?" but it was
generally recognized that all true prophets "had stood in the
council of Yahweh," therefore, in effect, received their revelation in heaven. However, as we have already noted, the
prophetic revelation was a conditional threat or promise which
called for obedience. The apocalyptic vision was a mystery
which called for wisdom. The prophetic message was explicitly
tied to the prophet's historical situation. The apocalyptic
revelation, in terms of the device of pseudepigraphy, could
refer to events long after the time of the alleged author and
therefore apparently remain a mystery for centuries. In short,
we find in apocalyptic an interest in the revelation of mysteries which is quite different from the revelation of the
prophets.

The transformation in the OT concept of revelation was not
entirely an innovation on the part of Daniel. It is at least
partially evident in early post-exilic prophecy. We have already noted some similarities between the court-tales of Daniel
and Deutero-Isaiah, both of which have an explicit Babylonian
setting.[54] Deutero-Isaiah speaks of revealing "hidden things
which you have not known" (48:6). Even though the events are
new, they have been predicted long ago--"who told this long
ago, who declared it of old? Was it not I, the Lord? And
there is no other god besides me" (45:21). In Deutero-Isaiah,
Yahweh's power to reveal secrets is tied to his power as creator. Yahweh can predict the future because he made it. In
short, the course of world history is built into creation.
Consequently, anyone who understands the workings of creation
can foretell the future. Deutero-Isaiah argues that only Yahweh understands the workings of creation since only he made
them.

Deutero-Isaiah was well aware that Chaldean wise men tried
to fathom both the universe and the future by divination and
omens. In fact, his oracles are explicitly directed against
them: "Let them stand forth and save you, those who divide the
heavens, who gaze at the stars, who at the new moons predict
what shall befall you" (47:13). However, in his polemic against
Chaldean wisdom, Deutero-Isaiah may have been influenced, if

only slightly, by the Chaldean idea of revelation. The world
runs a fixed course from creation. This idea was safely within
the bounds of Yahwistic faith, even if it could also be shared
by other religions. Deutero-Isaiah comes no closer than this
to Chaldean wisdom. He does not go on to say that the pre-
determined mysteries of the universe and of history are concealed in certain cryptic signs. He does, however, open the
way for this possibility.

Writing in the first century B.C., Diodorus Siculus described the mantic art of the Chaldeans as follows:

> The Chaldeans say that the nature of the world is
> eternal...and that the order and arrangement of the
> whole has come to be by a certain divine providence,
> and now the individual things in heaven are completed,
> not at random or by themselves, but by a certain
> determined and firmly set judgment of the gods. By
> making lengthy observations of the stars...they
> foretell to men many of the things which will happen.
> (2.30)

The logic of this art is that creation follows a fixed order,
and therefore this order is reflected in nature, especially in
the stars. This was evidently the logic of the "star-gazers"
also in the time of Deutero-Isaiah. Further, it is the logic
which underlies all use of omens. Neither Deutero-Isaiah nor
Daniel espouse the Chaldean cosmology, or interest in the
stars, but in both the world and history follow a set pattern,
which is mysterious to men but can be predicted with the aid of
revelation. In Daniel, but not in Deutero-Isaiah, the mysteries are revealed in cryptic symbols, which require interpretation, like the stars and omens of the Chaldeans.

Another aspect of the transition from prophetic to apocalyptic revelation can be seen in Ezekiel 38.[55] The mysteries
of the future are hidden in older prophecies: "Are you (Gog) he
of whom I spoke in former days by my servants the prophets of
Israel" (38:17). Here as in Daniel 9 an ancient prophecy only
yields its meaning after it has been available for many years.
The concern for the fulfillment of prophecy reflects an attitude similar to the *pesharim*, and marks an important transition
in the religion of Israel from the spontaneous oracles of the
earlier prophets to a more learned reflection on received texts.

The closest biblical parallel to the form of the visions of Daniel is found in proto-Zechariah.[56] In Zech 1:7-6:8, the prophet sees a series of visions which are interpreted to him by an angel. The introduction of this *angelus interpres* places a significant distance between the prophet and his god and gives the vision a certain measure of autonomy. Zechariah wrote after the Babylonian exile and may himself have been influenced by the model of Chaldean dream and omen interpretation. To some extent the need for interpretation could be said to be implied already in the widespread use of allegories by the earlier prophets, especially Ezekiel. However, both in Daniel and in Zechariah, the explicit introduction of the angelic interpreter marks a significant shift towards a *pesher* model of revelation, as the interpretation of mysteries.

There were, then, some biblical precedents for the understanding of revelation as we find it in Daniel. The *pesher* of visions and scriptures in chs. 7-12 is most directly based on the model of the court-tales. These in turn reflected Chaldean wisdom as observed by the Jews in Babylon, but Daniel was probably also familiar with the post-exilic prophets and there may be some influence from that quarter too. The post-exilic prophets may themselves have been influenced by Babylonian wisdom to some extent. Throughout the post-exilic period the difference between the Jewish and Babylonian understanding of revelation was not as sharp as it had been in the days of the classical prophets.

The concept of revelation as the interpretation of mysteries does not in itself characterize a work as apocalyptic, or even fully distinguish apocalyptic from prophecy. This understanding of revelation is found in many diverse forms of religious literature, some of which, such as the allegorical commentaries of Philo, are vastly different from Daniel. Again, Daniel is generically distinguished from proto-Zechariah by its contents, in particular by the nature of its eschatology.[57] Despite their similar understanding of revelation, Jewish apocalyptic and Babylonian (or Egyptian) dream interpretations can obviously not be simply classified together. Nevertheless, this style of revelation is one very important dimension of the

phenomenon we call apocalyptic. The insistence which we find
in Daniel on interpretation and deciphering of texts and visions shows that the visionary is not a prophet. He is a wise
man concerned with interpreting and applying signs and symbols.
He is not, of course, a collector of proverbs, or a sage of Ben
Sira's type, but he is a practitioner of mantic wisdom.

The Determinism of Apocalyptic

We have noted that one implication of this style of revelation is a deterministic view of history. Events can be foretold centuries before their time only if they are pre-
determined. For that reason, apocalyptic revelations take on
an informational character foreign to classical prophecy.
There is no question of averting that which is to be. The
apocalypses can only mediate a knowledge and understanding of
the inevitable. They cannot change it.

For both of these reasons, the implication of determinism
and the "informational" aspect, apocalyptic has been criticized
as an inferior religious form. Since such criticism has come
from no less a figure than Martin Buber, it deserves some comment. Writing on the subject of pseudonymity, Buber says:

> Such a literary fiction, common to most of the
> apocalyptic writers, is by no means a secondary phe-
> nomenon; the actual historical biographical situation
> of the speaker is deliberately replaced by an alien
> scene taken over as analogous to his own. That fic-
> tion plunges us already into the depths of the prob-
> lematic. The time the prophetic voice calls us to
> take part in is the time of the actual decision....In
> the world of the apocalyptic, this present historical-
> biographical hour hardly ever exists, precisely be-
> cause a decision by men constituting a factor in the
> historical-suprahistorical decision is not in question
> here. The prophet addresses persons...to recognize
> their situation's demand for decision and to act
> accordingly. The apocalyptic writer has no audience
> turned towards him; he speaks into his notebook.[58]

Again with reference to 4 Ezra: "Everything here is pre-
determined, all human decisions are only sham struggles."[59]

Buber, of course, is concerned about the apparent denial
of human freedom, and sees apocalyptic degenerate into idle
speculations which do not influence life decisions. Such a

critique, however, completely overlooks the historical situations in which apocalypses were actually written, and misrepre-
sents the function of the literary device of pseudonymity. The
apocalyptic writer did not speak to his notebook, but to people
involved in a historical crisis.

The fiction of pseudonymity, while important, is only a
fiction. The apocalyptic books were not intended for some distant time in the future, but for the immediate situation. The
attribution to an ancient sage was designed to add persuasive-
ness to the predictions. While it is true that no human decision could change the course of events, the fate of the individual was not predetermined.[60] In Daniel, it is possible to
either hold fast to the covenant or to betray it, and the
people can be led to justice. The wise can be tested by God,
and the testing implies that they are free to decide. In short,
only the course of the universe and of events is predetermined.
These form a framework within which the individual must take
his stand. The fact that external events can not be changed
serves to add urgency to the individual's decision.

We will return in Chapter VII to discuss the function of
Daniel and the purpose its literary form was meant to serve.
For the present we must note that the determinism implied was
not absolute. The individual was still free to make a decision
within the context of the inevitable unfolding of events. In
this respect Daniel did not fully embrace the implications of
Chaldean wisdom. However, that wisdom influenced the form of
Daniel to a considerable extent. The model of cryptic revelation followed by interpretation distinguishes Daniel from the
classical prophets. It shows the continuity of the book with
the Chaldean wisdom, and also with post-exilic Judaism, and to
some extent the Hellenistic world which shared that model of
revelation.

NOTES

CHAPTER III

[1]See B. M. Metzger, "Literary Forgeries and Canonical Pseudepigrapha," *JBL* 91 (1972) 3-24 and the literature there cited.

[2]So most recently Hanson, *Dawn*, 252.

[3]Collins, *The Sibylline Oracles*, 38-44.

[4]Martyrdom is explicitly advocated in the Testament of Moses, ch. 9. In Daniel 11, martyrdom is not deliberately sought, but is not avoided either. See below, Chapter VII.

[5]This was a standard opinion in the rabbinic writings. See G. F. Moore, *Judaism* (Cambridge: Harvard, 1929) 1. 237-41, 421; Collins, *The Sibylline Oracles*, 136 n. 124.

[6]Also 1 Macc 4:46. Judas ordered that the altar of holocausts, which had been profaned, should be pulled down and the stones kept in a special place until the appearance of a prophet who should give a ruling about them. In 1 Macc 14:41, the Jews appointed Simon as their leader until a trustworthy prophet should arise.

[7]See R. Meyer, "Prophecy and Prophets in the Judaism of the Hellenistic-Roman Period," *TDNT* 6 (1968) 812-28.

[8]*Ant.* 13.11.2(311-13); 15.10.5(373-79); 17.13.3(345-48). Cf. *JW* 2.7.3(112-13).

[9]*Ant.* 17.2.4(41-45). For further examples, see Collins, *The Sibylline Oracles*, 16-18, 134-36.

[10]See J. Reiling, "The Use of Pseudoprophētēs in the LXX, Philo and Josephus," *NovT* 13 (1971) 156; J. Blenkinsopp, "Prophecy and Priesthood in Josephus," *JJS* 25 (1974) 239-62.

[11]In *Ant.* 13.10.7(299), Josephus uses the term *propheteia* of John Hyrcanus, but he does not attribute any prophecies to him and does not indicate how his gift of prophecy gained expression.

[12]Collins, *The Sibylline Oracles*, 16-17.

[13]Charles, *APOT*, 2. ix.

[14]On these and other Hellenistic oracles, see Collins, *The Sibylline Oracles*, 6-15. On the Oracle of Hystaspes, see now J. R. Hinnells, "The Zoroastrian doctrine of salvation in the Roman world," *Man and His Salvation: Studies in Memory of S. G. F. Brandon* (E. J. Sharpe and J. R. Hinnells, eds; Manchester: Manchester University, 1973) 125-48.

[15]Collins, *The Sibylline Oracles*, 1-4.

[16]So especially D. S. Russell, *The Method and Message of Jewish Apocalyptic* (Philadelphia: Westminster, 1964) 127-39; also E. Osswald, "Zum Problem der vaticinia ex eventu," *ZAW* 75 (1963) 27-44.

[17]Russell, *Method*, 132-39. Cf. H. Wheeler Robinson, *Corporate Personality in Ancient Israel* (Facet Books, Biblical Series 11; Philadelphia: Fortress, 1964); T. Boman, *Hebrew Thought Compared with Greek* (London: SCM, 1960) 148-49.

[18]Russell, *Method*, 133.

[19]Ibid., 135.

[20]J. W. Rogerson, "The Hebrew Conception of Corporate Personality: A Re-examination," *JTS* 21 (1970) 1-16; J. Barr, *Biblical Words for Time* (SBT 33; Naperville: Allenson, 1962) 96, 130-31.

[21]Russell, *Method*, 133.

[22]Cf. A. D. Nock, "Oracles Théologiques," *Revue des études anciennes* 30 (1928) 280-90 and "Religious Attitudes of the Ancient Greeks," *Proceedings of the American Philosophical Society* 85 (1942) 472-82.

[23]Cf. J. C. H. Lebram, "Apokalyptik und Hellenismus im Buche Daniel," *VT* 20 (1970) 516-22.

[24]Dan 12:4; cf. 8:26, 11:35, 12:9.

[25]On the "esoteric" character of apocalyptic, see Russell, *Method*, 107-18; M. E. Stone, "Apocalyptic Literature," *Compendia Rerum Judaicarum ad Novum Testamentum* 2b (Philadelphia: Fortress, forthcoming).

[26]*JW* 2.8.7(142), 12(159).

[27]J.-T. Milik, *Ten Years of Discovery in the Wilderness of Judaea* (London: SCM, 1959) 115; Cross, *Ancient Library*, 45-46.

[28]A. Szörenyi ("Das Buch Daniel," 278-94) has argued that the entire book of Daniel is an implicit commentary on older material. He systematically brackets off all references to Maccabean times as later interpretations. This procedure is not legitimate. There is no doubt that older material is used as a source of imagery in the visions, but there is no reason to suggest that the book as a whole is conceived as a *pesher*.

[29]Cf. J. J. Collins, "The Symbolism of Transcendence in Jewish Apocalyptic," *BR* 19 (1974) 15-16.

[30]In Akkadian, the word *pasaru* refers not only to the decoding of the dream but also to the removal of its threat by a sort of therapeutic magic. See Oppenheim, "Dreams," 217.

[31]See F. F. Bruce, *Biblical Exegesis in the Qumran Texts* (Grand Rapids: Eerdmans, 1959); O. Betz, *Offenbarung und Schriftforschung in der Qumransekte* (WUNT 6; Tübingen: Mohr, 1960) 75-82.

[32]This was already noted by O. Eissfeldt, "Die Menetekel-Inschrift und ihre Deutung," *ZAW* 63 (1951) 105-14; K. Elliger, *Studien zum Habbakuk-Kommentar vom Toten Meer* (BHT 15; Tübingen: Mohr, 1953) 156-57. See now Mertens, *Das Buch Daniel*, 114-44.

[33]Betz, *Offenbarung*, 55-56, 61-67, 88-91; G. Jeremias, *Der Lehrer der Gerechtigkeit* (SUNT 2; Göttingen: Vandenhoeck und Ruprecht, 1963) 140-66.

[34]CD 6:7. Betz, *Offenbarung*, 23-25.

[35]See R. E. Brown, *The Semitic Background of the Term "Mystery" in the New Testament* (Facet Books, Biblical Series 21; Philadelphia: Fortress, 1968) 22-30; Betz, *Offenbarung*, 82-86.

[36]See Hengel, *Judaism and Hellenism*, 1. 236-39.

[37]See F. Nötscher, "Himmlische Bücher und Schicksalglaube in Qumran," *RevQ* 1 (1958/59) 405-11; E. F. Bishop, "Qumran and the Preserved Tablets," *RevQ* 5 (1964/65) 253-56; A. Yarbro Collins, *The Combat Myth in the Book of Revelation* (HDR 9; Missoula: Scholars Press, 1976) ch. 5.

[38]Cf. Russell, *Method*, 110-11; Notscher, "Himmlische Bücher," 410-11.

[39]The books which are opened in Dan 7:10 may derive from a different complex of ideas, that of actual court procedure. Cf. Montgomery, *Daniel*, 299.

[40]See S. Holm-Nielsen (*Hodayot* [Aarhus: Universitetsforlaget, 1960] 25) who disputes the relevance of the heavenly tablets for this passage. The "book of life" or related concepts appear in a number of OT passages, e.g., Pss 139:16, 69:29; Exod 32:32; Mal 3:16. See Delcor (*Daniel*, 152) for references to the heavenly tablets in the intertestamental writings.

[41]Cf. F. Boll, *Aus der Offenbarung Johannis* (Berlin: Teubner, 1914) 9 n. 1. In Isa 34:4 and Rev 6:14, the heavens are said to be rolled up like a scroll. The reference is primarily to the folding up of the heavens, but the comparison with written material is suggestive.

[42]See Mertens, *Das Buch Daniel*, 114-44.

[43]See the lengthy excursus of Hengel, *Judaism and Hellenism* 1. 210-18: "'Higher wisdom through revelation' as a characteristic of religion in late antiquity."

[44]A.-M. J. Festugière, *La Révélation d'Hermès Trismégiste* 1, *L'Astrologie et les Sciénces Occultes* (Paris: Gabalda, 1950) 309-24, following Boll, *Offenbarung*, 4-11.

[45]See F. Daumas, "Littérature prophétique et exégétique égyptienne et commentaires esséniens," *A la Rencontre de Dieu* (Mem. Gelin; Paris: Le Puy, 1961) 203-11.

[46]Trans. C. C. McCown, "Hebrew and Egyptian Apocalyptic Literature," *HTR* 18 (1925) 389.

[47]J. Wellhausen, "Zur apokalyptischen Literatur," *Skizzen und Vorarbeiten* 6 (1899) 225-34. For a more recent example, see L. Hartman, *Prophecy Interpreted* (Lund: Gleerup, 1966).

[48]E. Riess, "Nechepsonis et Petosiridis fragmenta magica," *Philologus Supplementband* 6 (1892-93) 345. See the study of W. Kroll, "Nechepso," PW 16. 2160-67.

[49]See especially F. Cumont, *Astrology and Religion among the Greeks and Romans* (New York: Dover, 1960; reprint of 1912 edition by G. P. Putnam's Sons); Festugière, *Révélation*, 89-186; E. R. Dodds, *The Greeks and the Irrational* (Berkeley and Los Angeles: University of California, 1966) 245-49.

[50]E.g., *Jub.* 12:17; *Sib. Or.* 3:218-30.

[51]See A. Caquot, "Sur les Quatre Bêtes de Daniel VII," *Semitica* 5 (1955) 5-13.

[52]See especially the description of the Chaldeans by Diodorus Siculus 2.29-31; Jansen, *Henochgestalt*, 13-21.

[53]For discussion of dreams in the OT, see Ehrlich, *Traum*; Andreas Resch, *Der Traum im Heilsplan Gottes* (Freiburg: Herder, 1964).

[54]Cf. von der Osten-Sacken, *Die Apokalyptik*, 13-34.

[55]See Wellhausen, "Zur apokalyptischen Literatur," 227.

[56]R. North, "Prophecy to Apocalyptic via Zechariah," VTSup 22 (1972) 47-71. On the historical setting of proto-Zechariah, see Hanson, *Dawn*, 209-79.

[57]See Hanson, *Dawn*, 251-59.

[58]M. Buber, "Prophecy, Apocalyptic and the Historical Hour," *Pointing the Way* (New York: Harper, 1957) 200.

[59]Ibid., 201.

[60]The Qumran scrolls offer a possible, but debatable exception to this point. See P. Wernberg-Moeller, "A Reconsideration of the Two Spirits in the Rule of the Community (1Q Serek III,13-IV,26)," *RevQ* 3 (1961) 413-41.

CHAPTER IV

SYMBOLS, MYTHS AND ALLEGORIES: THE MODE OF THE VISIONS

In the preceding chapter we noted the importance of interpretation, whether of scriptures, visions or other mysteries,
as a medium of revelation in Daniel. However, only in Daniel 9
do we find the actual interpretation of a traditional text, in
this case Jeremiah's prophecy of the seventy years. Chapters 7
and 8 do not begin with a scriptural text, but with an allegorical vision account, which is then explained, at least partially, in the interpretations. We do not wish to prejudge the
question whether the author of Daniel had genuine visionary experiences in which he "saw" these visions, or whether he composed them as literary works.[1] There is in fact no criterion by
which we can establish the author's state of mind. For our
purpose, the difference between the two alternatives is not
significant. In either case, the visions are imaginative con-
structs which arise out of the author's experience of historical events. They are not simply given to the author, in the
same sense as the prophecy of Jeremiah. Whether or not the
vision accounts describe actual ecstatic experiences, they are
products of the author's imagination. Even if we were to argue
that the visions were objectively revealed from a supernatural
source, it would still be clear that the vision accounts depend
on the descriptive abilities of the visionary's imagination.

The vision accounts, however, do not derive from the private, subjective consciousness (or subconscious) of an individual. They are formulated in traditional language, much of
which is drawn ultimately from ancient Near Eastern mythology.
The mythic character of apocalyptic imagery was perceived already at the end of the nineteenth century by Hermann Gunkel.[2]
Gunkel especially stressed the affinities of the Book of Revelation with Babylonian myth. With the recovery of the mythological texts from Ugarit since 1929, scholars have come to realize
that Canaanite myth is more directly relevant than Babylonian.
However, Gunkel's insight remains fundamental. Canaanite and
Babylonian myths were closely related in any case. The

significant point is that much apocalyptic language is mythic in origin and content. We cannot begin to appreciate a work such as Daniel until we become aware of the mythological echoes with which it rings.

We will begin our study of the visions, then, by reviewing the mythological ingredients of which they are largely composed.

The Mythological Imagery of Daniel 7: The Sea and Its Monsters

The mythic elements in Daniel are perhaps most obvious in ch. 7. The vision bristles with ancient motifs. First, Daniel saw a great sea, churned up by the four winds of heaven, from which four great beasts emerged (7:2). The turbulent sea is familiar from the OT, both as the abode of mythical chaos monsters and as an embodiment of chaos in its own right.[3] In Job 26, we are given a description of God's works of creation:

> He stretches out the north over the void,
>   and hangs the earth upon nothing...
> By his power he stilled the sea,
>   by his understanding he smote Rahab.
> By his wind the heavens were made fair,
>   his hand pierced the fleeting serpent.[4]

Here the sea, with Rahab and the serpent, is one of the chaotic forces which the creator must subdue. Again in Ps 89:9-11, the power of the creator is hymned:

> Thou dost rule the raging of the sea;
>   when its waves rise, thou stillest them.
> Thou didst crush Rahab like a carcass,
>   thou didst scatter thy enemies with thy mighty arm.
> The heavens are thine, the earth also is thine;
>   the world and all that is in it, thou hast founded
>   them.

and in Ps 74:13-17:

> Thou didst divide the sea by thy might;
>   thou didst break the heads of the dragons on the
>   waters.
> Thou didst crush the heads of Leviathan....
> Thou hast fixed all the bounds of the earth.

In each of these passages, the sea and the various monsters (dragons, Rahab, Leviathan) are conceived as forces of chaos

which were subdued in the course of creation and are now held
in check by the creator's power. The monsters are located in
the sea. They are "the dragons on the waters" (Ps 74:13) or
"the dragon that is in the sea" (Isa 27:1). It is not clear
how far a distinction can be maintained between the sea and its
monsters, since they repeatedly recur in parallelism to each
other. We should probably regard them all as embodiments of
the same primordial force of chaos.

The imagery of the sea and its monsters is used in the OT
not only with reference to the primordial battle of creation
but also to describe historical crises. Not surprisingly, the
Israelites saw an analogy between the conquest of the sea in
creation and the crossing of the Red Sea at the Exodus. So
Deutero-Isaiah asks:

> Was it not thou that didst cut Rahab in pieces
>   that didst pierce the dragon?
> Was it not thou that didst dry up the sea,
>   the waters of the great deep;
> that didst make the depths of the sea a way
>   for the redeemed to pass over? (Isa 51:9-10)

The reference is obviously to the Exodus, but that event is
seen as a re-enactment of the primordial defeat of the dragon.

More generally, the imagery of the chaotic sea could be
applied to Israel's historical enemies at any time. We read in
Isa 17:12-14:

> Ah, the thunder of many peoples,
>   they thunder like the thundering of the sea!
> Ah, the roar of the nations,
>   they roar like the roaring of many waters!
> The nations roar like the roaring of many waters
>   but he will rebuke them, and they will flee away.

The roaring of many waters should not be taken as a simple
metaphor, but must be viewed as another manifestation of primordial chaos.

Finally, Yahweh's defeat of the sea and its monsters can
be projected into the future, as the ultimate act of divine
deliverance. In the so-called Apocalypse of Isaiah we read:

> In that day the Lord with his hard and great and
> strong sword will punish Leviathan, the fleeting ser-
> pent, Leviathan the twisting serpent, and he will
> slay the dragon that is in the sea. (Isa 27:1)

Centuries later the author of the NT book of Revelation envisaged a new creation where "the sea was no more" (Rev 21:1).

This imagery of the sea and its monsters was obviously not
derived from anything in Israel's own history. It is only intelligible against the background of ancient Near Eastern myth.
The sea and its inhabitant monsters are prominent symbols of
chaos in both Canaanite and Babylonian mythology. There is no
doubt that the Canaanite myths have most directly influenced
the biblical tradition. In the Ugaritic texts we read how
Baal, the young god who stands at El's right hand, is challenged for the kingship by Yamm, Sea.[5] El abandons Baal into
the power of Sea, but Baal takes up two clubs fashioned by
Kothar, craftsman of the gods, and assaults and overcomes Sea:

> Sea fell, he sank to earth,
> His joints trembled, his frame collapsed.
> Baal destroyed, drank Sea!
> He finished off Judge River.[6]

In a variant of this myth we read:

> When you (Baal) smote Lotan, the ancient dragon,
> destroyed the crooked serpent,
> Shilyat with the seven heads,
> (Then) the heavens withered (and) drooped
> Like the loops of your garment.[7]

Lotan is clearly the Canaanite ancestor of the biblical Leviathan.

In another variant of the myth, we are told that Anat slew
Yamm and/or the serpent:

> Did I (Anat) not smite the beloved of El, Sea?
> Did I not destroy El's River, Rabbim?
> Did I not muzzle the dragon?
> I smote the crooked serpent
> Shilyat of seven heads.[8]

Here *Rabbim* (many, mighty) is directly reminiscent of the "many
waters" of the Psalms. The seven-headed monster reappears in
Revelation 12, 13 and 17.

We have seen that the defeat of the sea and its monsters
is presented in some OT texts as part of the work of creation.
Similarly in the Babylonian epic, the Enuma Elish, the battle
of Marduk with the monster Tiamat is directly related to the

creation of the world.[9] There is no reference to creation in
the Ugaritic myths, but Cross has rightly insisted that the
conflict of Baal and Yamm, and its variants, is cosmogonic.
The myth records the events which "constitute cosmos," and show
how order is imposed and chaos subdued.[10] Since the conflict
of creation and chaos is perennial, such a cosmogonic myth describes how the order of the world is constantly maintained.
It need not refer explicitly to the first reduction of chaos at
the creation of the world. The conflict with the sea-monster
has a central place in Canaanite myth. The allusions which we
find scattered through the bible are only intelligible against
this background.

From the preceding discussion it should be clear that when
the apocalypticist in Daniel 7 describes the sea churned up by
the winds and four huge beasts coming up out of the sea, he was
using traditional imagery. As we have seen, the stormy sea is
ubiquitous in the OT as a symbol of chaos--an image derived
from the Sea, Yamm, of Canaanite myth. The four beasts are
variants of Leviathan and Rahab and the monsters which inhabit
or are associated with the sea. The expression "great sea"
(*yammā' rabbā'*) recalls the many waters (*mayim rabbîm*) of the
Psalms. It is noteworthy that the third beast has four heads
and the fourth beast ten horns. We have seen that the dragon
in the Ugaritic texts had seven heads. The sea and the beasts
are, then, what Philip Wheelwright has called "symbols of ancestral vitality," that is, symbols which acquire their force
and richness from their traditional associations.[11]

The "Ancient of Days" and "One Like a Son of Man"

The sea and the beasts in Daniel 7 might be derived and
understood adequately from the scattered references to this
imagery in the Hebrew bible. The representation of the Ancient
of Days and the one like a son of man is more problematic. The
clustering of images which we find in Dan 7:9-14 can only be
understood directly against a background of Canaanite myth.[12]

The central problem of this imagery is the presentation of
the "one like a son of man" who comes "with the clouds of

heaven." As Emerton and others have realized, the entourage of clouds, in OT imagery, implies divinity.[13] In Deut 33:26, it is Yahweh who "rides the heavens to your help, the clouds in his majesty." In Psalm 104, Yahweh makes the clouds his chariot. Yet in Daniel 7, this "one like a son of man," who is accompanied by clouds, is apparently inferior to the "Ancient of Days," since kingship "is given" to him, presumably by the latter. At least the "one like a son of man" and the "Ancient of Days" appear as two distinct divine beings.

The idea that there is another God superior to Yahweh is foreign to the OT. O. Eissfeldt has argued that a few passages in the OT show Yahweh as distinct from and subordinate to El Elyon.[14] His main examples are Deut 32:8-9 where Elyon divides up the nations, and Israel falls to Yahweh's lot, and Psalm 82 where Yahweh speaks in the divine council and reminds the other gods that they are all sons of Elyon. However, in Deuteronomy 32, it is at least possible that Yahweh and Elyon are identified. In Psalm 82 "sons of Elyon" is a general traditional designation for the gods, and does not imply the acknowledgment of Elyon as a superior deity. Nowhere in the OT is Yahweh juxtaposed with another heavenly being in the way the "one like a son of man" and the "Ancient of Days" are juxtaposed here.

The imagery of Yahweh riding on the clouds is itself derived from the storm-imagery of the theophanies of Baal, who is repeatedly called the "rider of the clouds" in the Ugaritic texts.[15] The Canaanite myths also show striking parallels to the Ancient of Days. El, the father of gods and men, is depicted as a venerable whitehaired old man. The goddess Asherah addresses him:

> Thou art great O El, verily thou art wise,
> thy hoary beard indeed instructs Thee.[16]

In Daniel the hair of the Ancient is like cleanest wool.

Elsewhere El is called *abu shanima*, father of years, a phrase which instantly calls to mind the Ancient of Days.[17]

In the Ugaritic texts, El presides over the heavenly council:

> Then the two set their faces toward the mountain of El
> Toward the gathered council.
> Indeed the gods were sitting at table...
> Baal stands by (enthroned) El.[18]

El is also said to *judge*[19] and he is the final authority to
whom the other gods appeal. In Daniel 7:9-10, the Ancient of
Days took his seat, and

> Thousands upon thousands served him
> and myriads upon myriads attended his presence.
> The court sat and the books were opened.

Here we have the venerable high god presiding over a judicial
session of the divine council.

In all, the imagery of Dan 7:9-14 is unmistakeable. It
derives from a Canaanite enthronement scene in which Baal,
rider of the clouds, approaches El, the whitehaired father of
years who confers kingship on him. The OT passages which come
closest to this scene are found in the psalms which speak of
the enthronement of the Davidic king, especially Psalms 2 and
110. The Davidic king was said to be a son of God (Psalm 2)
and could be called simply *'elōhîm* "god" (Psalm 45) but he is
never described as riding on the clouds, nor as a heavenly
being. The imagery of Dan 7:9-14 cannot be explained from the
royal psalms. We must suppose that the author of Daniel had
access to independent traditions. The best parallels to the
"Ancient of Days" and the "one like a son of man" are found in
the Ugaritic texts. While we do not have a description of the
enthronement of Baal, which might provide a direct parallel to
Daniel 7, we find that, when Baal is supposed dead, El offers
to make one of the sons of Asherah king.[20] Although the sons
of Asherah prove inadequate and are rejected, the text shows
that kingship was in fact conferred by El. Similarly it is
conferred by the "Ancient of Days" in Daniel 7.

EXCURSUS: The Availability of Ancient Mythology

The imagery of the "Ancient of Days" and the "one like a
son of man" in Daniel 7 can not be derived from the OT, but
presupposes independent mythological traditions. These traditions are best represented by the Ugaritic texts from the second millenium B.C.

We have no solid evidence as to how or in what form the traditions represented by the Ugaritic texts were available in the second century B.C. A few suggestions can be made:

(1) In pre-exilic Israel, many old Canaanite traditions were transmitted in the royal cult in Jerusalem. An enthronement scene such as we find in Daniel 7 would seem especially appropriate for a royal cult.[21] The transmission of such traditions in post-exilic Judaism remains problematic, but it is possible that they survived either as folk traditions or in learned circles.

(2) About the end of the first century A.D., Philo of Byblos translated the ancient "Phoenician theology" of Sakkunyaton (Sanchuniathon). There have been doubts as to the authenticity of Philo's translation, but recent studies have shown that his work has much in common with the Ugaritic myths.[22] Philo does not provide parallels to Daniel 7, but his work shows that ancient Canaanite lore was accessible in the Roman period.

The use of ancient mythology in a Jewish apocalyptic work such as Daniel must be seen in the context of the interest in old traditions throughout the Hellenistic world. Despite the fact that Babylon no longer enjoyed a native monarchy, the myths and rituals associated with Babylonian kingship were still copied by scribes in the Hellenistic age. All our copies of the Akitu ritual date from the Seleucid period.[23] A lament for Uruk, a Sumerian work composed in the third millenium B.C., was recopied in the early Hellenistic period, when Babylon had again been overrun by foreigners.[24] Berossus translated the Babylonian cosmogony into Greek in the third century B.C. This persistent recopying of ancient materials suggests that the scribes looked to the old myths for meaning and guidance in the Hellenistic age.

Ancient myth is strikingly utilized in political prophecy in the Potter's Oracle, an Egyptian document from the Hellenistic age. Although this oracle is extant in Greek and was probably composed in that language, it reflects the sentiments of Egyptian nationalism. It looks forward to a "king from the sun" who will be sent by Isis--presumably a descendent of the

Pharaohs. It also predicts the destruction of the city by the sea (Alexandria). Ludwig Koenen has shown that the oracle draws on the structure of Egyptian cosmogonic myths:

> It is obvious that the savior-king of the prophecies plays the role of Horus. In this role he overwhelms the chaos of Seth, as does every Egyptian king, and he restores equilibrium to Egypt.[25]

Many of the Potter's predictions correspond closely to the prophecy of Neferty, which dates from 1991 B.C.

It appears, then, that the use of ancient myths and traditions in Jewish apocalyptic writings was not exceptional. Rather, we find that throughout the Hellenistic Near East ancient materials were re-copied and used. This interest in ancient materials may be considered complementary to the widespread use of pseudepigraphy. Antiquity was thought to be superior to the present. Therefore writings and traditions which either were or claimed to be ancient enjoyed special prestige. We have already noted, with reference to the four kingdoms oracle in Daniel 2, that Babylonians in the Hellenistic period looked back to the time of Nebuchadnezzar as a golden age. The reason, in some part at least, was that Babylon was no longer ruled by a native king, but by a Greek, Seleucid monarch. The demise of native kingships in the Near East was undoubtedly an important factor in the esteem for antiquity in the Hellenistic age.[26]

At least in Babylon, the transmission of the ancient myths was the work of learned scribes who had mastered the difficulties of Akkadian writing. It is most likely that the use of ancient myths in Jewish apocalyptic writing was also the work of learned men. The Jews who wrote (and read) sibylline oracles in epic Greek hexameters were not the rank and file of the peasantry. The eschatological prophecies of Qumran were produced by prolonged study of biblical prophecy. We have already seen that the author of Daniel belonged to a class of *maskîlîm* or wise men, and that his hero, Daniel, was learned in "the letters and language of the Chaldeans" (Dan 1:4). It is probable then that the mastery of archaic traditions displayed in Daniel 7 was the product of learning, rather than simple folk-traditions.

We are still uncertain as to how the author of Daniel came
by his material. There is no reason, however, to doubt that
ancient traditions closely related to the Ugaritic myths were
available in the second century B.C. Such traditions were certainly available to Philo of Byblos in the first century A.D.
It is possible that there were similar traditions within Judaism, which had once been associated with the royal cult.
There can be no doubt that Israelite traditions were more extensive than what we now find in the Hebrew bible. In any
case, the Ugaritic material furnishes the only clear background
against which the clustering of motifs which we find in Daniel
7 is intelligible. (End of Excursus)

Further Traditions in Daniel 7

Not all the imagery of Daniel 7 derives from Canaanite
myth. The sequence of the four kingdoms, as we have seen, was
a widespread feature of political oracles in the Hellenistic
Near East. In Daniel 7, it is presumably derived from Daniel 2.
The description of the individual beasts is not related to the
traditional chaos imagery. The use of animal imagery is, of
course, widespread in apocalyptic. The most famous example is
perhaps the Animal Apocalypse in 1 Enoch. Such imagery is a
natural device in allegorical writing and is probably universal.
The fact that the beasts in Daniel 7 represent kingdoms may reflect the traditional Hebrew and Ugaritic use of the names of
male animals to designate nobility.[27] The specific list of
beasts in this vision finds its closest parallel in Hosea 13:7:

> So I will be to them like a lion,
>   like a leopard I will lurk beside the way.
> I will fall upon them like a bear robbed of her cubs,
>   I will tear open their breast,
> and there I will devour them like a lion,
>   as a wild beast would rend them.[28]

In other biblical passages (Isa 11:6, Jer 5:6) the wolf, leop-
ard and lion are singled out as representative wild beasts. As
a further instance of imagery which is derived from a biblical
source rather than older mythology, we may note that the throne
of God in Dan 7:9 is fiery and has wheels, like the throne of
God in Ezekiel 1.

Like all apocalyptic writings, Daniel draws imagery from
various sources. He does not simply take over an ancient myth,
but he uses old images to construct his new vision. We are reminded of the famous comment of Franz Boas on the nature of
mythology:

> It would seem that mythological worlds have been
> built up, only to be shattered again, and that new
> worlds were built from the fragments.[29]

So Daniel uses the fragments of older mythology to build his
own mythological world.

A Mythic Pattern in Daniel 7

However, the new vision of Daniel derives more than fragmentary motifs from Canaanite mythology. We have noted that,
while the imagery of the sea and the beasts is found frequently
in the OT, it ultimately derives from the Canaanite cosmogonic
myth. Again, the imagery of the "Ancient of Days" and "one
like a son of man" finds its closest parallels in the Ugaritic
references to Baal, rider of the clouds, and El, father of
years. The conferral of kingship on the "one like a son of
man" most probably derives from a Canaanite myth of the enthronement of Baal. However, in the Ugaritic myth of the conflict of Baal and Yamm, Baal attains his kingship precisely by
his defeat of Yamm, sea. Therefore the eruption of chaos with
the emergence of the beasts and the conferral of kingship on
the "one like a son of man" are not isolated motifs, but are
part of a pattern. The sequence of events in the Canaanite
myth may be summarized as
(a) the revolt of Yamm, sea, who demands the surrender of Baal,
    and kingship over the gods;
(b) the defeat of Yamm by Baal;
(c) the manifestation of Baal's kingship.[30]
In Daniel 7, we find the revolt of the sea (a) through the
beasts which rise from it and the final kingship of a Baal-like
figure (c). The defeat of Yamm in the Ugaritic myths is
achieved by battle. In Daniel, the beasts are destroyed by the
judgment of the divine council. However, the similarity to the

Canaanite myth on points (a) and (c) leaves no room for doubt
that Daniel 7 is modelled on the same mythic pattern as the
conflict of Baal and Yamm.

The confrontation between the forces of chaos, represented
by the sea and the beasts, and the heavenly figures of the
"Ancient of Days" and "one like a son of man" is the main focus
of Daniel 7. Other symbolism is made subordinate to this confrontation. Even though the four beasts presumably represent
four successive kingdoms, they are all judged together, since
they are manifestations of the same chaotic power of the sea.
The vision is focused on this confrontation of the beasts from
the sea with the heavenly figures, not on the temporal succession of world-kingdoms.[31]

Daniel 7 is not, of course, simply another variant of the
Canaanite cosmogonic battle of Baal and Yamm. We will return
in the following chapters to examine the vision within the context of the book of Daniel. However, the mythic pattern is one
important factor which determines the meaning of the vision.

The Mythic Elements in Daniel 8

Despite its manifold similarities to ch. 7, Daniel 8 is
modelled on a different myth. The heart of the vision lies in
vss. 8-12. The little horn "grew great even to the host of
heaven, and it cast down to the ground some of the host and
some of the stars and trampled on them." It then proceeds to
threaten the prince of the host. This attempt to raise himself
above the stars and thereby attain to divine status, inevitably
reminds us of Isa 14:12-15:

> How you are fallen from heaven, O Day-star, son of Dawn,
> How you are cut down to the ground, you who laid the
>   nations low!
> You said in your heart, 'I will ascend to heaven;
> above the stars of God I will set my throne on high;
> I will sit on the mount of assembly in the far north;
> I will ascend above the heights of the clouds.
> I will make myself like the Most High.'
> But you are brought down to Sheol, to the depths of
>   the Pit.

Helal ben Shachar, Day-Star son of Dawn, makes only this enigmatic appearance in the Hebrew bible. He serves here as a

metaphor for the king of Babylon, but he is obviously a mythical character in his own right. The reference to the "mount of assembly in the far north" (Isa 14:13) suggests that we are dealing with a Canaanite myth. In fact, there is a fragmentary Ugaritic myth which tells how Athtar, the morning star, attempted to take over Baal's throne but proved inadequate. This abortive attempt of Athtar to rule over the divine council is probably the ultimate source of the imagery of Isaiah 14 and of Daniel 8.[32]

Here again we have no evidence as to how this material was transmitted. Motifs of this myth still circulated long after the time of Daniel. In Revelation 12, the dragon sweeps down a third of the stars with his tail. While this passage does not appear to depend on Daniel 8, it presupposes the same myth of a revolt against the stars. In the Greek mythographer Nonnos of Panoplis (in Egypt), who wrote in the fifth century A.D., we find an account of the revolt of Typhon (Typhoeus) against Zeus. There, as in Daniel 8, one of the major acts of revolt was an attack on the stars. At least one of Typhon's motives was to rise above the stars and gain the throne of Zeus. There is no question of a literary relationship between the story in Nonnos and that in Daniel. Both testify to an ancient myth which was found in both the Greek and the Semitic worlds.[33]

Not all the imagery of Daniel 8 must be related to the revolt of the Day Star. It has long been realized that the choice of symbols for the kingdoms of Greece and Persia is determined by the astral geography of the Hellenistic age. The ram is the constellation Aries which presides over Persia, according to the astrologer Teucer of Babylon. The goat represents Capricorn in the Zodiac, and according to Teucer, Capricorn presided over Syria. The author of Daniel was obviously familiar with the system of Teucer or one of its antecedents.[34]

It remains true, however, that the pattern by which the main action of the chapter is described is derived from the myth of Helal ben Shachar. While this vision is different from what we found in Daniel 7 in its motifs and associations, it nevertheless is basically similar to it. In both chapters *kingship* is at stake. In both a *threat* is posed by a rebellious king (or kings). This threat is removed by a supernatural power. Daniel 8 makes no reference to what follows the defeat of the little horn. We must presume that it is some state of salvation, analogous to the kingdom which is conferred on the one like a son of man in Daniel 7.

The Mythic Elements in Daniel 10-12

In chs. 10-12, we meet again familiar mythic motifs. Each people on earth is represented by an angelic prince in heaven. The conflicts between peoples on earth is only a manifestation of the more important conflicts between their patron angels in heaven. So the angel Gabriel fights in turn against the "princes" or patron angels of Persia and Greece and is assisted by Michael, "one of the chief princes" who is also described as "your prince" the prince of Israel.

This mythic system is a Jewish adaptation of the common world-view of the ancient Near East. Each people has its own patron deity. This world-view is vividly expressed in the message which the Assyrian commander sent to the people of Judah in Isa 36:18-20:

> Beware lest Hezekiah mislead you by saying, "The Lord will deliver us." Has any of the gods of the nations delivered his land out of the hand of the king of Assyria? Where are the gods of Hamath and Arpad? Where are the gods of Sepharvaim? Have they delivered Samaria out of my hand? Who among all the gods of these countries have delivered their countries out of my hand, that the Lord should deliver Jerusalem out of my hand?

The king of Assyria, in turn, attributed his success to the power of his god who fought for him.[35]

This polytheistic system which identified each people with a particular god was accepted with slight modification in Israel. The classical formulation is found in Deut 32:8:

> When the Most High gave to the nations their inheritance
> when he separated the sons of men,
> he fixed the bounds of the peoples
> according to the number of the sons of God.
> For the Lord's portion is his people,
> Jacob his allotted heritage.[36]

Here each of the nations is assigned to a god. Israel is assigned to Yahweh. In Daniel 10-12, the old national gods of Deuteronomy are presented as the angelic princes of the nations.

This mythological system forms the framework of Daniel 10-12. The narrative of ch. 11 consists of a review of the history of the Hellenistic age. Within this narrative, no reference is made to the angelic princes. Instead the account of Antiochus Epiphanes in Dan 11:36-45 reflects a pattern similar to Daniel 8. The king "shall exalt himself and magnify himself above every god and shall speak astonishing things against the God of gods" (11:36), just as Helal ben Shachar, and the little horn, had attempted to set themselves above the stars. This revolt of Antiochus and his subsequent fall bring the review of history in Daniel 11 to a conclusion. There follows an eschatological consummation in Dan 12:1-3, which includes an account of the resurrection.

The history narrated by the angel in Daniel 11 is not described in mythological terms, except for the battle in heaven which serves as a framework. Yet it is built on a pattern similar to what we found in Daniel 7 and 8. First, there is the threat posed especially by Antiochus Epiphanes. Then this threat is removed by the death of the king (11:45) and the victory of Michael (12:1). The triumphant conclusion is not described in terms of a kingdom, but as a resurrection of the dead.

In summary, then, the visions of chs. 7 and 8, and the angelic narrative in chs. 10-12, all draw heavily on traditional, and in large part mythological, materials. Each section draws on a different complex of mythological motifs. Daniel 7 draws on the old Canaanite myth of the conflict of Baal and Yamm; Daniel 8 on the myth of the revolt of Helal ben Shachar; Daniel 10-12 on the mythic system of the national deities. Yet within each section, we found a similar pattern of events. In each, the kingship over heaven and earth is at stake. First, there is a *threat* posed by a rebellious king or kings. Then that *threat is removed* by some supernatural power. Finally, there follows a *state of salvation*, expressed as a kingdom in Daniel 7, as resurrection in Daniel 12, and only

implied in Daniel 8. These three sections of Daniel are further bound together by the fact that they all focus on the
career of the Seleucid king Antiochus IV Epiphanes.

A similar sequence of events, also focused on Antiochus
Epiphanes, can be found in the interpretation of Jeremiah's
prophecy in Dan 9:24-27. There again the king figures as a
threat and he is removed by a supernatural power. As in Daniel
8, the state of salvation is only implied. Unlike the other
chapters, Daniel 9 makes little use of mythical motifs.

How the Mythic Elements Sould be Read: the Visions as Allegories

In the preceding pages we have attempted to list the main
mythological features which we find in the visions of Daniel.
These features are mythological, in the sense that they refer
to superhuman beings and powers, and are derived from ancient
Near Eastern myths. The mythic elements are not isolated metaphors. Rather, in chs. 7, 8 and 10-12 they constitute a pattern
or a system which forms the framework of the message of the visions.

Yet it is clear that the visions of Daniel are not simply
stories about gods and heavenly beings. The author leaves no
room for doubt on this point. The visions in chs. 7 and 8 are
followed by interpretations. The interpretations typically
translate the vision in terms of human history. So we are told
in Dan 7:17: "These four great beasts are four kings who shall
arise out of the earth." Again, in Dan 8:20-21: "As for the
ram which you saw with the two horns, these are the kings of
Media and Persia. And the he-goat is the king of Greece, and
the great horn between his eyes is the first king." In Daniel
10-12 the heavenly battle of the angels is paralleled by human
wars on earth. In short, the visions of Daniel can not be read
purely as mythical formulations of timeless truths, but as allegories of specific events in human history.

The Allegorical Mode

The term "allegory" is frequently used by literary (and
biblical) critics in a pejorative sense, which suggests that

allegory is somehow an inferior product of the imagination. It
has long been fashionable to distinguish between "allegory"
which is despised as an artificial and contrived mode of speech,
and "symbol" which is respected as an authentic poetic and
religious form of expression. In the words of Edwin Honig:
"allegory suggests something obvious and old fashioned, like
Sunday-school religion, but symbolism suggests something esoteric and up-to-date, like higher mathematics."[37] The preju-
dice against allegory has been encouraged by the fact that
allegories have often been used crudely in the service of edu-
cation or propaganda. However, any literary mode can be used
badly, and we should not reject the entire style of writing for
that reason.

Etymologically, "allegory" means saying one thing when you
mean something else. As such it is one kind of metaphoric or
symbolic language. The distinctive character of allegory is
that it contains some explicit indication of the second level
of meaning, while in other symbolic language the allusion may
be only implicit.[38] However, we should not make too sharp a
distinction between allegory and other forms of metaphorical
writing, since the explicit allusions to a second level of
meaning may be rare and ambiguous on occasion.

There is in fact a range of writings which can be considered allegorical. First we may distinguish between allegorical commentaries--such as the Qumran *pesharim* and the works of
Philo--and literary allegories, such as the visions of Daniel.
In the case of actual commentaries, a meaning is attached to
the text which has no necessary intrinsic relation to its original meaning. Literary allegories are composed with their interpretation in view. Yet, even here, too sharp a distinction
should not be made. Both the commentaries and the literary
allegories are based on the assumption that language has more
than one level of meaning. A literary allegory is a translation of the data or events it describes, even as an allegorical
commentary is a translation of its text. In a sense, a literary
allegory is the inverse of a commentary, since it creates a more
obscure, rather than a clearer, formulation.

Within the range of literary allegory we also find significant differences. At one end of the spectrum there is
naive allegory--what Northrop Frye has described as "a dis-
guised form of discursive writing which belongs chiefly to
educational literature on an elementary level: school-room
moralities, devotional exempla, local pageants and the like."[39]
On this end of the spectrum we should locate all use of allegory as a simple code, when the message can be stated *fully* and
more clearly without the allegory. Philip Wheelwright has described this type of allegory as "steno-symbols."[40] A steno-
symbol has a one-to-one relationship with what it represents,
such as the mathematical symbol *pi*, or is transparent of meaning, and can be exhausted by its first or literal intentional-
ity.

It is noteworthy that Wheelwright resorts to mathematics
for an example of steno-symbols. In fact it is difficult to
imagine a literary allegory which can be fully exhausted by one
referent, or can be translated without any loss of meaning.
However bad an allegory may be, it always adds some new nuance
or association to the "literal" meaning. Perhaps the nearest
literary approximation to Wheelwright's "steno-symbols" can be
found in a certain type of political allegory. In an occupied
country, a writer who wishes to express rebellious sentiments
may well couch them in a code language which will be understood
by sympathizers but not by the occupying forces. If allegory
of this type consists of purely steno-symbols which add nothing
to what could be said in plain prose, then it becomes easily
outdated. Its relevance does not transcend the immediate situation for which it is written.

The allegories which we find in apocalyptic, and specifically in Daniel, have often been understood as naive allegories
of this sort. Most recently the distinguished NT scholar
Norman Perrin has argued that apocalyptic is dependent on "a
view of myth as allegory and upon the treatment of symbols as
steno-symbols. Typically the apocalyptic seer told the story
of the history of his people in symbols where each symbol bore
a one-to-one relationship to that which it depicted. This
thing was Antiochus Epiphanes, that thing was Judas Maccabeus,

the other thing was the coming of the Romans, and so on....Once
the symbols have been correctly identified, the allegory itself
can be abandoned and the story retold in steno-language."[41]

Perrin does not speculate as to why the apocalypticist
uses allegorical language. Two explanations might be proposed
which would be consonant with this understanding of the visions
as steno-symbols. First, they might be political allegories.
The author may have wished to conceal his message from his enemies. This explanation breaks down, however, since the interpretations which follow the visions speak openly of kings and
kingdoms. Ultimately the political character of the visions is
concealed from no one. Second, the author may simply have
wished to give his work an aura of mystery. The fact that an
interpretation is necessary underlines the difficulty of the
vision and makes its attribution to a divine source credible.
We are reminded of the comment of Plutarch:

> In days of old, what was not familiar or common,
> but was expressed altogether indirectly and through
> circumlocution, the mass of the people imputed to
> the assumed manifestation of divine power and held
> it in awe and reverence. (*De Pythiae Oraculis*, 25)

This is undoubtedly one factor in the use of allegorical language, but it does not adequately account for the mythic character of the language used.

Allegory and Mythic Patterns

However, not all allegory is naive allegory, or consists
of steno-symbols. Few if any literary allegories have specific
referents for every detail of their imagery. Typically an allegory corresponds to its referent only in its outline and a
few key details. Edwin Honig defines the "allegorical quality"
as "a twice-told tale written in rhetorical, or figurative,
language and expressing a vital belief....The twice-told aspect
of the tale indicates that some venerated or proverbial ante-
cedent (old) story has become a pattern for another (the new)
story."[42] The word *pattern* is of crucial importance in this
definition. A literary allegory does not consist merely of a
set of isolated correspondences, but tells its story in such a

way that it reflects the pattern of a venerated older story.
The relevance of this understanding of allegory for the use of
mythic patterns which we have noted in Daniel 7-12 is obvious.

The use of venerated patterns to construct allegories for
new events and experiences is a typical characteristic of myth,
which has been expounded in classical form by Mircea Eliade.
For "archaic man," "objects or acts acquire a value, and in so
doing become real, because they participate after one fashion
or another in a reality that transcends them."[43] The participation in transcendent reality may be formulated in various
ways: by imitation of celestial archetypes, by the "symbolism
of the center," or by the repetition of primordial events.

The use of motifs and patterns from Canaanite myth in the
OT, which we noted with reference to the imagery of the sea and
its monsters, is a striking instance of the repetition of primordial events. For example, in Isa 51:9-10, the parting of
the Red Sea at the Exodus is identified with the victory over
Rahab and the dragon. Now the victory over the dragon was the
primordial event by which order was established over chaos.
The meaning and significance of the Exodus was expressed by
presenting it as a re-enactment of that primordial battle. The
ancient myth serves as a paradigm which is manifested again in
historical events. The allegorical language of Daniel 7 similarly gives meaning and significance to the events it describes
by assimilating them to a primordial pattern.

The four kings/kingdoms are presented in Daniel 7 as manifestations of the ancient chaos monster. It should be quite
clear that we are not dealing here with a code which can be
discarded when it is deciphered. We cannot say that the statement in Dan 7:3, "four great beasts came up out of the sea," is
adequately paraphrased in Dan 7:17, "these four great beasts
are four kings who shall arise out of the earth." Even a reader who is ignorant of, or chooses to ignore the echoes of
Canaanite mythology and of the biblical Leviathan in the beasts
which rise from the sea must concede that the vision has an
evocative power, which is lacking in the interpretation. In
fact, the interpretation only offers two terse verses as against
thirteen verses of the vision, and in many respects it fails to

clarify. So, for example, the sea is not even mentioned, and the 'saints of the Most High' are mentioned without clarification in both vision and interpretation. We need not conclude with Ginsberg and others that we are dealing with distinct layers in Daniel 7.[44] Even if this were true, we should still have to ask why the redactor only partially interprets the vision. Whether the interpretation was written by the author of the vision or not, it is not intended to replace the vision or to provide an adequate substitute for it. It tells us only enough to make clear that Daniel was not witnessing a mythical drama unrelated to particular earthly events but an interpretation of contemporary history. That interpretation is provided by showing that the events in question conform to a mythic pattern. We find exactly the same process in Daniel 8.

The understanding of allegory as the application of an ancient pattern enables us to understand further the relation between actual interpretations of an ancient text, such as we have in Daniel 9, and the literary allegories of the visions. In both cases ancient traditions are used as paradigms to interpret the new situation. The difference lies in the explicitness with which the ancient paradigm is cited.

Celestial Archetypes in Daniel 10-12

Daniel 10-12 differs from chs. 7 and 8 insofar as the historical/eschatological prophecy is not presented as a vision of Daniel but as a narrative by the angel. However, the relation between the heavenly battle of Michael and the "princes" of Persia and Greece in ch. 10 and the historical battles of the kings of Persia and Greece in ch. 11 is clearly analogous to the relation between the beasts which arise out of the sea and the kings which arise out of the earth in ch. 7. We can not say that the "princes" of Persia and Greece are simply poetic metaphors for their countries or that Michael is simply a metaphor for Israel. These angelic figures are intrinsic to the visionary's world-view. This world-view is mythical and imaginative, but the angels can not be dispensed with here any more than the mythic imagery can be dispensed with in ch. 7. The angelic patrons are conceived as distinct from their nations but inseparable from them. They represent a metaphysical dimension of the nations which is not fully actualized in any human king. They give imaginative expression to the author's belief that each nation has a significance which goes beyond its manifest earthly reality. In this case, transcendent reality is represented by reference to celestial archetypes rather than to primordial paradigms.

We will find in the following chapter that celestial imagery also plays an important role in Daniel 7 and 8. This imagery is important for the understanding of Daniel 7-12, as it shows that the visionary is working with a two-story universe where the angelic world represents a metaphysical level which cannot be discounted.

Non-allegorical Symbols in Daniel 7-12

The beasts in Daniel 7 and 8 and the angelic patrons in Daniel 10 have at least an allegorical aspect insofar as they refer or can be directly related to identifiable historical entities. There are other symbols in Daniel which do not have historical referents, but represent events which lie beyond human experience, such as the final judgment or the resurrection of the dead. These eschatological formulations are not interpretations of actual events, and so cannot in any sense be understood as literal descriptions.

There is no sharp break in Daniel between the parts which are allegories of specific historical events and the eschatological conclusions. Rather, the allegories are designed to show that the historical events participate in a mythic pattern, of which the eschatological conclusion is an integral part. The partial and confusing experience of the present is shown to have meaning in terms of the larger paradigmatic story.

The Significance of Recapitulation

The visions of Daniel 7-8, the prophecy and interpretation of Daniel 9, and the angelic narrative of chs. 10-12 are each descriptions of the career of Antiochus IV Epiphanes and its consequences. These chapters are very closely related to each

117

other, as we have seen, and show no significant difference of
viewpoint. Yet they are formulated differently.

The juxtaposition of parallel accounts is a very common
characteristic of apocalyptic writings. The most striking example is the NT book of Revelation.[45] Other examples have recently been noted in 4 Ezra and the Jewish Sibylline Oracles.[46]
Critics of a former generation tended to see in such reduplica-
tions the signs of multiple authorship. It is now apparent
that recapitulation is an integral characteristic of these
books.

In fact, the juxtaposition of different formulations of
the same narrative or message is an essential characteristic of
myth. The English anthropologist Edmund Leach has explained
this phenomenon by the analogy of electronic communications.[47]
If a message has to be communicated in the face of distrac-
tions, or "noise," the communicator must resort to "redundance."
He must repeat the message several times in slightly different
ways. In this way the basic structure which the different
formulations have in common gets through. This basic structure
cannot be exhausted or fully expressed by any one formulation.
It is essentially an apprehension of the total meaning of life
and the world, and such total meaning can never be fully ar-
ticulated. In the words of Paul Ricoeur:

> This intuition of a cosmic whole, from which man is
> not separated...(is) not *given*, but simply *aimed at*.
> It is only in intention that the myth restores some
> wholeness; it is because he himself has lost that
> wholeness that man re-enacts and imitates it in myth
> and rite....There does not exist, in fact, any act
> of signifying that is equal to its aim.[48]

The use of recapitulation in a book like Daniel reflects
the difference between religious myth and religious dogma.
Dogma demands the affirmation of definite propositions. Myth
allows for a variety of formulations. Myth, like dogma, requires a commitment, but the commitment is not tied to any one
formulation but rather to the underlying view of life. Myths,
of course, are often transformed into dogmas in the history of
religion, but the manner in which different mythic patterns are
juxtaposed in Daniel shows that that stage had not yet been
reached.

Conclusion

Daniel 7-12 draws heavily on traditional language, much of which finds its closest parallels in Ugaritic myths. Daniel does not use this language merely for embellishment, but rather uses ancient mythic patterns to interpret and show the significance of the events of his own time. Needless to say, Daniel does not simply repeat the ancient myths but used them to construct his own new vision. We will examine some of these mythic materials within the context of the book of Daniel in the following chapter.

NOTES

CHAPTER IV

[1] On the psychology of the visionary experiences of the OT prophets, see the fascinating, but inconclusive, discussion of J. Lindblom, *Prophecy in Ancient Israel* (Oxford: Blackwell, 1962) 122-48; Russell (*Method*, 158-72) argues that apocalyptic visionaries had "genuine psychical experience."

[2] H. Gunkel, *Schöpfung und Chaos* (Göttingen: Vandenhoeck und Ruprecht, 1895).

[3] See the review of this material by H. G. May, "Some Cosmic Connotations of *Mayim Rabbim*, "Many Waters," *JBL* 74 (1955) 9-21, and for a detailed analysis of its Canaanite roots, F. M. Cross, *Canaanite Myth and Hebrew Epic* (Cambridge: Harvard, 1973) 112-44. All the relevant passages are collected in M. K. Wakeman, *God's Battle with the Monster* (Leiden: Brill, 1973) 56-105.

[4] Job 26:7, 12-13. M. H. Pope (*Job* [AB 15, 3rd edition; Garden City: Doubleday, 1973] 180-86) finds a further explicit reference to sea in vs. 13a, which he translates "By his wind he bagged the Sea."

[5] *CTCA*, 2. English translation in *ANET*, 129-31.

[6] Trans. Cross, *Canaanite Myth*, 115.

[7] *CTCA*, 5.1.1-5. Trans. Cross, *Canaanite Myth*, 119.

[8] *CTCA*, 3.3.35-39. Trans. Cross, *Canaanite Myth*, 119.

[9] See A. Heidel, *The Babylonian Genesis* (Chicago: University of Chicago, 1951; reprinted 1972).

[10] Cross, *Canaanite Myth*, 120.

[11] P. Wheelwright, *Metaphor and Reality* (Bloomington: Indiana University, 1962) 105.

[12] For a review of the various religio-historical parallels which have been proposed, see C. Colpe, "Ho Huios tou Anthropou," *TDNT* 8 (1972) 408-20.

[13] J. A. Emerton, "The Origin of the Son of Man Imagery," *JTS* 9 (1958) 225-42. Cf. 231-32: "The act of coming with clouds suggests a theophany of Yahweh himself. If Dan. vii. 13 does not refer to a divine being, then it is the only exception out of about seventy passages in the OT."

[14] O. Eissfeldt, "El and Yahweh," *JSS* 1 (1956) 25-37.

[15] See Emerton, "Son of Man Imagery," 232.

[16]*CTCA*, 4.5.66. Cross, *Canaanite Myth*, 16.

[17]*CTCA*, 6.1.36; 17.6.49. Cross, *Canaanite Myth*, 16; M. Pope, *El in the Ugaritic Texts* (VTSup 2; Leiden: Brill, 1955) 32.

[18]*CTCA*, 2.1.19-21. Cross, *Canaanite Myth*, 37.

[19]"El sits as judge with Haddu his shepherd." *Ugaritica* 5, Text 2. Cross, *Canaanite Myth*, 21.

[20]*CTCA*, 6.1.53-67; *ANET*, 140.

[21]Bentzen (*Daniel*, 64) saw in Daniel 7 traditions which had been associated with the (alleged) festival of Yahweh's enthronement. J. Morgenstern ("The King-god among the Western Semites and the meaning of Epiphanes," *VT* 10 [1960] 138-97 and "The 'Son of Man' in Dan 7,13f," *JBL* 80 [1961] 65-77) has argued that Daniel 7 was influenced by a hypothetical cult of Antiochus Epiphanes at Tyre, but his thesis has no solid evidence to support it.

[22]See L. R. Clapham, *Sanchuniathon: The First Two Cycles* (Unpublished dissertation; Cambridge: Harvard, 1969). For a review of the problems associated with Philo and a good bibliography, see J. Barr, "Philo of Byblos and his Phoenician History," *BJRL* 57 (1974) 17-68.

[23]*ANET*, 331. See J. Z. Smith, "Wisdom and Apocalyptic," *Religious Syncretism in Antiquity* (B. Pearson, ed.; Missoula: Scholars Press, 1975) 131-56.

[24]T. G. Pinches, *The Old Testament in the Light of Historical Records and Legends of Assyria and Babylonia* (London: SPCK, 1908) 477-78.

[25]L. Koenen, "The Prophecies of a Potter: A Prophecy of World Renewal becomes an Apocalypse," *Proceedings of the Twelfth International Congress of Papyrology* (D. H. Samuel, ed.; Toronto: Hakkert, 1970) 250. See further his "Die Prophezeiungen des 'Töpfers,'" *Zeitschrift für Papyrologie und Epigraphik* 2 (1968) 178-209.

[26]See further below, Chapter VII.

[27]Cross, *Canaanite Myth*, 4-5; P. D. Miller, "Animal Names as Designations in Ugaritic and Hebrew," *UF* 2 (1971) 177-86.

[28]So also W. Baumgartner, "Ein Vierteljahrhundert Danielforschung," *TRu* 11 (1939) 218-19; A. Caquot, "Sur les Quatre Bêtes de Daniel VII," *Semitica* 5 (1955) 5-13, has attempted to find indications of astral symbolism in the four beasts, but his parallels are too indirect to be convincing.

[29]Quoted by C. Lévi-Strauss, *The Savage Mind* (Chicago: University of Chicago, 1966) 21.

[30]For a detailed analysis of the pattern of the cosmogonic combat myth at Ugarit and throughout the ancient Near East, see P. D. Hanson, "Zechariah 9 and the Recapitulation of an Ancient Ritual Pattern," *JBL* 92 (1973) 37-59; A. Yarbro Collins, *Combat Myth*, ch. 2.

[31]So also M. Noth, "The Understanding of History in Old Testament Apocalyptic," in *The Laws in the Pentateuch and Other Essays* (Philadelphia: Fortress, 1967) 214. See further below, Chapter VI.

[32]*CTCA*, 6.1.53-67; *ANET*, 140. See M. Pope, "Attar," in *Wörterbuch der Mythologie* 1. *Götter und Mythen im vorderen Orient* (H. W. Haussig ed.; Stuttgart: Klett, 1965) 249-50.

[33]Nonnos, *Dionysiaca* 1.154, 2.361. For the text of Nonnos, see W. H. D. Rouse, *Nonnos: Dionysiaca* (LCL; Cambridge: Harvard, 1940) 3 vols. See further A. Yarbro Collins, *Combat Myth*, ch. 2.

[34]F. Cumont, "La plus ancienne géographie astrologique," *Klio* 9 (1909) 263-73; A. Caquot, "Sur les Quatre Bêtes," 10. Teucer of Babylon is thought to have lived in the first century A.D. but Cumont argues that his astrological system is older.

[35]Cf. *The Annals of Sennacherib* (ed. D. D. Luckenbill; Chicago: University of Chicago, 1924).

[36]The MT reads "sons of Israel," but the LXX reading, "sons of God," is now supported by evidence from Qumran. See P. W. Skehan, "A fragment of the 'Song of Moses' (Deut 32) from Qumran," *BASOR* 136 (1954) 12-15.

[37]E. Honig, *Dark Conceit* (Evanston: Northwestern University, 1959) 3.

[38]See N. Frye, *Anatomy of Criticism* (Princeton: Princeton University, 1957) 90; T. Todorov, *The Fantastic* (Cleveland: Case Western Reserve, 1973) 63.

[39]Frye, *Anatomy*, 90.

[40]Wheelwright, *Metaphor and Reality*, 93-94.

[41]N. Perrin, "Wisdom and Apocalyptic in the Message of Jesus," *Proceedings of the Society of Biblical Literature* (1972) 558; "Eschatology and Hermeneutics: Reflections on Method in the Interpretation of the New Testament," *JBL* 93 (1974) 11. For a detailed critique of Perrin, see J. Collins, "The Symbolism of Transcendence," 12-22.

[42]Honig, *Dark Conceit*, 12.

[43]M. Eliade, *The Myth of the Eternal Return* (New York: Pantheon, 1954) 3-4.

[44]Ginsberg, *Studies*, 5-23.

122

[45]See especially A. Yarbro Collins, *Combat Myth*, ch. 1. Also A. Farrer, *A Rebirth of Images: The Making of St. John's Apocalypse* (London: Dacre, 1949) 36-58.

[46]E. Breech, "These Fragments I have Shored against my Ruins: the Form and Function of 4 Ezra," *JBL* 92 (1973) 267-74; J. Collins, *The Sibylline Oracles*, 37, 74.

[47]E. Leach, "Genesis as Myth," *Myth and Cosmos* (John Middleton, ed.; Garden City: Natural History Press, 1967) 1-13. Cf. W. Meeks, "The Man from Heaven in Johannine Sectarianism," *JBL* 91 (1972) 48.

[48]P. Ricoeur, *The Symbolism of Evil* (Boston: Beacon, 1969) 167-68.

THE 'SAINTS OF THE MOST HIGH' AND 'ONE LIKE A SON OF MAN'

We have considered in broad outline the mythological
framework of the visions and the different patterns which are
applied in chs. 7, 8, and 10-12. We must now examine the
imagery in greater detail and see how it is adapted within the
book of Daniel. In particular, we will attempt a closer correlation of the chapters with each other, and focus on the aspects of the imagery which run throughout the visions and serve
to bind them together. The most important of these aspects are
those which refer to angelic beings and to the "saints of the
Most High."

The 'Son of Man' and the 'Saints of the Most High'

The most problematic details in the imagery of Daniel are
surely the "one like a son of man" and the "saints of the Most
High" in ch. 7. These terms have given rise to an immense
secondary literature,[1] much of which deals with the religio-
historical background of Daniel 7, which we have already discussed. In this chapter we want to leave aside the religio-
historical question and ask in what way these phrases are used
within the book of Daniel. We want to establish the meaning of
these phrases in the terms of Daniel itself, that is, to see
whether they can be correlated or equated with any other figures or expressions within the book.

Basically, two interpretations of the "saints of the Most
High" have been put forward. Traditionally, the phrase has
been taken to refer to the faithful Jews at the time of the
Maccabean revolt. This is still the view of the majority of
scholars. It has not, however, gone unchallenged. In 1927,
Otto Procksch pointed out that the "saints" or "holy ones"
(qdwšym) in the Hebrew bible usually referred to angels, not
men. Consequently, he suggested that, in Daniel, they should
also be understood as angels.[2] This position was revived by
Martin Noth, and has found an increasing number of adherents,[3]
while it has also occasioned lively debate.[4] The angelic sense

of the term "saints" is now known to be derived from the
Canaanite use of *qdšm*, holy ones, to refer to the divine council of El.[5]

The interpretation of the "one like a son of man" is inevitably closely tied to the "holy ones." According to the
most widely held view, the "one like a son of man" is a collective symbol for Israel, the holy ones of the Most High. In the
words of Sigmund Mowinckel:

> In the present form of Daniel's visions of the
> beasts, the Son of Man is a pictorial symbol of
> the people of Israel, not a personal Messiah of
> any kind.[6]

There is, however, a dissenting tradition of scholarship which
sees the "one like a son of man" as an individual figure. The
traditional view, which identified the "Son of Man" with the
Messiah, has scarcely any scholarly support now, as it is
widely recognized as the product of a Christian interpretation,
in the light of the NT. A number of scholars, however, have
identified the "one like a son of man" with an individual
angel.[7] An angelic interpretation is most clearly compatible
with Noth's understanding of the "holy ones" but the two interpretations do not necessarily imply each other. Many of the
scholars who have identified the "son of man" as an angel have
assumed that the "holy ones" referred to Israel.

It is not possible to resolve either of these problems by
purely philological considerations. The phrase "son of man" is
simply a Semitic idiom for a human being.[8] The fact that
Daniel sees "one *like* a son of man" clearly suggests that "son
of man" is not a title here and is not the name of a well-
known figure. "Son of Man" becomes a title in the NT and
probably also in the Similitudes of Enoch, but there is nothing
to suggest that it was so used before the first century B.C.[9]
Again, the preposition "like" might suggest that what Daniel
saw was not in fact a human figure, but this is less than certain, in view of the generally symbolic character of the vision.
Ultimately, the identity of the "one like a son of man" can
only be established from its context in Daniel.[10]

The same is true of the "holy ones of the Most High." The substantive adjective $q^e d\hat{o}\check{s}\hat{i}m$, holy ones, is used in the OT nearly always to refer to angels--but even Noth admits one undisputed exception in Ps 34:10. Besides, he freely admits that the adjective "holy" is often applied to human beings, and that Israel can be called a "holy people." Even on this evidence we could not preclude the possibility that Daniel 7 follows Psalm 34 and refers to the Jews. The evidence from Qumran is similarly inconclusive. The one phrase which precisely parallels Daniel 7--"the holy ones of the Most High," in CD 20:8--is unfortunately ambiguous:

> Let no man agree with him in property or work,
> for all the holy ones of the Most High have cursed him.

This passage is in Hebrew, $q^e d\hat{o}\check{s}\hat{e}$ '$el y\hat{o}n$, and it clarifies the Aramaic of Daniel, $qadd\hat{i}\check{s}\hat{e}$ '$el y\hat{o}n\hat{i}n$, which could conceivably be translated as "the holy ones among the heavenly beings" or "the heavenly holy ones," but it does not tell us whether the reference is to angels or human beings. Undoubtedly, most of the substantive uses of "holy ones" at Qumran refer to angels but here again there is at least one case where the term, most probably, is used with reference to human beings. This is 1QM 10:10: "Who is like Thy people Israel...the people of the holy ones of the covenant," but even here we should note that the phrase is "people of the holy ones" not simply "holy ones." A few other passages are ambiguous. In the Apocrypha and Pseudepigrapha, where in large part we must rely on translations of Hebrew or Aramaic originals, the term "holy ones" is used frequently of both angels and men.[11]

In summary we may say that the Hebrew, $q^e d\hat{o}\check{s}\hat{i}m$, used substantively, refers in the great majority of cases to angelic or heavenly beings. However, there is one undisputed text in the OT where $q^e d\hat{o}\check{s}\hat{i}m$ refers to human beings, and there are some passages in the Qumran scrolls where a human reference is possible. Further, since the adjective "holy" could be used attributively of human beings, at any time, the substantive use could conceivably have been developed from it. The philological evidence must therefore be regarded as inconclusive.

Equally, the problem cannot be solved by a source critical analysis which would understand the "holy ones" as angels in some verses but as humans in other verses from a different source. Noth considered vss. 21-22 a later addition, primarily because he thought vs. 21, "this horn made war on the saints and prevailed over them," incompatible with his interpretation of the "saints" as angels in the rest of the chapter.[12] This procedure is clearly illegitimate. Since we are trying to establish the identity of the "saints," it will not do to begin by bracketing out the verses which create problems for one interpretation. Dan 7:25b, "and shall wear out the saints of the Most High," was also problematic for Noth, as it suggested that "saints" could be overcome. Here he avoided the problem by suggesting that the verb usually translated "wear out" (*blʾ*) be derived from an Arabic root *bala*, to test or to offend. This suggestion has been widely rejected and must be considered unlikely.[13] In any case, we will show below that none of these verses is incompatible with the understanding of "saints" as angels.[14]

Further, no distinction can be made between the "saints" in vss. 21-22 and the "saints of the Most High" in the rest of the chapter. The two phrases are clearly synonymous in vs. 22. The horn makes war successfully against the "saints" in vs. 21 but equally against the "saints of the Most High" in vs. 25. It is possible that the phrase "people of the saints of the Most High" in vs. 27 has a different referent than the other phrases, but this does not require the hypothesis of a separate source.

Ultimately, the identity of the "holy ones" and the "one like a son of man" within the book of Daniel can only be established from their present context. Before we proceed to examine the relationship of these phrases to other imagery in the book, it is necessary to address more thoroughly the question of the unity of ch. 7. If that chapter were composite, as many scholars have held, we would have to reckon with the possibility that some of its language has a different meaning in Daniel than it had in its source. Daniel 7 is the only one of the visions whose internal unity has been seriously questioned in this way.

EXCURSUS: The Unity of Daniel 7

Objections to the unity of Daniel 7 have focused on two blocs of material: (a) the enthronement vision, vss. 9-10, 13-14 and (b) the references to Antiochus Epiphanes, vss. 8, 11a, 20-21, 24-25.

(a) The references to the heavenly scene in vss. 9-10, 13-14 stand out in their context, as they seem to be poetic fragments inserted in a prose narrative. There is no doubt that the imagery of these verses is traditional, and it is quite possible that the visionary simply incorporated a few verses from a poem. This in itself is not an argument against the unity of the chapter. The question is whether the vision of the four beasts in Dan 7:2-8 ever existed without the enthronement scene. So, for example, Dequeker has argued that the bulk of Daniel 7 consists of a pre-Maccabean vision of four beasts which represent four kingdoms, and is another specimen of the anti-Hellenistic use of the four kingdoms schema found in Daniel 2. A Maccabean redactor enlarged this vision "by use of the apocalyptic materials he took from another source which provisionally can be labeled: the Myth of the Enthronement of the Son of Man by the Ancient God."[15] Dequeker admits that there is nothing in the enthronement scene which points specifically to Maccabean times but insists that the vision of the "Son of Man" comes from a different source than the four kingdoms passage which precedes it.

Dequeker seems quite unaware of the mythological references in Daniel 7. As we have seen in the preceding chapter, the beasts which rise from the sea belong to the same complex of mythic material as the enthronement of the "one like a son of man"--specifically the Canaanite myth of the conflict between Baal and Yamm for kingship. Apart from Daniel 7, we never find the sea or beasts associated with the four kingdoms. Equally, the number four is never associated with the sea and its monsters. In Daniel 7, the two traditions--the Canaanite conflict myth and the four kingdoms--are inseparably fused since the kingdoms are described as beasts. The vision of the four beasts cannot be understood without reference to the

Canaanite conflict myth, and the enthronement of the Baal-like
figure of the "one like a son of man" is an integral part of
that myth. Accordingly, in its most original form, Daniel uses
the Canaanite conflict myth as an allegory for the popular
schema of the four kingdoms. The verses which refer to the
enthronement of "one like a son of man" cannot be regarded as
later additions.

(b) Dequeker's thesis that Daniel 7 consists primarily of
a pre-Maccabean vision rests on his conviction that all references to Antiochus Epiphanes, the eleventh horn of the fourth
beast, are secondary. He then regards the present form of
Daniel 7 as a "pesher" on the older vision.[16] The term "pesher"
is obviously inappropriate as it refers to explicit commentary,
whereas the references to Antiochus Epiphanes are integrated in
the vision. However, the point at issue is whether these verses
are a later addition. The verses in question are 8, 11a, 20-21
and 24-25.

A number of scholars have regarded the references to the
eleventh horn as secondary, because in vs. 7 the beast is said
to have ten horns, and the eleventh seems added as an after-
thought. Some scholars have even rejected the reference to ten
horns (vss. 7, 24) as secondary.[17] However, even H. L. Ginsberg, the great champion of fragmentation, realized that the
horns are an integral part of the vision, analogous to the four
wings of the third beast and the three ribs in the mouth of the
second.[18] It is not certain whether the visionary had ten specific kings in mind, or simply used a round number, suggested,
perhaps, by the toes of the statue in ch. 2.[19] In any case,
he clearly wanted to emphasize that Antiochus IV Epiphanes was
different from all his predecessors. It is not therefore surprising that Epiphanes is not numbered with the others but is
singled out as a special phenomenon.

Some confusion has been caused by the relationship between
Antiochus and the Greek kingdom, the eleventh horn and the
beast. Since the visionary wished to use the schema of the
four kingdoms, the entire Greek empire, the fourth beast, is
ultimately condemned. Within the Greek kingdom, Antiochus is
singled out for special mention. He is, nonetheless, a

representative of Hellenistic dominion, a manifestation of the beast. The schema of the four kingdoms was, of course, independent of the career of Antiochus, but there is no reason to believe that the form of that schema presented in Daniel 7 ever existed without the eleventh horn. We may conclude, then, that the content of ch. 7 does not require the hypothesis that any verses were inserted by an editor other than the original author.

However, certain arguments have been brought against the unity of the chapter, on the basis of stylistic inconsistencies. It is well to begin by reviewing the literary structure of the chapter.

The Literary Structure of Daniel 7

As Noth and Dequeker have noted, the vision of Daniel consists of a number of scenes, marked by two formulaic expressions.[20] The first, "I was seeing...and behold" (*ḥzh ḥwyt ...w'rw*) usually introduces the scene. The second, "I was seeing until..." (*ḥzh ḥwyt 'd dy*) introduces the dynamic action of the vision. So the first scene, vss. 2-4, begins: "I was seeing in my vision by night, and behold..." Then the sea and the four beasts are introduced and the first beast described. In 4b we find the second formula: "I was seeing until its wings were plucked off..." The second and third scenes, vss. 5 and 6, describe the second and third beasts. In each case the second formula is omitted, presumably for the sake of brevity. In vs. 7, the fourth beast is introduced by the usual formula "I was seeing in visions of the night, and behold..." At this point, however, complications arise.

The conclusion to the vision of the fourth beast is given in vs. 11b: "I was seeing until the beast was slain..." Between vss. 7 and 11b we find a number of introductory formulae: In vs. 8, the eleventh horn is introduced by the phrase "I was considering the horns and behold..." (*mstkl ḥwyt bqrnyy' w'lw*). In vs. 9, the vision of the "Ancient of Days" and the heavenly court is introduced: "I was seeing until..." (*ḥzh ḥwyt 'd dy*). In vs. 11, the scene returns to the eleventh horn.

The formula is abbreviated: "I was seeing..." (*ḥzh hwyt*), without either "behold" or "until." After vs. 11, we find a new visionary scene in vs. 13: "I was seeing...and behold" (*ḥzh hwyt w'rw*) introducing the "one like a son of man." Finally in vs. 21, when Daniel is seeking clarification from the angel, he elaborates part of his vision, and uses the formula "I was looking until."

We should emphasize that these recurring formulae in Daniel 7 do not indicate a rigid structure which is strictly observed. Only in one case, the first scene in vss. 2-4, do we find the two formulae clearly juxtaposed. Even there we cannot speak of a neatly bipartite vision. The first formula ("I was seeing and behold") introduces (a) a description of the sea, (b) an action--four beasts "came up out of the sea," and (c) a description of the first beast. The second formula only introduces the action related to the first beast. The second and third scenes omit the second formula ("I was seeing until") as also does the vision of "one like a son of man" in vss. 13-14. In view of this variation, we should hesitate to infer editorial activity because of apparent deviations from a supposed formal structure.

Scholarly debate has focused on vss. 8-11a, that is, on the verses which intervene between the introduction of the fourth beast in vs. 7 and his destruction in 11b. We have seen already that the scene of the heavenly court and Ancient of Days (vss. 9-10), and the scene of the "one like a son of man," are intrinsically related to the beasts from the sea and cannot be regarded as later additions. The reason for the position of vss. 9-10 before the destruction of the beast is obvious. The beast is destroyed by the judgment of the court which is introduced in these verses. Now the most obvious basis for the judgment of the court is the blasphemy of the eleventh horn in vss. 8 and 11a. Accordingly these verses which refer to the horn are not conspicuously intrusive.

The stylistic peculiarities of vss. 8 and 11a are not sufficient to brand them as editorial insertions: vs. 8 is introduced by the formula "I was considering and behold..." Three objections have been brought against this phrase.[21]

First, it is repetitive after the introductory formula for the fourth beast in vs. 7. In fact, however, the repetition is a natural way to single out the horn for special attention. Second, it uses the term *mstkl* (considering) instead of the usual *ḥzh* (seeing). This variation, however, is explicable precisely as a device to avoid undue repetition of the previous verse. Third, the word for behold is *'lw* instead of the usual *'rw*. This detail is insignificant. Both forms of the word were current; *'lw* is also found in Dan 2:31 and 4:7, 10. It was not exceptional to interchange two forms of the same word. In Jer 10:11, we find two forms of the Aramaic word for land, *'arqā'* and *'ar'ā'*, within the same sentence. Other examples are found in the Elephantine papyri.[22]

Finally, no significance can be attached to the use of the perfect tense after "behold" in vs. 8, instead of the usual participle. This again may be simply a way to emphasize the advent of Antiochus Epiphanes.

The objections against vs. 11a are even weaker. Dequeker argues that "the difficulty of vs. 11 lies in the fact that the regular transitional formula *ḥzh hwyt 'd dy* is first interrupted, then extensively repeated."[23] This is simply not the case. The phrase *ḥzh hwyt* (I was seeing...) in vs. 11a is not to be read as part of the formula *ḥzh hwyt 'd dy* (I was seeing until...) in vs. 11b. It is a distinct formula which reintroduces the horn after the digression on the heavenly court.

There is no reason, then, to see either vs. 8 or vs. 11a as an editorial addition. In fact, vss. 7-11 present a coherent literary unit, describing the fourth beast. The unit is framed by the introduction of the beast in vs. 8, with the formula "I was seeing...and behold," and its destruction in vs. 11b, with the formula "I was seeing until..." Within this framework, we find another bi-partite vision. The phrase "I was considering...and behold" introduces the horn in vs. 8. This is followed by the formula "I was seeing until" which introduces the heavenly court. Verse 8 and vss. 9-10 belong together as they describe the protagonists in the confrontation. Verse 11a re-introduces the horn and so frames the heavenly court scene within two references to the horn. The

phrase *ḥẓh ḥwyt* by which this verse is introduced is not found
in this abbreviated form elsewhere in the book. Therefore, it
should not be confused with the regular introductory formulae.
There is no reason to posit editorial insertions in this
passage.

Verses 20-21 and 24-25 have been rejected by Dequeker and
others because they presuppose the introduction of the eleventh
horn in vss. 8 and 11a. Accordingly, they stand or fall with
these verses. Other objections against the unity of the chapter have been based on discrepancies between the vision and
interpretation. As we have seen in the previous chapter, few
if any allegories have specific referents in every detail.
Typically, they correspond to their referents in outline and
in a few key details. This is also the case in Daniel 7. The
fact that there is a second vision and interpretation in Dan
7:19-27 cannot be taken as an editorial revision either. It
is simply a way of emphasizing the fourth beast and the eleventh
horn.

In short, despite the persistent efforts of critics to
drive wedges between the sentences of Daniel 7, there is no
reason to posit that this vision existed in any form before
Maccabean times or that it includes any later editorial insertions. (End of Excursus)

The Parallelism of the Visions

The "holy ones of the Most High" and the "one like a son
of man" cannot be explained by purely philological arguments,
nor by a source-critical analysis of Daniel 7. Rather we must
determine how they function in Daniel 7-12. The question cannot be confined to Daniel 7, because the "holy ones" also appear in Daniel 8. Further, we have already seen that the individual visions in Daniel 7-12 are variant formulations of the
same complex of events, the persecution of Antiochus Epiphanes.
As such, they complement each other and may be used to clarify
each other. The interpretation of Jeremiah's prophecy in Dan
9:24-27 is one formulation among the others but it contains
none of the mythological elements found in the other accounts

and no description of the eschatological events. Accordingly,
it has no parallels to the "one like a son of man" or the judgment scene. We may therefore leave it aside for the present.
Apart from Daniel 9, we find four accounts in Daniel which
focus on the career of Antiochus Epiphanes:

(1) the vision in 7:1-14 and its interpretation in 7:17-18;
(2) the elaboration of this vision in 7:19-22 and its inter-
    pretation in 7:23-27;
(3) the vision in 8:1-12 and its interpretation in 8:20-25;
(4) the narrative account in 10:20-12:3.
      These accounts share a common pattern:
(a) Review of history prior to the time of Antiochus Epiphanes:
    7:1-7 and its interpretation in 7:17; 7:19 and its inter-
    pretation in 7:23-24a; 8:1-8 and its interpretation in
    8:20-22; and 10:12-11:20.
(b) The career of Antiochus, which is presented as a revolt
    against God: 7:8, 11; 7:20-21 and its interpretation in
    7:24b-25; 8:9-12 and its interpretation in 8:23-25; 11:
    21-45.
(c) The intervention of a supernatural power: 7:9-12; 7:22 and
    its interpretation in 7:26; 8:25; 12:1.
(d) The eschatological state of salvation: 7:13-14 and its
    interpretation in 7:18; 7:22 and its interpretation in
    7:27; 12:1-3. There is no description of the final salva-
    tion in Daniel 8.

      If we may categorize the career of Antiochus as a *threat*
(to the faithful Jews and heaven), then we may conveniently
summarize this pattern as Past History--Threat--Supernatural
Intervention--Salvation. At least in Daniel 7 the "past history" is subsumed under the category "threat" as all four kingdoms are beasts from the sea.
      Since the first three accounts (i.e., chs. 7-8) are com-
plicated by the alternation of vision and interpretation, we
may begin our analysis with the fourth section (chs. 10-12).

The Angelic Narrative, Dan 10:12-12:3

      As we have noted earlier, the narrative of the angel in
Daniel 10-12 is set in the common mythical system of the Ancient

Near East. Over each nation there is a patron deity, or in this case, angel. When two nations fight on earth, it is because their patrons are fighting in heaven.

The framework within which the historical events of Daniel 11 take place is outlined in Dan 10:13-11:1. An angel, who may be identified as Gabriel by analogy with Dan 8:16 and 9:21, explains how he was obstructed for 21 days by the prince of Persia, until Michael, "one of the first princes," came to his aid (10:13) and how he must now return to fight with the prince of Persia, and after him with the prince of Greece. In these battles, Gabriel's only ally is Michael, "your prince" (10:20-21).

These verses set the stage for the following account of the hellenistic wars, which are then described in terms of battles between kings on earth. The introductory verses have, however, made clear that the earthly battles are only one dimension of what is happening in a two-story universe. Corresponding to the kings on earth and their conflicts are the patron angels of the peoples and the battles waged between them.

Heavenly battles were frequent between the gods of the various nations in pagan polytheistic mythologies. In biblical writings Yahweh's heavenly adversaries are usually ignored, but he still acts as a divine warrior. When Israel went out to battle on earth, Yahweh also marched out with his heavenly armies. The victory was primarily achieved by the heavenly, not the earthly forces.[24]

The earthly and heavenly battles were really two dimensions of the same battle. Accordingly we find angelic hosts in direct confrontation with human enemies. The pattern can be illustrated from Judges 5. When Deborah and Barak went out to fight against Sisera, Yahweh also marched out from Seir. The two dimensions of the battle are evident in Judg 5:19-20:

> The kings came, they fought, then fought the kings
> of Canaan....From heaven fought the stars, from their
> courses they fought against Sisera.

Similarly in the Qumran War Scroll, the angelic host mingles freely with the army of Israel. We read in 1QM 12:7-8:

> Mighty men and a host of angels are among those
> mustered with us, the mighty one of war is in our
> congregation, and the host of his spirits is with
> our steps.

It is not necessary to assume that the battle between Michael
and the prince of Greece on the heavenly level is strictly
single combat. At least Michael is accompanied by Gabriel. It
is likely that both princes were thought to be accompanied by
their hosts. This is certainly the case in the similar, though
much later passage in Rev 12:7-8. There we read that "war
arose in heaven, Michael and his angels fighting against the
dragon; and the dragon and his angels fought." Similarly in
the Qumran War Scroll, both Michael and Belial are accompanied
by their hosts. If, as seems likely, both Michael and the
prince of Greece are implicitly accompanied by their hosts in
Daniel, then we must take it that the individual figures are
representatives of the hosts they lead. The "princes" of
Greece and Persia certainly represent a number of kings at the
human level.

In Dan 11:2b-45, we find a description of the hellenistic
wars on the human level. However, in the account of the career
of Epiphanes the two spheres merge. In 11:36

> the king will do according to his will; he will
> magnify and exalt himself above every heavenly
> being, and he will speak astonishing things against
> the highest god and he will prosper.

The pattern here corresponds directly to what we found in
Judges 5. There the heavenly host fought against Israel's enemies. Here Israel's enemy comes into direct conflict with the
heavenly host and with God himself.

The phrase which we translated "above every heavenly being" is *'al kol 'ēl* in Dan 11:36. The word *'ēl* is normally
translated "god" but since the term is grouped here with *'ēl
'ēlîm*, god of gods, or Yahweh, and since the pagan gods are
mentioned separately in vs. 37, we must conclude that it refers
to Yahweh's angelic host. In fact, *'ēlîm* is a common synonym
for angels, especially in the Qumran scrolls. Accordingly,
Yadin even translates *'ēl 'ēlîm* as "god of angels" in the War
Scroll, a rendering which can be supported by analogy with

Yahweh Sabaoth, lord of hosts, in the bible, and the expression
"lord of spirits" in the Similitudes of Enoch (1 Enoch 37:4;
38:2, 6, etc.).[25] The statement that the king prospered shows
that he was successful for a time not only in his persecution
of the Jews (11:33-35) but also in his attacks on God and the
heavenly host. The explicit mention of Antiochus' disregard
for pagan gods in vs. 37 is surprising. It is mentioned after
the supreme blasphemy against the highest god as an addendum to
show the completeness of the king's impiety.

The scene returns explicitly to the heavenly realm in 12:1,
"at that time Michael the great prince will arise." The precise connotation of ya'^amod, will arise/stand is not clear.
The context suggests a military victory, but the reference to
"everyone who is found to be written in the book" (12:1d) might
suggest a judicial setting.[26] The two connotations are not incompatible with each other.

The result of Michael's intervention, whether it is military or judicial or both, is that Israel will be rescued and a
resurrection will follow. Then "the wise will shine like the
splendor of the firmament, and those who lead the many to justice will be like the stars forever." Many scholars have regarded this passage as a simple comparison. This however is
unlikely. The stars had long been identified with the angelic
host in Israelite tradition. In Judg 5:20 the stars fought
against Sisera. In Job 38:7 the stars are linked with the sons
of God shouting for joy at creation.[27] Ultimately this tradition can be traced back to Canaanite mythology where the stars
appear as members of the divine council in the Ugaritic texts.[28]

We shall see that the identification of stars and the angelic host is clear in Dan 8:10. Now in 1 Enoch 104 the righteous are promised that they "will shine as the lights of
heaven, and the portals of heaven will be opened to you" (vs.
2) and a few verses later, that they will "become companion to
the hosts of heaven" (vs. 6).[29] In this case there can be no
doubt that the identification of stars and angels is assumed
and that "to shine like the stars" means "to join the angelic
host." In intertestamental Judaism, the righteous were frequently thought to become companions to the angels after death.

So in the Similitudes of Enoch (39:5), "the dwelling-places of the righteous are with the holy angels." In Mark 12:25 (par Matt 22:30, Luke 20:36), Jesus tells the Sadducees that when men rise from the dead they are like the angels in heaven. In the Qumran scrolls, the members of the community mingle with the angels even before death.[30]

We see from 1 Enoch 104 that fellowship with the angels could be expressed as "shining like the stars." This is also the case in a passage closely contemporary with Daniel, the Testament of Moses 10:9:

> and he will cause thee to approach the heaven of the
>   stars
> in the place of their habitation,
> and thou shalt look from on high
> and see thy enemies in Gehenna.

Here the spatial imagery is very definitely emphasized. Israel does not merely resemble the stars by shining but is elevated to the place of their habitation. The fact that Israel collectively is raised up does not seriously affect the relevance of this text as a parallel for Daniel. In view of this evidence from intertestamental Judaism, we should conclude that in Daniel 12 the wise who "shine like the stars" become assimilated to, or join, the heavenly host.

The formulation of resurrection by reference to stars inevitably suggests a relation to the widespread Hellenistic belief in astral immortality. The idea that exceptional individuals, such as Castor and Pollux, could be immortalized as stars was current in Greece from a very early stage. In the fifth century B.C. a belief in astral immortality was sufficiently widespread to become the butt of Aristophanes' jokes.[31] By the first century B.C., Cicero could speculate that the heaven was nearly filled with mortals.[32] We have no clear evidence that the idea of astral immortality was popular in the Hellenistic Near East in the early second century B.C., but it must at least have been known. In any case, Daniel does not simply accept the Hellenistic idea. If he was influenced by it at all, he adapted it to fit traditional Israelite concepts. Just as the Jews did not regard the stars as gods but as members of Yahweh's long-revered angelic council, so astral immortality was not the return of a fiery soul to the fiery regions of heaven, nor a form of apotheosis, but the admittance of the faithful just to Yahweh's angelic host.

Daniel 10-12, then, makes explicit the conceptual framework within which the apocalypticist saw the career of Antiochus Epiphanes. This framework is primarily a heavenly battle between the angelic princes, and, presumably, the hosts they lead. However, humans participate in this battle and so Epiphanes can be said to come into confrontation with God and the 'ēlîm, angels, and even be successful against them for a time. After the battle has come to an end, the faithful Jews who suffered in the battle (Dan 11:35) will be rewarded by sharing the splendor of the heavenly host.

Nothing is said explicitly in Daniel 12 with reference to an eschatological kingdom. Accordingly, it provides no direct parallel to the "holy ones" or the "one like a son of man." However, we should note that if Israel mingles with the heavenly host in the eschatological era, a kingdom which is given to one must be given to both.

The Vision in Daniel 8

The vision in Daniel 8 describes the career of Epiphanes in vss. 9-12 and 23-25. Here we are given no introduction to the heavenly background of the events and there is no eschatological conclusion. However, we have already seen that a mythic pattern is applied. This is the pattern of the revolt of the day-star, which is familiar from Isaiah 14. The little horn rose up against the host of heaven, cast some of the host and some of the stars to the ground and trampled on them, and then proceeded in its onslaught on the lord of the host.

We have already noted the frequent identification of stars and angels in the biblical world. The parallelism of the stars here with the host of heaven makes quite explicit that supernatural heavenly beings are referred to. Here, as in Daniel 11, Epiphanes passes over from the purely human domain and launches an attack on the heavenly host. This is precisely parallel to

Dan 11:36 where Epiphanes elevated himself *'al kol 'ēl*,
against every heavenly being.

The parallel passage in the interpretation of the dream is
unfortunately obscured by textual difficulties. The Hebrew
reads (Dan 8:24-25):

> *wᵉhisḥît 'ᵃsûmîm wᵉ'am qᵉdôšîm*
> *wᵉ'al siklô wᵉhiṣlîaḥ mirmāh bᵉyādô*

> He will destroy mighty ones and a people of holy
> ones and against his plotting, and deceit will
> prosper in his hand.

The above is plainly corrupt. The LXX reads:

> He will destroy powerful ones and a people of holy
> ones and his plotting shall be against the holy
> ones.

which presupposes a Hebrew reading

> *wᵉhisḥît 'ᵃsûmîm wᵉ'am qᵉdôšîm*
> *wᵉ'al qᵉdôšîm siklô.*

This is a possible reading, but the phrases *'am qᵉdôšîm* and *'al*
qᵉdôšîm are so similar that we must suspect dittography, especially since *'am qᵉdôšîm* (the people of the holy ones) appears
to be superfluous. Consequently the reference to the people of
the holy ones must be regarded as textually suspect and no conclusions as to its meaning can be based on this verse.

In any case, there is at least a reference here to the
qᵉdôšîm, holy ones. The parallelism with the dream requires
that the holy ones be taken as equivalent to the host and the
stars in the dream. Since 'host' and 'stars' refer unequiv-
ocally to heavenly, angelic beings, the natural inference is
that the holy ones are angels too. In both dream and interpretation, the apocalypticist is speaking of an attack on the
heavenly host.

There are two possible objections to this interpretation.
First, Delcor has argued ingeniously that the casting down of
the stars refers not to an attack on Yahweh's angelic host, but
parallels Dan 11:37, where mention is made of Antiochus' disregard for the gods of his fathers.[33] On this interpretation,
the stars and the host of heaven would refer to pagan deities.

Undoubtedly both terms are used in this sense in the bible,
notably in Deut 4:19 where Israel is warned to "beware lest you
lift up your eyes to heaven, and when you see the sun and the
moon and the stars, all the host of heaven, you be drawn away
and worship them and serve them, things which the Lord your god
has allotted to all the peoples under the whole heaven."[34] But
the patron angels or gods of the gentiles were not the only
angelic beings who could be represented by the stars. Yahweh
also had a faithful heavenly host attendant on him, which could
also be portrayed in astral terms, as is evident in Judg 5:20,
where the stars fight with Israel against a pagan people. The
host of the good angels is considerably more prominent in intertestamental literature, closer to the time of Daniel, than
in the OT, a fact amply illustrated by the Qumran War Scroll,
to which we have referred above. In view of the parallelism
with the $q^e d\hat{o}\check{s}\hat{i}m$ in the interpretation, it is surely more
likely that the host here is Yahweh's host rather than the
pagan gods. Delcor fails to find any correlative to this part
of the vision in the interpretation and any parallel to the
$q^e d\hat{o}\check{s}\hat{i}m$ in the vision. Yet this parallelism is crucial for the
understanding of Daniel, as it shows that when Epiphanes
'destroys' the holy ones, his activity need not be confined to
the earthly realm, but can include violence to the angelic host
in the heavenly battle. We cannot reduce the reference to the
stars to a purely imaginative description of the arrogance of
Epiphanes. Undoubtedly the passage is imaginative, but like
all the symbolism of Daniel, it is grounded in a particular
metaphysics and cannot be dismissed as "mere" metaphor.[35]

A second objection to the foregoing interpretation of
Daniel 8 might arise from the uncertainty of the relation of
the interpretation to the vision. Even if the host of heaven
and the stars in the vision are understood as the angelic host,
might they still be only a symbolic representation of the human
holy ones? Here again we must bear in mind the metaphysical
dimension of the symbolism. A reference to humans cannot exhaust the meaning of language which describes angels or heavenly beings. In the author's own terms, angels are not symbols
but real beings. Accordingly, in the author's terms, it is

unthinkable that humans would be symbolized by angels, or depicted in language which is normally understood to refer to
heavenly beings.[36] The only way in which Dan 8:24-25 can be
read as a reference to Israel is by assuming that here Israel
has merged with the heavenly host, as is the case in the Qumran
War Scroll. This is possible, and may be the correct interpretation of the passage, especially if the word 'am (people) is
original in the text. It should be noted that in Daniel 12 the
faithful Israelites do not join the heavenly host until after
the resurrection, but this is not conclusive as the host may be
thought to mingle with the Israelites in the time of battle.[37]
In view of the corruption of the text, it is not possible to
decide whether or not Israel is included in the interpretation.
However, it should be clear that the term $q^e d\hat{o}\hat{s}\hat{i}m$ at least includes a reference to the angelic host.

The Visions in Daniel 7

We can now turn to the most obscure account of the career
of Antiochus Epiphanes, that found in Daniel 7. The main vision extends from vss. 1-14 and is interpreted in vss. 17 and
18. The vision is further elaborated in vss. 19-22 and this in
turn is interpreted in vss. 23-27. The interpretation of the
first vision is very brief and passes over several elements of
the vision without comment. We are merely told that the four
beasts are four kings who will arise from the earth, and that
the "holy ones of the Most High" will receive the kingdom,
which, in the vision, was given to the "one like a son of man."
The second vision and interpretation are more detailed. In the
vision the horn makes war on the "holy ones" until the Ancient
of Days comes and judgment is given to the "holy ones," who
receive the kingdom. In the interpretation we are told that
the horn wears down the "holy ones," but that the kingdom is
given to the "people of the holy ones."

The symbolic nature of the visions has been rightly emphasized. Accordingly, Delcor repeats the traditional argument
that the figure of "one like a son of man" is used here merely
to contrast with the animal figures. While the contrast with

the animals is real, this does not exhaust the significance of the choice of a human figure. In the Animal Apocalypse of 1 Enoch 83-90, Israel was adequately represented by animal figures, while, significantly, human figures were reserved to represent angels. The usage in the book of Daniel elsewhere points to an angelic identity. In Dan 8:15 an angel appears "like the appearance of a man" ($k^emar'\bar{e}h$ $g\bar{a}ber$) and 9:21 refers to "the man Gabriel" ($h\bar{a}-'\hat{\imath}\check{s}$ $Gabr\hat{\imath}'el$); in 10:5 an angel appears as '$\hat{\imath}\check{s}$ '$ehad$ $l\bar{a}b\bar{u}\check{s}$ $badd\hat{\imath}m$, a man clothed in linen, and this description is repeated in Dan 12:6. The human figure is symbolic, but significantly chosen. In view of the usage in the other visions of Daniel, it is most probable that the figure of "one like a son of man" represents the angelic host and/or its leader.

No argument as to the identity of the "one like a son of man" can be derived from the fact that the earthly character of the kings is emphasized--they will arise from the earth (vs. 17) or on the earth (vs. 23). As Noth has already observed, in Daniel 2 the sequence of earthly kingdoms which apparently provided the model for Daniel 7 is replaced by a kingdom of heavenly origin.[38]

Furthermore, in the light of our exegesis of Daniel 8, Dan 7:21-22 and 25, which speak of the horn prevailing over the holy ones, cannot be considered incompatible with understanding "holy ones" as angels. Rather, those verses strengthen that interpretation, since they provide a close parallel to 8:10, where angels must be meant. This remains true even if we accept the traditional meaning of bl' (7:25) as "wear away" or destroy. Both Daniel 7 and 8 can be understood in the light of the heavenly battle explicitly described in 10:12-11:1 and in 12:1. The angelic patrons of the Seleucids are not explicitly mentioned in Daniel 7 or 8, but then they were omitted in Dan 11:36-37 too, when the human Antiochus Epiphanes was said to launch an attack on heaven.

The only serious objection to a purely angelic interpretation of the "holy ones" in Daniel comes from the expression "people of the holy ones" in 7:27. Despite the argument of Noth, that 'am (people) should be translated "host," Coppens'

reasoning is more convincing. Just as Michael is prince of
Israel (Michael *your* prince, 10:21), so Israel is the people of
the holy ones.[39] But the "people of the holy ones" receives
the kingdom just as did the holy ones and the "one like a son
of man." This can be explained in either of two ways. First,
it may indicate that the heavenly host has already mingled with
Israel, and so the people can no longer be distinguished from
its patrons. Alternatively, we may emphasize the fact that in
vs. 27 the kingdom given to the people consists of all *under*
heaven, and conclude that the kingdom is being realized at once
on two levels. Since we have seen in Daniel 12 that the just
would join the stars or heavenly host after the final judgment,
either interpretation may appear appropriate. In either case,
the people shares in the kingdom of the angels and so the interpretation in 7:27 is merely a spelling out of the human dimension of the more complete reality mentioned in the vision in
vs. 22 and in the interpretation in vs. 18.

C. W. Brekelmans has argued "that the kingdom is given to
the holy ones in Dan. 7 points strongly to the equation of the
holy ones with the people of God, because the eschatological
kingdom of the angels is practically unknown in this period."[40]
However, the kingdom of the angels appears in the one other
great work of the period which describes the final battle for
the kingdom--the Qumran War Scroll, in 1QM 17:6-8. In fact,
this passage may be an excellent formulation of the conception
underlying Daniel--"to raise up among the angels the authority
of Michael and the dominion of Israel among all flesh." It is
precisely Michael's rule over the heavenly realm which makes
possible the dominion of Israel on the human level. We are
dealing with two dimensions of the same reality. The elevation
of Israel is recognized to be dependent on a broader, metaphysical order of the universe represented by Michael and his angels. In the terms of the War Scroll or of Daniel, Israel is
allowed to share in the dominion of the angelic host. The re-
ception of the kingdom by the people of the holy ones in Dan
7:27 is a symbolic formulation, equivalent to the assimilation
of the wise to the stars in Dan 12:2.

H.-W. Kuhn has pointed out that "holy ones" is a frequent term for the faithful in the eschatological community.[41] However, it is precisely their association with the angels in the eschatological community which warrants use of the title "holy ones" for human beings. In the Qumran scrolls it appears that the community is already admitted to fellowship with the angels. More usually, where the eschatological period was not yet thought to have arrived, this fellowship was regarded as future.[42] In Daniel, the faithful Jews are not yet described as "holy ones" but they are "the people of the holy ones" and will join with their heavenly counterparts in the eschatological victory.

The "One Like a Son of Man"

What then of the figure of the one like a son of man? There are two possible interpretations. He may be a symbolic figure, representing the angelic host collectively, or he may represent their leader, specifically. Since the four beasts are interpreted as four kings (Dan 7:17) and in view of the prominence of Michael in Daniel 10-12, the latter is the more likely. Of course the leader represents the collective unit in any case, and there is considerable fluidity between the two. In Dan 7:17, the four beasts are kings. In 7:23, the fourth beast is a kingdom. It seems most likely that the figure of the "one like a son of man" represents the archangel Michael, who receives the kingdom on behalf of his host of holy ones, but also on behalf of his people Israel.

If this interpretation is accepted, then the later development of the "Son of Man" in the Similitudes of Enoch becomes much more readily intelligible.[43] In 1 Enoch 46:1, the "Son of Man" "had the appearance of a man and his face was full of graciousness like one of the holy angels." This figure can no longer be identified with Michael, head of the host (cf. Enoch 40:9), but is at least a heavenly being of an angelic type. Other remnants of this tradition which understood the "Son of Man" figure as the head of the angelic host can be found in NT passages which refer to the coming of the Son of Man "with his angels." In Matt 16:27, the Son of Man will come "in the glory of his father with his angels" and in Mark 8:38, he will come "in the glory of his father with his holy angels" (also Luke 9:26 and Matt 25:31). In Matt 13:41, "the Son of Man will send his angels" thereby showing his authority over the host. This idea is repeated in Matt 24:31 and Mark 13:27. In Rev 14:14, "one like a son of man" appears riding on a white cloud as one of a series of destroying angels.

The "one like a son of man" in Daniel is a variant of the belief in a heavenly, angelic savior figure which we find in a number of other Jewish intertestamental works. We have already mentioned the role of Michael in the Qumran War Scroll, especially in 1QM 17:7-8, where God raises up "among the angels the authority of Michael and the dominion of Israel among all flesh." Michael in the War Scroll leads a host which includes both men and angels, and his role is purely military.

In other documents of the period, the angel's role is more diversified. In the Melchizedek scroll from Qumran, Melchizedek appears as an angelic figure who plays a role which is military, priestly and judicial.[44] In 11QMelch vs. 10, Ps 82:1 is applied to Melchizedek: "The heavenly one stands in the congregation of God, among the heavenly ones he judges." The scene is reminiscent of Daniel 7. While the "one like a son of man" is not actually said to judge his opponents in Daniel, he receives his kingdom in a judgment scene. At least the exaltation of the figure of Melchizedek and the fact that his opponents are judged can be paralleled in Daniel 7. There is also evident parallelism between Melchizedek's battle with Belial (vss. 13-15) and Michael's heavenly battle with the princes of Greece and Persia (Daniel 10). Melchizedek in the scroll is assisted by the angelic host--vs. 14, "and to his help are all the heavenly ones (on high)." He may also be assisted by a human force if the reference to "the men of the lot of Melchizedek" is correct (vs. 8).

In the Testament of Moses, ch. 10, an angel executes God's vengeance on the world. Here the angel's role is primarily destructive but the statement that "the hands of the angel will be filled" (vs. 2) may mean that he is also a priestly figure.

In Revelation 12, the battle of Michael and his angels with the dragon and his angels is explicitly portrayed. However, when the dragon has been defeated the kingdom is awarded, not to Michael and his angels, but to Christ--Rev 12:10: "Now is the salvation and the power and the kingdom of our God and the authority of his Christ." We have here an example of angelic Christology. The role allotted to Michael or another angelic figure in Jewish texts is transferred by the Christian redactor to Christ.[45]

This is paralleled by other NT texts in which Christ appears as leader of the heavenly host. In addition to the "Son of Man" passages in Matt 16:27 and Mark 8:38, 2 Thess 1:7 speaks of "the revelation of the lord Jesus from heaven with the angels of his power," and 1 Thess 4:16 says that Christ will descend from heaven "at the voice of an archangel." The identification of Christ with the archangel Michael was explicitly made in the Shepherd of Hermas.[46]

Conclusion

In summary, the "holy ones" and the "holy ones of the Most High" in Daniel refer to the angelic host. The "people of the holy ones" refers to the faithful Jews who share in the eschatological triumph of the host. The manner in which the Jews share in the eschatological triumph can be variously expressed as assimilation to the host (Daniel 12) or as enjoying dominion over "everything under heaven" (Daniel 7). The "one like a son of man" is the archangel Michael who leads and represents both the heavenly host and their human counterparts, the faithful Jews.

The significance of this conclusion is that the two-story universe which is explicit in chs. 10-12 is also presupposed in Daniel 7 and 8. It is therefore the common metaphysical framework of the visions. This means that throughout Daniel 7-12 (with the exception of ch. 9), the symbolism has a vertical dimension--that the correlation of earthly and heavenly realities must be considered in addition to the plot of the story and in addition to the traditional connotations of the imagery. In Eliade's terms, transcendent reality is symbolized not only by the repetition of primordial events, but also by the imitation of celestial archetypes.

"Vertical" or spatial symbolism is evidently not oriented to future expectation or political events, in the sense that "horizontal," temporal symbolism, such as the schema of the four kingdoms or the seventy weeks of years, is. Instead, it illuminates dimensions of present experience. The ancient writers use vertical, "height" language where we should speak of *depth* experiences. Consequently, such vertical, spatial imagery is particularly prominent in the Wisdom literature, which is notoriously ahistorical. [47] The Gospel of John also provides many striking examples of the use of vertical symbolism to express dimensions of experience--one must be born *from above*, eat bread *from heaven*, etc.

The spatial imagery of Daniel is not derived from Wisdom literature, but, as we have seen, from the mythological traditions it uses. However, such imagery plays a far more prominent role in Daniel than in prophetic books such as Deutero-Isaiah, which often draw on similar mythological traditions. The prominence of this imagery in Daniel should alert us that the visions are not only concerned with chronological history, but also with dimensions of present experience. We will consider how this vertical symbolism relates to the temporal language of Daniel, and to the treatment of history, in the following chapter.

CHAPTER V

[1]See Colpe, "Ho huios tou anthropou," 400; J. Coppens et
L. Dequeker, *Le Fils de l'homme et les Saints du Très-Haut en
Daniel VII* (Louvain: Publications Universitaires, 1961) 55-56.

[2]O. Procksch, "Der Menschensohn als Gottessohn," *Christentum und Wissenschaft* 3 (1927) 429.

[3]Noth, "The Holy Ones of the Most High," *The Laws in the
Pentateuch and other Essays*, 215-28 (= "Die Heiligen des
Höchsten," *NorTT* 56 (1955) 146-61; H. Kruse, "Compositio libri
Danielis et idea filii hominis," *VD* 37 (1959) 147-61; J. Barr,
"Daniel," *PCB* (London: Nelson, 1962) 597; L. Dequeker, "Dan VII
et les Saints du Très-Haut," *ETL* 36 (1960) 353-92; J. Coppens,
"La vision daniélique du Fils d'Homme," *VT* 19 (1969) 171-82;
and Z. Zevit, "The Structure and Individual Elements of Daniel
VII," *ZAW* 80 (1968) 385-96.

[4]See the criticisms of Noth's article by C. W. Brekelmans,
"The Saints of the Most High and their Kingdom," *OTS* 14 (1965)
305-29; H. W. Kuhn, *Enderwartung und Gegenwärtiges Heil* (SUNT 4;
Göttingen: Vandenhoeck und Ruprecht, 1965) 92; R. Hanhart, "Die
Heiligen des Höchsten," *Hebräische Wortforschung* (Fs. Baum-
gartner; VTSup 16; Leiden: Brill, 1967) 90-101; U. Müller,
*Messias und Menschensohn in jüdischen Apokalypsen und in der
Offenbarung Johannes* (Gütersloh: Mohn, 1972) 25. The recent
articles of G. F. Hasel, "The Identity of the 'Saints of the
Most High' in Daniel 7," *Bib* 56 (1975) 173-92 and V. S. Pothyress, "The Holy Ones of the Most High in Daniel VII," *VT* 26
(1976) 208-13 add nothing of significance to the arguments of
Brekelmans. Both argue that "holy ones" *can* refer to human
beings but neither provides an analysis of Daniel to establish
the meaning here.

[5]See Pope, *El in the Ugaritic Texts*, 14; L. Dequeker,
"Les Qedôšîm du Ps LXXXIX a la lumière des croyances sémitiques," *ETL* 39 (1963) 469-84.

[6]S. Mowinckel, *He That Cometh* (Nashville: Abingdon, 1959)
350.

[7]N. Schmidt ("The Son of Man in the book of Daniel," *JBL*
19 [1900] 22-28) identified the "Son of Man" with the archangel
Michael. So also T. K. Cheyne, W. E. Barnes, G. H. Box, F.
Stier, J. A. Emerton (tentatively), U. Müller. Z. Zevit identifies him with Gabriel. J. Coppens identifies the "Son of
Man" with the angelic host, but allows for the possibility that
he is the leader of that host. See J. J. Collins, "The Son of
Man and the Saints of the Most High in the Book of Daniel," *JBL*
93 (1974) 64.

[8]See G. Vermes, "The Use of Bar-Nāsh/Bar-nāshā in Jewish Aramaic," in M. Black, *An Aramaic Approach to the Gospels and Acts* (3rd ed.; Oxford: Clarendon, 1967) 310-30.

[9]The view that the "Son of Man" was a well-known traditional figure taken over by Daniel is elaborated by Mowinckel, *He That Cometh*, 346-450.

[10]Two other isolated opinions should be noted. H. Sahlin ("Antiochus IV Epiphanes und Judas Mackabäus," *ST* 23 [1969] 41-68) identifies the "one like a son of man" as Judas Maccabee. H. Schmid ("Daniel, der Menschensohn," *Judaica* 27 [1971] 192-221) identifies him with Daniel. Neither identification has any basis in the text.

[11]The evidence on the use of "holy ones" is set out clearly by Brekelmans, "The Saints of the Most High." In the case of the Qumran scrolls, not all the instances which Brekelmans classifies as referring to humans necessarily do so. See the criticisms of S. Lamberigts, "Le sens de $qdw\check{s}ym$ dans les textes de Qumrân," *ETL* 46 (1970) 24-39; L. Dequeker, "The 'Saints of the Most High' in Qumran and Daniel," *OTS* 18 (1973) 133-62.

[12]Noth, "Holy Ones," 226. His arguments that these verses are a later addition from a literary point of view are not compelling.

[13]See Hanhart, "Die Heiligen," 93; Brekelmans, "The Saints of the Most High," 329.

[14]So now also Dequeker, "Saints," 180, in revision of his earlier opinion.

[15]Ibid., 123.

[16]Ibid., 126. Cf. Szörenyi, "Das Buch Daniel," 278-94.

[17]Hölscher, Scott, et al. For references, see Dequeker, "Saints," 114.

[18]Ginsberg, *Studies*, 16.

[19]Plöger (*Das Buch Daniel*, 116-17) identifies the ten kings as seven Seleucid monarchs (Seleucus I, II, III, IV; Antiochus I, II, III) plus Antiochus Hierax, brother and rival of Seleucus II, and two sons of Seleucus IV, Demetrius and Antiochus. The latter two and their father were the horns plucked up in vs. 8. Alexander the Great might be counted instead of Antiochus Hierax.

[20]Dequeker, "Saints," 116. Precedent for these formulae can be found in Dan 2:31, 34; cf. Dan 4:7, 10.

[21]Ibid., 115-16.

[22] E. Sachau, *Aramäische Papyrus und Ostraka aus einer jüdischen Militär-Kolonie zu Elephantine* (Berlin: Königliche Museen, 1911) 262.

[23] Dequeker, "Saints," 120.

[24] See in general, P. D. Miller, Jr., *The Divine Warrior in Early Israel* (HSM 5; Cambridge: Harvard, 1973).

[25] Y. Yadin (*The Scroll of the War of the Sons of Light against the Sons of Darkness* [Oxford: Oxford University, 1962] 230) lists instances where 'ēlîm should be read as angels.

[26] So Nickelsburg, *Resurrection*, 11.

[27] Cf. also *1 Enoch* 80:6; *2 Apoc. Bar.* 51:10. See J. Collins, "Son of Man," 57.

[28] Miller, *Divine Warrior*, 21-23; see also 66-69 for the divine council in the OT.

[29] On the text of this passage, see Nickelsburg, *Resurrection*, 119 n. 30. The phrase from vs. 6 is missing in the Greek.

[30] See Kuhn, *Enderwartung*, 113-17; Nickelsburg, *Resurrection*, 144-69.

[31] Aristophanes, *Peace*, 832-41. See in general, F. Cumont, *Lux Perpetua* (Paris: Geuthner, 1949) 142-88.

[32] Tusculan Disputations 1.12, 28.

[33] Delcor, *Daniel*, 173.

[34] See also Jer 8:2, 2 Kgs 21:3-5, where the worship of the host of heaven is also condemned.

[35] Delcor (*Daniel*, 173) appeals to 2 Macc 9:10, where it is said that Antiochus had tried to reach the heavenly stars, but that is in quite a different context and besides it may be a reinterpretation of this passage in Daniel for a hellenized audience.

[36] Against this, R. Hanhart ("Die Heiligen des Höchsten," 94) draws attention to 2 Macc 7:34 where the expression *ouranious paidas* (heavenly children) is used of the Jews, and to 3 Macc 6:28, where the Jews are called "sons of God." Hanhart has been aptly refuted by Nickelsburg (*Resurrection*, 104 n. 53), who points out that both of these passages have an apocalyptic background in which these terms originally referred to angels. Only when the traditions were removed from their apocalyptic context were the titles transferred to the righteous. For a parallel to Dan 8:10, see *1 Enoch* 46:7.

[37]Apart from the merging of angels and men in the Qumran scrolls, we should note that angels are said to come to the aid of Jews in battle in 2 Macc 10:29-30. The term $'^a s\hat{u}m\hat{i}m$ in Dan 8:24 might be considered an equivalent of $gibb\hat{o}r\hat{i}m$, mighty men, which is used to describe angels in the War Scroll (see Yadin, *The Scroll of the War*, 230), but, of course, it could also refer to humans.

[38]Noth, "The Saints of the Most High," 228.

[39]Ibid., 223; Coppens, *Le Fils de l'homme*, 63.

[40]Brekelmans, "The Saints of the Most High," 329. His argument has been accepted by Kuhn, *Enderwartung*, 92 and Müller, *Messias und Menschensohn*, 25-26.

[41]Kuhn, *Enderwartung*, 92.

[42]E.g., *1 Enoch* 39:5; 48:1; 104:2, 4.

[43]On the "Son of Man" in *Enoch*, see Colpe, "Ho huios tou anthropou," 423-27. The identification of Enoch with the Son of Man in ch. 71 is surely a secondary addition in view of the pre-existence attributed to the Son of Man in *1 Enoch* 48:6. For a contrary view, see N. Perrin, *A Modern Pilgrimage in New Testament Christology* (Philadelphia: Fortress, 1974) 28-31.

[44]I follow the interpretation of 11Q Melchizedek proposed by A. S. van der Woude, "Melchizedek als himmlische Erlösergestalt in den neugefundenen eschatologischen Midraschim aus Qumran, Hohle XI," *OTS* 14 (1965) 354-73; also M. de Jonge and A. S. van der Woude, "11QMelchizedek and the New Testament," *NTS* 12 (1966) 301-26; J. A. Fitzmyer, "Further Light on Melchizedek from Qumran Cave 11," *JBL* 86 (1967) 22-41. For parallels between Melchizedek and Michael, see van der Woude, "Melchizedek," 367-73. The two figures are identified in the medieval *yalkut ḥadash* and other texts.

[45]The survival of the mention of Michael in Rev 12:7-9 is probably a remnant of a Jewish work; see A. Yarbro Collins, *Combat Myth*, ch. 3.

[46]*Herm. Vis.* 3; *Herm. Sim.* 8:3, 3; 9:12, 7-8. For this and other implicit identifications of Christ and Michael in early Christian literature, see J. Danielou, *The Theology of Jewish Christianity* (London: Darton, Longman and Todd, 1964) 1. 121-27.

[47]J. G. Gammie ("Spatial and Ethical Dualism in Jewish Wisdom and Apocalyptic Literature," *JBL* 93 [1974] 356-85) has a good collection of passages which use spatial imagery in both Wisdom and Apocalyptic, but seems to be unaware of the mythical background of apocalyptic symbolism.

CHAPTER VI

HISTORY AND ESCHATOLOGY

The visions of Daniel are not simply reformulations of
ancient myth or speculations about the heavenly world. They
are primarily interpretations of an historical situation. Much
of Daniel deals explicitly with history and chronology. Each
vision includes a review of history. In Daniel 7, the four
beasts represent the supposed succession of world empires,
Babylon, Media, Persia and Macedonia. Daniel 8 deals with the
Macedonian empire, from the time of the overthrow of Persia.
Daniel 9 divides the post-exilic period into seventy weeks of
years, and chs. 10-12 begin from the time of the Persians and
provide a detailed account of the Hellenistic period. Further,
each vision includes a calculation of the "time of the end."
In Dan 7:25, the holy ones will be delivered into the power of
the fourth beast for a "time and times and half a time." In
Dan 8:13-14, an angel asks explicitly how long the period of
the vision will last, and is told: "For two thousand, three
hundred evenings and mornings; then the sanctuary shall be restored." According to Dan 9:26-27, half one week of years
(3-1/2 years) will elapse between the time the temple is profaned and its restoration. Finally, in 12:5-13, we get a
series of calculations: "It shall be for a time, times and a
half a time"; "And from the time that the continual burnt
offering is taken away and the abomination that makes desolate
is set up, there shall be a thousand two hundred and ninety
days"; "Blessed is he who waits and comes to the thousand
three hundred and thirty five days."

Chronological Predictions

The author of Daniel obviously regarded chronology as
something of considerable importance. Already in antiquity
this was regarded as the distinctive feature of his prophecy.
Josephus (*Ant.* 10.11.7[267]) wrote that Daniel "was not only
wont to prophesy future things, as did the other prophets, but
he also fixed the time at which these would come to pass."

This concern for chronology is undoubtedly important in Daniel but it cannot be taken as the primary interest of the book. The most striking aspect of the predictions of the end is the discrepancy between them. In all, four calculations of the end-time are given. One of these, 3-1/2 years (a time, times and half a time, or half of a week of years) is given three times--in 7:25, 9:27 and 12:7. The other figures (1150, 1290 and 1335 days) all fall between three and four years and seem to be different calculations of the 3-1/2 years. There is a wide consensus that the different dates should be understood as revisions due to the delay of the expected event.[1] When each predicted date passed, a new one was calculated. Some of these calculations may have been added later, by someone other than the original author. In any case, the point to note is that the visions were not thought to be disproved by the non-fulfillment of the predictions.[2] Further, it was not even thought necessary to delete the incorrect figures. The different calculations could stand juxtaposed in consecutive verses. The attitude of Josephus is significant. Daniel was still read and cherished in the first century A.D. because of his precise predictions, which could be re-calculated to fit any period. Ultimately the chronological predictions were regarded as cryptic signs, similar to the mythic symbolism of the visions. They could not be taken as clear definitive indications of the timing of an event.

The fact that such predictions were made remains significant. They added urgency and realism to the prophecies. They expressed the conviction that the eschatological event would really happen in the future and would happen soon. The precise timing of that event might have to be recalculated, but at least there was the conviction that the event would really take place. This event could be plotted chronologically and would be at least in this sense an historical event. This chronological dimension of the eschatological happening has obvious significance for the understanding of history in Daniel.

Eschatology as "Goal" or "End" of History

Despite the conspicuous prominence of chronological data in Daniel, no less an authority than Gerhard von Rad could

categorize it as "fundamentally unhistorical thinking."[3] Von
Rad's reasoning is based on the lack of references to the history of Israel and the saving acts of God. The salvation event
is purely eschatological and future. History itself is void of
salvation. The course of history is indeed subject to God,
even determined by him. However, by directing attention to the
totality of history and its predetermined goal, Daniel is di-
verting attention from particular historical events and their
significance. Von Rad sees an irreconcilable difference between prophecy and apocalyptic in their respective attitudes
to concrete historical events.

Von Rad's position represents one extreme of the spectrum
of scholarly opinion. The other extreme may be illustrated by
Klaus Koch's interpretation of Daniel.[4] Koch starts from virtually the same observations as von Rad. He notes the remarkable lack of interest in specifically Israelite history. He
also agrees that Daniel is concerned with universal history
rather than particular events. However, Koch argues that these
peculiarities of Daniel are not due to a loss of interest in
history. The book of Daniel may rightly be categorized as
"history" or "world-history" because it is concerned to show
the "irreversability" (*Unumkehrbarkeit*) and "teleology" or
quality of "striving towards a goal" (*Zielstrebigkeit*) in the
course of events. While there is no explicit interest in the
early history of Israel, Koch argues that it is presupposed.
Daniel is working with a three-fold schema of history. First
there is the pre-exilic period, the specific history of Israel.
Then there is the period of the world kingdoms. Within this
period there is a gradual deterioration, as the kings become
increasingly arrogant. However, this period also represents an
advance in the development of world-history, as the horizons of
the visionary expand to include not only Israel, but all the
kingdoms of the world. Finally, there is the eternal eschatological kingdom, "in which the humanity of mankind first attains its true state." The history of Israel is caught up in
universal history in the later periods. Its religion and its
God are directed to the interests of universal humanity.[5] In
this way the "legacy of the prophets" is fulfilled. Whereas
the prophets were concerned with particular situations, Daniel

has a comprehensive view of universal history. The eschatological period is presented as the goal towards which all history
is moving and in which Israel and all humanity will be fulfilled.[6]

The sharp divergence in viewpoint between von Rad and Koch
is due in part to the vagueness and ambiguity of the category
"historical thinking."[7] Both scholars agree that eschatology,
the expectation of a decisive event in the future, is of central importance in Daniel. We have seen that this future event
is "historical" insofar as it can be the subject of chronological predictions. Further, the expectation of an eschatological
event is an obvious point of continuity between prophecy and
apocalyptic. The references in Dan 12:1 to "that time," "a
time of affliction," are reminiscent of the prophetic "Day of
the Lord."[8] Accordingly, von Rad's assertion that apocalyptic
is "fundamentally unhistorical," and unrelated to the prophetic
view of history, requires at least some modification.

Eschatological expectation must be considered "historical"
insofar as it reflects a concern with human events and their
temporal unfolding. It does not necessarily follow that the
eschatological event is a goal towards which history is striving as Koch suggests. It can, alternatively, be understood as
an *end*, which cuts off and terminates a historical development.
So in Rudolf Bultmann's understanding of apocalyptic:

> This end of history no longer belongs to history as
> such. Therefore it cannot be called the goal of
> history towards which the course of history moves
> by steps. The end is not the completion of history
> but its breaking off, it is, so to speak, the death
> of the world due to its age. The old world will be
> replaced by a new creation, and there is no contin-
> uity between the two Aeons. The very memory of the
> past will disappear, and, with that, history van-
> ishes.[9]

The difference between the conceptions of the "end of history" and the "goal of history" are not absolute. Both point
beyond the present order to an eschatological state of salvation. What is at issue is the degree of continuity (or lack of
it) between the eschatological state and the present or past.
The question is whether the state of salvation is understood as

a continuation and fulfillment of previous history, or rather
stands over against it as a radically different order of
things, which must replace rather than perfect the present
order.

We will argue in this chapter that the second of these
alternatives is the more accurate description of Daniel. The
visionary is concerned with universal history only insofar as
it provides a framework within which the urgency of the present
crisis can be appreciated. Daniel is not concerned to extend
salvation beyond the borders of Israel to all humanity. On the
contrary, salvation is restricted to a smaller group within
Israel. The history of the gentile kingdoms culminated not in
fulfillment, but in judgment and destruction. Even the history
of Israel cannot be said to reach fulfillment in unbroken continuity with the past. While the state of salvation is described in language drawn from OT prophecy, that language is
radically reinterpreted. The eschatological community of the
elect is not defined as the people of Israel or the state of
Judah, but primarily as the "wise teachers," the *maskîlîm*, and
those of the Jews who follow them.

Daniel's view of history, which emphasizes the discontinuity between the present and the eschatological order, is not
without its antecedents in biblical prophecy. Already in the
eighth century Amos of Tekoa did not envisage the harmonious
development of salvation history towards a goal, but rather
threatened that "the end has come upon my people Israel; I will
never again pass them by" (Amos 8:2) and warned that the day of
the Lord would be a day of darkness and not light.[10] More
clearly, some of the post-exilic prophets stressed that the
eschatological state will not fulfill the present order, but
replace it:

> For behold I create new heavens and a new earth;
> and the former things shall not be remembered or
>   come into mind. (Isa 65:17)[11]

We will find, however, that the gulf between the eschatological
state and the present order is much greater in Daniel than in
any of the post-exilic prophets. Even in Trito-Isaiah the new
creation is still a human condition, although it is freed from

many of the defects of the old order. In Daniel, however, the
maskîlîm are transformed to an angelic state and will not only
"fill out their days" (Isa 65:20) but will enjoy eternal life.

Past History in Daniel

The reviews of history which we find in Daniel are strikingly silent on the specific history of Israel. The only allusions to pre-exilic Israel are found in the prayer of Daniel in
ch. 9, which is widely thought to be a later addition. The
apparent lack of interest in pre-exilic Israel can in part be
explained by Daniel's supposed date. Whereas Enoch lived before the flood, and so had occasion to prophesy all of Israel's
history, Daniel lives in the Babylonian exile, so his prophecies start from there. Accordingly, Koch assumes that Daniel
fails to refer to earlier history only because he has no occasion to do so. The earlier period is presupposed. Therefore,
according to Koch, Daniel is working with a three-fold division
of history: (a) Israel's history of salvation up to the time of
the exile, (b) the period of gentile domination, and (c) the
eschatological era.[12]

This three-fold division of history is nowhere explicit in
Daniel. No reference is made to pre-exilic Israel. If the
author had really wished to present a three-fold schema, we
must presume that he could have found a way despite the supposed exilic date of Daniel, or if necessary, attributed his
visions to a more ancient sage.

Instead, Daniel's vision of history begins with the four
beasts which rise from the sea, and which, we are told, represent four kingdoms. The sequence of four kingdoms followed by
a fifth is taken over from the anti-Hellenistic resistance
literature of the Near East. The proximate source is undoubtedly Daniel 2 where we have found the schema in a Babylonian oracle, adapted to the Jewish polemic against idolatry. As used
in political propaganda, the schema was directed primarily
against the fourth kingdom. The first three had already passed
away. They may have been good or bad, depending on the viewpoint of the oracle. In Daniel 2, the first kingdom is clearly

approved, as the "head of gold." The point of the schema was
to assert that the present fourth kingdom would be overthrown
like its predecessors. We should expect then that the fourth
kingdom would be the chief object of the author's animosity.
The fact that Daniel 2 shows no particular hostility towards
the final kingdom indicates that it was not primarily concerned
with a real political situation. Daniel 7, on the contrary,
was written in the heat of persecution. There is no doubt
about the visionary's feelings towards "the fourth beast which
was different from all the rest" (7:19) and, more specifically,
the little horn which is its final representative.

In Daniel 7, however, this pattern of the four kingdoms is
combined, as we have seen, with a mythic pattern now familiar
from Ugaritic texts. The four kingdoms are beasts which rise
from the sea, therefore monsters of chaos. All four rise from
the same sea, because all ultimately represent the same primordial force of chaos. The greater prominence given to the
fourth, which is said to be different from all the others, indicates that he is the supreme exemplar. However, all the
beasts and horns belong together as embodiments of the chaotic
power of the Sea, which is confronted by the heavenly figure
riding on the clouds and by the judgment of God.

There is an obvious tension between the pattern of the
four kingdoms, which clearly implies chronological succession,
and the mythic pattern, which is concerned with the instantaneous confrontation of the heavenly God with the forces of the
Sea. It is crucial for the understanding of the vision that
the mythic pattern takes precedence over the sequence of the
four kingdoms. All four kingdoms are judged simultaneously
(7:11-13). Further, the fourth beast is killed and its carcass
destroyed, while the three which preceded it historically are
allowed to remain alive.

H. L. Ginsberg has argued that the survival of the earlier
beasts reflects the survival of the Median and Persian empires
in the "residual" kingdoms of Atropatene and Persis.[13] Even
Ginsberg, however, cannot find a historical explanation for the
survival of the first kingdom. He tries to avoid the difficulty by claiming that Dan 7:4, "it was lifted from the earth"

($n^e t\hat{\imath} lath$ min 'ar'$\bar{a}$'), means that the first beast was destroyed.
The fallacy of this suggestion is clear to anyone who reads the
whole verse--"it was lifted from the earth and made to stand on
two feet like a man." Dan 7:12 says explicitly that an extension of life was given to all the beasts except the fourth.

Since the judgment scene is plainly set in the future, it
cannot refer to actual historical data. The fact that the
fourth beast is destroyed while the others are allowed to sur-
vive can only be a literary way of expressing the relative
evaluation of the four kingdoms. The fourth beast is punished
more severely because of its greater wickedness. The predicted
destruction of the fourth beast before the others frustrates
our expectation of chronological development. Instead we are
shown the confrontation of human history of every era with the
judgment of God.[14] In this respect, the viewpoint of Daniel 7
is essentially similar to Daniel 2.

Instantaneous confrontation, rather than chronological
development, is also the focus of ch. 8. Here again, the mythic pattern typified by the revolt of Helal ben Shachar in Isaiah 14 does not provide scope for a chronological development.
Accordingly, the four kingdoms schema is abbreviated. The
first two kingdoms are omitted and the third is quickly dis-
patched. Thus the visionary is free to focus on the fourth
kingdom, and more particularly on the little horn, in which
that kingdom and indeed all human aspirations to dominion,
culminate. The horn represents a king who appears "at the
latter end of their rule when the transgressors have reached
their full measure" (8:23). This sentence might be thought to
imply a gradual crescendo in the sins of the gentiles. However,
Daniel nowhere suggests that each succeeding kingdom is worse
than its predecessor. The final king, Antiochus IV Epiphanes,
clearly represents the peak of wickedness. He is the ultimate
representative of sinful human dominion, and therefore the
confrontation with God takes place in his time. No differen-
tiation between the other kings of the Greek empire, or between
the first three kingdoms, is implied.

Despite the greater historical detail, the review of history in Daniel 11 is essentially based on the same model as

ch. 8. The history prior to Antiochus IV Epiphanes is passed over without evaluation. The heart of the review lies in the king's revolt against God (11:36). The career of Epiphanes is spelled out in a chronological succession of events. However, these have significance only insofar as they represent his revolt against heaven, whether by attacking the covenant, ignoring his ancestral gods, or directly blaspheming the Most High God himself. While Daniel is aware of the chronological extension of history, so that the "prince of Greece" succeeds the "prince of Persia," and Antiochus is successful for a time, the meaning of history lies in its vertical dimension, in the revolt of the world-kingdoms, embodied by Antiochus, against the kingship of God.[15]

In Daniel 7, 8, and 10-12, then, we find the main emphasis on the confrontation of God and all worldly kingdoms, with minimal attention to any chronological development within history. The fact remains that Daniel uses historical schemata, such as the four kingdoms, repeatedly inserts chronological data, and at least in ch. 11 pays considerable attention to historical detail. This aspect of Daniel can be seen most clearly in ch. 9. In the prophecy of the seventy weeks of years, no use is made of mythological patterns or motifs. Consequently we are left with a bare chronological outline of a few important events in the history of post-exilic Judaism, culminating in a prediction of the "time of the end."

It is important to note that there is no gradual development in this portrayal of Jewish history. Seven weeks pass before the restoration of Jerusalem after the exile. Then sixty two of the remaining sixty three pass without event, or any development whatsoever. History can scarcely be said to be striving towards a goal. In fact, the focus of the prophecy falls again sharply on the career of Antiochus Epiphanes in the final week. The purpose of the schematization of the seventy weeks of years is to assert that Antiochus Epiphanes figures in the *last* period. The schema of the four kingdoms has a similar function in the rest of the book. Since Antiochus figures in the last period, the intervention of God must be expected soon.

This lends urgency to the present situation. The chronological
predictions intensify the urgency and so further sharpen the
focus on the present. In short, the chronological factors in
Daniel are not designed to convey a sense of development in
universal history but to focus attention on the brief period of
the present in which the confrontation between God and the
kingdoms of the earth takes place.

In this way the chronological framework is made to complement the vertical antithesis between heaven and earth. By
means of the chronological schema, one period of history is
designated as the last, and this period is set in immediate
contrast to the eschatological kingdom which will follow it.
The antithesis between the world kingdoms and the kingdom of
God is therefore expressed on two axes. The vertical spatial
imagery contrasts heaven and earth, the kingdom of "one like a
son of man" who comes on the clouds of heaven, and that of the
beasts which come up out of the sea. The horizontal, chronological framework contrasts present and future, the kingdom of
Antiochus and whatever will follow its overthrow. On both
axes, the focus is on the sharp antithesis between the two
poles. History is not an unbroken development towards a goal.

The Eschatological Future

Daniel is not only concerned with the world empires and
their judgment by God. He also looks beyond the judgment to
an eschatological kingdom.[16] The aftermath of the judgment is
described in three passages: (1) Dan 7:13-14, 22, 27; (2) Dan
9:24, and (3) Dan 12:1-3.

There are basically two ways in which scholars have interpreted the eschatological kingdom. It has been seen as the
definitive restoration of the national kingdom of Israel. In
this case, the kingdom is explicitly located on earth. In the
words of D. S. Russell:

> It is an earthly kingdom in which the surviving
> members of the nation will share together with some
> of the more illustrious dead who will be raised by
> resurrection to take part in it (12.2). This kingdom,
> unlike any that have gone before, will be an ever-
> lasting kingdom in which evil of every kind will be
> destroyed (7.18, 27).[17]

This kingdom is permanent in the sense that "it will never pass to another people" (2:44). However, it is essentially a continuation of human history. The kingdom of God is manifested by the dominion of Israel over the nations. This dominion may be more lasting and perfect than other kingdoms, but it is nevertheless an historical kingdom with a definite extension in space and time. The alternative to this interpretation sees the eschatological kingdom as a heavenly kingdom, which will break into this world at a particular time, but thereafter is not commensurate with space and time as we know them.[18]

The sharp divergence between these interpretations reflects the lack of any clear, detailed description of the kingdom in the text of Daniel. As we have seen in Chapter V above, the sequel to the demise of Antiochus is only discussed in Daniel 7 and 12. Daniel 8 simply concludes with a reference to the defeat of the king--"by no human hand, he shall be broken." Daniel 9 also concludes on a note of destruction--"until the decreed end is poured out on the desolator." However, in 9:24 we are given a brief proleptic statement of what the eschatological restoration involves:

> Seventy weeks of years are decreed concerning your
> people and your holy city, to finish transgression,
> to put an end to sin, and to atone for iniquity, to
> bring in everlasting righteousness, to seal both
> vision and prophet, and to anoint a most holy place.

The termination of sin and the ushering in of righteousness give no specific information about the nature of the final kingdom. The only significant point for our problem is that the temple will be re-consecrated. The restoration of the temple is also said to mark the end-time in 8:14.

The Temple and the End-time

A number of authors have suggested that the temple is the hinge on which Daniel's view of history turns.[19] The era of the four world kingdoms, and even the career of Daniel himself, begins from the time of the Babylonians, who destroyed the first temple. The restoration of the Persian period is apparently not significant enough to be regarded as the fulfillment of the prophecy of Jeremiah. That prophecy must be reinterpreted to refer to an eschatological restoration. So Enno Janssen argues that in Daniel the second temple is regarded as insignificant, and the restoration of Solomon's temple is expected as the culmination of history.[20] This interpretation is largely based on Koch's theory that Daniel implies a distinction of three periods. The post-exilic period is conceived as a temporary lapse in salvation history. The eschatological age will be an idealized restoration of pre-exilic Israel, the definitive fulfillment of the promises of the covenants.

This interpretation of history can possibly be documented elsewhere in intertestamental Judaism and apocalyptic literature.[21] It is not, however, supported by the explicit statements of Daniel.

First, the era of the world-empires does not, in fact, begin with the destruction of the temple by the Babylonians. That destruction is not even mentioned in any of the oracles which discuss the succession of kingdoms--chs. 2, 7, 8, or 10-12. Daniel 1 does not begin with the final fall of Jerusalem to Nebuchadnezzar, but with an enigmatic seige in the "third year of the reign of king Jehoiakim."[22] There is no reference to the destruction of the temple, although the king is said to have taken vessels from it. There is no basis for Janssen's statement that Daniel's history begins with the destruction of the temple in 587 B.C.[23] The Babylonians are never denounced for destroying the temple. Nebuchadnezzar is depicted in very positive terms in ch. 2. Even in ch. 9, the seventy weeks of years are not calculated from the destruction of the temple but "from the going forth of the word to restore and build Jerusalem" (9:25).

Second, there is no indication in Daniel that the second temple was insignificant or negatively regarded. On the contrary, the defilement of that temple by Antiochus Epiphanes was precisely the climax in that king's confrontation with God (8:11, 9:26, 11:31). By contrast, in several closely contemporary writings, the second temple is either completely ignored (in the Apocalypse of Weeks) or thought to be impure and unfit for sacrifices (in the Animal Apocalypse, *1 Enoch* 89:73, and the

Testament of Moses 4:8). In Daniel 11:22, the High Priest is described as the "Prince of the Covenant." A writer who regarded the second temple as defiled or even insignificant would hardly have spoken of its priesthood with such respect.

The role of the temple in Daniel 9 cannot be used to support the theories of Koch or Janssen. Nothing is said of the role which the temple is to play in the eschatological age. Koch assumes that worship in the Jerusalem temple will be a vital necessity for mnakind, and compares the prophetic vision of the nations flocking to Zion in the eschatological period.[24] However, the motif of the eschatological pilgrimage is simply not found in Daniel. No interest is expressed in the ongoing worship in the temple. While the author of Daniel may have tacitly assumed that temple-worship would be important, we cannot interpret the book on the basis of tacit assumptions. It is at least clear that the state of salvation is not defined in terms of an ongoing temple cult.

The fact remains that the restoration of the temple is connected with the *eschaton* in 9:24 and 8:14. Two reasons for this may be suggested. First, for a Jew in the time of Antiochus Epiphanes, the desecration of the temple was an obvious irritant. As we have noted, Daniel looked on the temple with respect. Whatever role the temple was to play in the eschatological age, it clearly could not be left desecrated. The re-consecration of the temple therefore removes an impediment to the state of salvation, but does not necessarily constitute that state.

Second, Daniel 7 expresses the eschatological salvation in images drawn from a traditional complex which we have associated with the Canaanite mythology of Baal. Now in the myth of Baal, as in other Near Eastern myths which dealt with the theme of kingship, great importance was always attached to the house of the god.[25] The restoration of the temple could therefore be entailed by the mythology of the kingdom. The relation of this temple to empirical, "historical" reality should then be interpreted in the broader context of the kingdom.

In short, Daniel does not provide a clear picture of the role of the temple in the eschatological age. What is said of the temple must be assessed in the light of the eschatological expectation of the other chapters.

Daniel 7: The Future Kingdom

The statements about the future kingdom which we find in Daniel 7 do not amount to a clear description either. In Dan 7:14, the "one like a son of man" approaches the Ancient of Days and is given "dominion and glory and kingdom, that all peoples, nations and languages should serve him, his dominion is an everlasting dominion, which shall not pass away, and his kingdom one that shall not be destroyed." In 7:22, "judgment was given for the saints of the Most High and the time came when the saints received the kingdom." In 7:27, the angel explains:

> The kingdom and the dominion and the greatness of
> the kingdoms under the whole heaven shall be given
> to the people of the saints of the Most High.
> Their kingdom shall be an everlasting kingdom,
> and all dominions shall serve and obey them.

Many scholars understand the eschatological kingdom in Daniel as a messianic kingdom of Israel. Those who take the "one like a son of man" as simply equivalent to Israel naturally assume that an ongoing Israelite kingdom is intended. Even when we understand that the "saints of the Most High" are the angelic host under their leader Michael, we must note that "the greatness of the kingdoms *under* the whole heaven shall be given to the *people of* the saints of the Most High," and all dominions shall serve and obey them (7:27). The eschatological kingdom is not a purely angelic state. It includes a role for the "people of the saints" and these exercise sovereignty over all human dominions. The picture is similar to the two-dimensional culmination of the Qumran War Scroll, where God exalts "the authority of Michael over all the angels and the dominion of Israel over all flesh" (1QM 7:7-8). The problem of Daniel 7 is, then, to establish precisely the identity of the "people of the saints" and the manner in which they will exercise their dominion.

The Identity of the "People of the Holy Ones"

The eschatological kingdom in Daniel 7 must be understood in conjunction with Daniel 10-12. There the mythological framework is provided by the battle between Michael, "prince" of Israel, and the angelic patrons of the other nations. The eschatological kingdom is ushered in by the victory of Michael over his opponents and so, we might presume, by the victory of Israel over the other nations. In the specific context of Daniel, this would mean victory over the Seleucid kingdom of Antiochus IV Epiphanes. The patron angels in ch. 10 and the four kingdoms schema in ch. 7 both carry nationalistic implications and suggest that the eschatological kingdom will be primarily the restoration of the kingdom of Israel.

However, the matter is not quite so simple as that. We cannot simply identify the "people of the saints" with the Jewish state, or ethnically, with the Jewish people. Even before the Babylonian exile the prophets had realized that the messianic kingdom could not be simply identified with Israel. The comments of John Bright on the idea of the "remnant" in Isaiah are apposite:

> There will always be a Remnant! This does not mean, it must be repeated, that Isaiah was able to identify the existing state or any group in it with the true people of God, over whom God would establish his rule. On the contrary, the hope of the Kingdom of God is sharply divorced from the existing state.[26]

The post-exilic prophets distinguish sharply between the true people of God and the 'official' Israel:

> For Thou art our Father, though Abraham does not know us and Israel does not acknowledge us,

and God warns his "rebellious people": "Behold my servants shall eat but you shall be hungry, behold my servants shall drink but you shall be thirsty."[27] The servants of Yahweh cannot be simply identified with the people of Israel.

When Daniel was written, the Jewish state was rent by civil strife.[28] Dan 11:32 distinguishes clearly between the "violators of the covenant" and the "people which knows its God," both of which were parties within Israel. The latter

party of faithful Jews is further specified in 11:34 as "the
wise instructors of the people" (*maskîlê 'am*) and they are said
to give instruction to the "many" (*rabbîm*). The "many" appears
to be yet a third category within Israel, who are not accused
of violating the covenant, but lack the understanding to quali-
fy as *maskîlîm*. Accordingly the "wise instructors" have the
task of making the many "understand" (*yābînû lārabbîm*). In
this they meet with mixed success: "when they fall, they shall
receive a little help, but many shall join themselves to them
with flattery" (11:34). Ever since Porphyry commentators have
understood the "little help" as a slighting reference to the
Maccabees.[29] While this is possible, it is by no means evident. Rather the sentence seems to distinguish two groups
within the "many"--the minority who respond to the teaching and
example of the *maskîlîm* and so provide "a little help" and the
majority who only join them in appearance but are not truly
converted.

There is no doubt that the visionary identifies with the
maskîlîm. If the "people of the saints of the Most High" are
to share in the victory of Michael and receive a kingdom, this
"people" is not co-extensive with the state of Judah but is
confined to the wise teachers and the section of the populace
which responds to them and provides "a little help." It is
highly important to note how this elect group is defined. It
is not by race, geography or nationality, but by wisdom and
understanding. It is not enough to belong to the undifferentiated mass of the *rabbîm*, although these are not accused of
violating the covenant. Further, the *maskîlîm* do not guide the
people simply by exhorting them to loyalty, but by *making them
understand*.

Daniel 11 does not specify the nature of the understanding
to which so much importance is attached. There are two possible interpretations, and they are not mutually exclusive.
First we may compare the role of the *maskîlîm* to that of the
Levites in Ezra's reform. We read in Neh 8:7 that the Levites
were "making the people understand the Torah" (*mᵉbînîm 'eth-hā-
'am la-ttôrāh*) and also that they met with Ezra "to study the
words of the law" (*lᵉhaskîl 'el-dibrê ha-ttôrāh*) (Neh 8:13).

The verbs *bîn* (understand) and *skl* (understand, study) are both
used in the Hiphil or causative, both here and in Daniel 11.
The object of both verbs in Nehemiah is the Torah. The fact
that Daniel borrows terminology from earlier biblical books
does not guarantee that he wishes to use it in the same sense.
None the less, instruction in the Torah would make excellent
sense in the context of the Maccabean persecution.

The other interpretation is complementary to this, rather
than an alternative. The term *maskîlîm* is also used in Dan 1:4
to describe Daniel and his companions. The wisdom attributed
to Daniel in the court-tales includes learning in Chaldean language and literature, but above all refers to the interpretation of dreams and mysterious signs, the ability to give *pesher*.
We have already seen that the visionary in Daniel 7-12 presents
his revelation in the form of *pesharim*, interpretations, either
of visions or of scriptural prophecy. It is reasonable to assume that the instruction given by the *maskîlîm* was similar in
kind, and that the visions of Daniel are themselves samples of
that instruction.

The "wisdom" which is so important in Daniel 11 must then
be said to include understanding of scripture, but also other
revelations such as the visions of Daniel. Even in the case of
the Torah, the instruction cannot have been confined to famil-
iarizing the people with the statements found in the law, but
must have involved the "true understanding" and interpretation.
Now in each of the visions of Daniel and in the interpretation
of Jeremiah's prophecy in ch. 9, the interpretation given is
eschatological. Visions and scriptural prophecies are all
understood to refer to the future and to the final crisis of
the "end-time." The eschatological interpretation of scripture
is amply illustrated in the Qumran texts, where Torah and
prophecy alike are understood to refer to the last age. The
technique of eschatological interpretation is more fully developed at Qumran, but Daniel already shows the same presuppositions. Dreams, visions and scriptures are alike mysteries
and their true interpretation refers to the eschatological
period.

H. L. Ginsberg has clearly shown that the *maskîlîm* are described in terms of the suffering servant of Isaiah 53.[30] Like the servant, the *maskîlîm* are said to "justify the many." Like the servant, they submit to death, but at the end they are exalted. Even the term *maskîlîm* itself corresponds to Isa 52: 13: "Behold my servant *yaskîl*." The word "*yaskîl*" is usually translated "will prosper" in this passage. However, it more usually means "will understand," or "will cause to understand, instruct." The Maccabean visionary was not concerned with the historical-critical understanding of Isaiah, or with the meaning of the servant song in its own time. He read it as an eschatological prophecy which he saw fulfilled in the martyrs of his day. The *maskîlîm* were precisely those who had understanding and sought to justify the many by instructing them. They were therefore acting out the role of the servant and could hope for a like reward of exaltation.

The "wisdom" which the *maskîlîm* impart to the *rabbîm* is the eschatological understanding of history, derived from the interpretation of visions and scriptures. We will return in our final chapter to examine the purpose and function of this instruction. For the present, we wish to establish that the elect group in Daniel, "the people of the saints of the Most High," is identified as those who share this eschatological understanding.

The Exercise of Sovereignty

The manner in which this "people of the Holy Ones" will exercise its kingship is illuminated by Dan 12:1-3:

> At that time your people shall be delivered, everyone whose name shall be written in the book and many of those who sleep in the land of dust will awake, some to eternal life and some to shame and eternal abhorrence. And the wise instructors shall shine like the brightness of the firmament, and those who turn many righteousness like the stars for ever and ever.

The description of the resurrection draws heavily on the terminology of the prophets, and especially of Isaiah.[31] Isa 26:19 says that "dwellers in the dust" will awake. The word "abhorrence" (*dērā'ôn*) is also used to describe the fate of the

wicked in Isa 66:24. The exaltation of the servant in Isa
52:13--"he shall be exalted and lifted up and shall be very
high"--is suggestive for the star-imagery of Dan 12:3. Undoubtedly the visionary understood his prophecy of resurrection
as a fulfillment of the OT prophecies. It does not, of course,
follow that his conception of salvation was the same as theirs.

The terminology of resurrection is used in a number of
places in the prophets. In some of them it is purely metaphorical and refers to the restoration of Israel, not to the
resurrection of individuals who had actually died. This is the
sense of the famous passage in Hos 6:1-2: "Come, let us return
to Yahweh, for he has torn that he may heal us, he has stricken
and he will bind us up. After two days he will revive us and
on the third day he will raise us up, that we may live before
him." In the context of Hosea's preaching, the reference is
obviously to the restoration of the nation.[32] Ezekiel 37 is
more explicit. After the vision of the dry bones which are
restored to life, the Lord says to the prophet: "these bones
are the whole house of Israel. They say 'Our bones are dried
up, and our hope is lost.'"[33] Here again, there is no question
of bringing dead individuals back to life. Isa 26:19 is less
clear. This passage occurs in the context of the restoration
of Israel. The fate of the Israelites is sharply contrasted
with those who have been their overlords. The power of those
lords has passed away--"They are dead, they will not live; they
are shades, they will not arise" (26:14). By contrast, for
Yahweh's people: "Thy dead shall live, their bodies shall rise.
O dwellers in the dust, awake and sing for joy." There is no
reference to a judgment of those raised, and no description of
the risen life. While the interpretation must remain open, the
balance of probability suggests that nothing more than the
restoration of the people is involved.[34]

The late prophetic texts, sometimes called proto-
apocalyptic, clearly envisage the eschatological restoration as
a prolongation of history, though under ideal conditions often
expressed in mythological language. This type of eschatology
can best be illustrated from Isaiah 65. The prophet speaks of
a "new heavens and a new earth," imagery often repeated in

later apocalyptic (e.g., Rev 21:1). In this new creation,
life goes on in a way that is better, but not essentially different from the old creation:

> No more shall there be in it an infant that lives
>   but a few days,
> or an old man who does not fill out his days,
> for the child shall die a hundred years old,
> and the sinner a hundred years old shall be accursed.
> They shall build houses and inhabit them;
> they shall plant vineyards and eat their fruit.
> (Isa 65:20-21)

While the state envisaged here is very different from the
present order, history still continues to unfold by the succession of generations.

The resurrection envisaged by Daniel is vastly different
from any of these conceptions. First, it is clearly a resurrection of individuals: "many of those who sleep" will awake.
A universal resurrection is apparently not envisaged.[35] The
author of Daniel is not a systematic theologian who might feel
obliged to treat his subject exhaustively and clarify all aspects of the question. He only expresses what is of interest
and seems significant to him. There will be a resurrection,
and it will include both good and bad. It may be that there
will also be an undistinguished multitude who, in Kipling's
phrase, are "neither good enough to merit heaven nor bad
enough to merit Hell," and who are allowed to sleep on. The
visionary is primarily concerned with the protagonists in the
confrontation of his time. Of these, the good will be rewarded
and the bad punished.

Second, the resurrection involves a judgment, the distinction between the good and the bad. It serves to implement a
system of reward and punishment on the individual level after
death, which was not explicit in any previous OT text.[36]

Third, and most important, the astral imagery of 12:3 cannot be taken as simple comparison.[37] The stars, in Dan 8:10,
are the angelic host, and this identification is known in the
OT and can be traced back to the Ugaritic myths. In view of
the crucial role played by the heavenly host throughout Daniel
7-12, the use of this imagery cannot be accidental. Rather,

the *maskîlîm* are admitted to the angelic host and become like
them--a concept which is also found at Qumran and in many intertestamental and NT texts. This idea is radically different
from any resurrection language that we find in Isaiah. It
clarifies the relationship between the "Saints" and "the people
of the Saints" in ch. 7. There we found that judgment was
given in favor of the Saints of the Most High and the time came
when the Saints received the kingdom (7:22) but also "the
kingdom...shall be given to the people of the Saints of the
Most High" (7:27). The relation between these two statements
is clarified by the transformation of the *maskîlîm* in ch. 12.
The kingdom is given to the "Saints" or angels, but the
maskîlîm, "the people of the Saints," are transformed and become like the angels, and so are enabled to share in their
dominion.

This transformation is not confined to the resurrected
martyrs. Those who become like the stars are the *maskîlîm*, who
justify the many. Presumably they are all transformed, as no
distinction is made within that group. By contrast, we are
told in 11:35 that *some* of these wise instructors will fall,
but not all of them. Accordingly, we must assume that they
"will not all die, but will all be changed."[38] The transformation to an angelic state is not contingent on the death of the
individual but will happen to all the *maskîlîm* at the time of
the end.

It is more difficult to establish whether a distinction is
maintained between the *maskîlîm* and other members of the people
who are saved. It is possible that the transformation to an
angelic state is a special privilege, reserved for the elite.[39]
The fact is that the author of Daniel is primarily interested
in the *maskîlîm*. He is not sufficiently interested in any
other class to tell us what happened to the rest of humanity at
the time of the end. But even the lack of further information
is significant. The eschatological kingdom which is of interest to the visionary is the angelic kingdom in which the
maskîlîm share.

We have said that there are basically two options for the
interpretation of the eschatological kingdom. First, there is

the view of such scholars as Charles and Russell, who see it as a restored kingdom of Israel. Life goes on, on earth. The majority of humanity remains alive through the eschatological crisis, but is now politically subject to Israel. Resurrection is an exception, reserved for the elite of the Jews, who are raised to eternal life, and the elite of their enemies (including perhaps some renegade Jews) who are exposed to everlasting disgrace. For the majority of mankind, life goes on from generation to generation, while sin is no more, righteousness is restored and the Jewish temple becomes a center of cult for all nations. The second option views the *eschaton* as the end of history (Stauffer, Noth, Bultmann) which breaks in at a particular time, but is not thereafter commensurate with space or time.

The book of Daniel cannot be said to exclude either of these interpretations definitely. On the one hand, there is nothing to suggest that the world is destroyed or comes to an end (as we find in later apocalypses such as the NT book of Revelation). On the other hand, there is no description of an ongoing messianic kingdom, or of an eschatological state such as we find in Isaiah 65. Daniel simply does not present a fully developed systematic doctrine of eschatology.

It is not our purpose to use the book of Daniel to elaborate a system of beliefs which it does not contain, but simply to understand that which is presented in the book. The message of Daniel is centered on the *maskîlîm* and their eventual exaltation. The kingdom which is contrasted with the four beasts is the dominion of the angelic "one like a son of man" which comes on the clouds of heaven and which is shared by the *maskîlîm*. The messianic kingdom of the Jews is not explicitly denied, but it plays no part in the book. The traditional expectations of Israel are reinterpreted to refer to the destiny of the *maskîlîm*.

The reinterpretation of older tradition is evident in Dan 12:1. There we read that "there shall be a time of distress such as never has been since there was a nation till that time; but at that time your people shall be delivered." The language of this verse recalls Jer 30:7: "Alas! that day is so great,

there is none like it; it is a time of distress for Jacob; yet
he shall be saved out of it." The phrase '$\bar{e}t$ $\d{s}\bar{a}r\bar{a}h$, "time of
distress," is used in both passages to describe the period
which immediately precedes salvation.[40] The restoration which
follows in Jeremiah is the restoration of Israel from the exile.
In Daniel, the salvation in question is the resurrection of the
$mask\hat{\imath}l\hat{\imath}m$ and their adherents. The saved community is defined
differently from Jeremiah. The state of salvation is still
communal, as the $mask\hat{\imath}l\hat{\imath}m$ are not isolated individuals, but it
now involves the transcendence of individual death.

It appears, then, that the eschatological state which is
of importance to Daniel is not the fulfillment of world history,
or of the history of Israel, but a radically different order,
which is not commensurate with time or space. The rejection of
the present order is less developed here than in some later
apocalypses such as NT Revelation or 4 Ezra, which explicitly
envisage an end of this world. However, the break between the
eschatological period and the preceding history is much more
sharply defined in Daniel than in late prophetic or proto-
apocalyptic works such as Trito-Isaiah. Not only does Daniel
involve a rejection of the present order, but the salvation
enjoyed by the $mask\hat{\imath}l\hat{\imath}m$ is no longer of an earthly kind at all.
Rather, it involves the transcendence of death and assimilation
to an angelic state.[41]

The sharpness of the break between the eschatological
period and the preceding history is further emphasized by the
"vertical" spatial imagery in the visions.

The Significance of the Vertical Imagery

We have noted already that the book of Daniel is presented
on two axes. Most obviously there is the horizontal axis of
chronology. The heavenly kingdom of Yahweh's angelic host does
not govern the world in the present. Chronologically it is
future. However, the heavenly angelic world is already in existence. Therefore there is also the vertical spatial axis
that contrasts heaven and earth. This axis figures prominently
in each of the visions although it is less evident in ch. 9.

In ch. 7, the beasts rise from the sea, and represent kingdoms which arise from the earth. By contrast, the "one like a son of man" comes "on the clouds of heaven." In ch. 8, the career of Antiochus Epiphanes is represented as an attempt to elevate himself above the stars. Chapters 10-12 presuppose a heavenly battle parallel to the strife on earth. At the end, the *maskîlîm* become "like the stars."

Spatial imagery is widely used in biblical literature to express dimensions of experience. We have already referred to such usage in the Wisdom literature and the Gospel of John. Now the community which Daniel represents may be said to be defined by a dimension of experience. The *maskîlîm* are not identified primarily by race, nation or geography, but by their wisdom. We have seen that their wisdom consisted at least in part of the knowledge of eschatological mysteries, typified by the visions of Daniel. These mysteries are also heavenly mysteries, since they have to be interpreted for Daniel by an angel. So we may say that the *maskîl* who understands such heavenly visions is enjoying already, proleptically, a limited form of participation in the transcendent world of the angels.[42] The prominence of the heavenly world in Daniel permits a measure of incipient mysticism. Not only can the visionary hope to transcend the limitations of this life in the eschatological future, but he can already, in a limited way, attain transcendence in the present by his visions and his knowledge.

The main emphasis in the book of Daniel is still on future expectation--as is evident from the attention paid to chronology. However, the element of mysticism introduced by the vertical imagery, however limited, marks a significant transition in the development of Jewish eschatology. Some of the post-exilic prophets, such as Trito-Isaiah or Deutero-Zechariah, share the sharp rejection of the present order which we find in Daniel, to a considerable extent. Neither of these works, however, shows any interest in the heavenly world, and neither envisages that righteous humans can ever hope to transcend death and become like angels. Similarly, neither makes any use of the literary form of visions interpreted by an angel, which is used in Daniel to indicate the heavenly origins of the revelation.

Interest in the heavenly world is much more fully developed in later Jewish apocalypses.[43] Heavenly journeys and astral speculation are noted features of the Enochic literature. The implications of spatial imagery in apocalyptic writings are perhaps most clearly evident in the Qumran scrolls. The scrolls nowhere attest a belief in bodily resurrection, and do not explicitly formulate a belief in the immortality of the soul.[44] The reason, apparently, is that the sectarians believed that they had already passed over into the state of salvation. So we read in the *Hodayot*, or psalms of thanksgiving:

> I give Thee thanks, O Adonai,
> for Thou hast redeemed my soul from the Pit
> and from Sheol of Abaddon Thou hast made me rise
>   to *everlasting heights*,
>
> and I have walked in an infinite plain!
> And I knew there was hope for him whom Thou hast
>   shaped from the dust
> for the everlasting assembly.
>
> Thou hast cleansed the perverse spirit from great sin
> that he might watch with the army of the Saints
> and enter into community with the congregation of the
>   Sons of Heaven.
> and Thou hast cast an everlasting destiny for man
> in the company of the Spirits of Knowledge.
>   (1QH 3:19-23)

The author of this hymn was evidently convinced that he was already enjoying "life on the height," by which he very explicitly means life in the company of the "Saints" or angels. As such, he has, in the words of John's Gospel, already passed from death to life. This fellowship with the angels ("realized angelology," to adapt C. H. Dodd's famous phrase) is associated with the cult in the Manual of Discipline: "let no person smitten with any impurity whatever enter the Assembly of God... for the Angels of Holiness are in their Congregation" (1QSa 2: 3-10). However, it is also found in the War Scroll (1QM 12:9) and evidently embraced the entire life of the sectarians.

The Qumran sectarians, secluded near the Dead Sea, were apparently convinced that they already shared in the angelic life. Even here there was probably an expectation of further fulfillment. The War Scroll, at least, looks forward to a great battle with Belial and his forces. Evidently, then, salvation is not yet complete.[45] However, we find a much higher degree of mystic participation in the heavenly life in the Qumran scrolls than in any other apocalyptic writings.

The *maskîlîm* of Daniel are much more restrained in their relation to the heavenly world. We are repeatedly reminded that the end-time is still in the future. The state of salvation may be anticipated to a limited extent by heavenly visions but the *maskîlîm* are still unmistakeably earthbound, surrounded by afflictions, persecution and apostasy. The chronological axis of Daniel plays an important part by preserving the reality and importance of earthly events. At Qumran, we cannot but feel that the sectarians are losing touch with reality and are being caught up in a private world of fantasy. In Daniel, however, the heavenly vision is held in tension with historical events. The vision has significance insofar as it illumines the real-life situation of the *maskîlîm*. It reassures them of their ultimate values and gives them strength in their trials. In the concluding chapter of this book, we will examine in greater detail the function which the visions of Daniel were designed to fill.

Conclusion

Our examination of the treatment of history in Daniel has pointed to the conclusion that eschatology is envisaged as an end of history rather than a goal. While there is, of course, some continuity between history and eschatology, the emphasis falls on the discontinuity. Past history shows neither gradual improvement nor gradual decline. It serves primarily as a foil to highlight the short period of the present which is dominated by an evil king, Antiochus Epiphanes. The focus of history in Daniel is the revolt of this king against God, which is the consummation of all human pride and rebellion. The period of the present where this king rules is set in sharp contrast to the imminent eschatological heavenly kingdom.

The discontinuity between the present and the eschatological age is much sharper in Daniel than in the prophets of the early post-exilic period. The main novel feature in Daniel's portrayal of the eschaton is his belief that the *maskîlîm* will be resurrected to join the heavenly host. The antithesis between the present and the eschatological state is intensified by the use of vertical imagery, the contrast between heaven and earth, angels and humans. The imagery of the heavenly world suggests a limited form of mysticism, through the angelic revelations to Daniel. Later Jewish apocalyptic writings, especially the Qumran scrolls, develop the sense of present mystical participation in the angelic world. In Daniel, however, such participation is primarily reserved for the future. The heavenly and eschatological vision is held in tension with the present historical situation. For that reason it can be said to be a political document which determines the stance of the visionary in the crisis of his time.

[1]So Plöger (*Das Buch Daniel*, 143) argues that Daniel 9 was written later than ch. 8 and ch. 12 later than either. Recently Hans Burgmann ("Die vier Endzeittermine im Danielbuch," *ZAW* 86 [1974] 543-50) has argued that other considerations may also have been operative, involving the differences between solar and lunar calendars.

[2]Millenarian groups of all ages have reacted to the non-fulfillment of prophecies, not by losing faith, but by revising their calculations. For a fascinating modern example, see L. Festinger, *When Prophecy Fails* (New York: Harper, 1964).

[3]Von Rad, *Theologie*, 2. 321.

[4]K. Koch, "Spätisraelitisches Geschichtsdenken am Beispiel des Buches Daniel," *Historische Zeitschrift* 193 (1961) 1-32; also "Die Weltreiche im Danielbuch," *TLZ* 85 (1960) 829-32. A similar position is maintained by D. Rössler, *Gesetz und Geschichte* (WMANT 3; Neukirchen: Erziehungsverein, 1960).

[5]Koch, "Spätisraelitisches Geschichtsdenken," 28.

[6]Ibid., 31.

[7]B. W. Jones, "Ideas of History in the Book of Daniel," (Ph.D. Dissertation; Berkeley: Graduate Theological Union, 1972) 4-33, lists no fewer than twelve senses in which the word "history" is used in biblical studies!

[8]Many authors have stressed the importance of the "Day of Yahweh" for apocalyptic--e.g., J. Bloch, *On the Apocalyptic in Judaism* (Philadelphia: Dropsie College, 1952) 5-14; P. von der Osten-Sacken, *Gott und Belial* (SUNT 6; Göttingen: Vandenhoeck und Ruprecht, 1969) 34-41.

[9]R. Bultmann, *History and Eschatology* (New York: Harper, 1957) 30. Bultmann's description is based primarily on later apocalyptic works such as 4 Ezra.

[10]See J. J. Collins, "History and Tradition in Amos," *ITQ* 41 (1974) 120-33.

[11]On the conflicting viewpoints among the prophets of the post-exilic period, see Hanson, *Dawn*. Haggai and Zechariah looked for the definitive establishment of the hierocratic order which they supported. Trito-Isaiah and Deutero-Zechariah hoped for the eschatological overthrow of that order.

[12]Koch, "Spätisraelitisches Geschichtsdenken," 28. So also E. Janssen, *Das Gottesvolk und seine Geschichte* (Neukirchen-Vluyn: Erziehungsverein, 1971) 56-57.

[13]Ginsberg, *Studies*, 6-7.

[14]This is clearly seen by Noth, "The Understanding of History," 194-214, although he fails to give due attention to the mythic pattern involved.

[15]Koch is aware of this dimension of Daniel ("Spät-israelitisches Geschichtsdenken," 29). However, he mentions it only as a modification of his basic emphasis on "goal-directedness" (*Zielstrebigkeit*).

[16]The Jewish apocalypses are never purely concerned with the "end." They always look to another era beyond it. See J. J. Collins, "Jewish Apocalyptic as the Transcendence of Death," *CBQ* 36 (1974) 21-43.

[17]Russell, *Method*, 286-87. Cf. also Charles, *The Book of Daniel*, cxii: "its hopes are directed not to the afterworld... but to the setting up of a world-empire of Israel which is to displace the heathen, to a Messianic kingdom on earth."

[18]E. Stauffer, "Das theologische Weltbild der Apokalyptik," *ZST* 8 (1931) 203-15; Bultmann, *History and Eschatology*, 30.

[19]So especially Janssen, *Das Gottesvolk*, 51-54; also A. Jaubert, *La Notion d'Alliance dans le Judaïsme* (Patristica Sorbonensia 6; Paris: Seuil, 1963) 82-85; R. Hanhart, "Kriterien Geschichtlicher Wahrheit in der Makkabäerzeit," *Drei Studien zum Judentum* (Theologische Existenz Heute 140; München: Kaiser, 1967) 14.

[20]So Janssen, *Das Gottesvolk*, 51-54.

[21]Most plausibly the Animal Apocalypse in *1 Enoch*. For a discussion of the various attitudes to history in the apocalyptic writings, see G. Reese, "Die Geschichte Israels in der Auffassung des frühen Judentums" (Dissertation; Heidelberg, 1967). Reese notes that Daniel differs from most other apocalypses by its emphasis on the world-empires and lack of attention to the history of Israel (151).

[22]There is no evidence for such an event in the third year of Jehoiakim. Nebuchadnezzar had not even become king at the time. See Montgomery, *Daniel*, 113-14.

[23]Janssen, *Das Gottesvolk*, 51.

[24]Isa 2:2-4, Mic 4:1-4, Zech 14:16.

[25]See W. H. Schmidt, *Königtum Gottes in Ugarit und Israel* (BZAW 80; Berlin: Töpelmann, 1966) 68-70; A. S. Kapelrud, "Temple-building, a Task for Gods and Kings," *Orientalia* 32 (1963) 56-62; Cross, *Canaanite Myth*, 142-43.

[26]J. Bright, *The Kingdom of God* (Nashville: Abingdon, 1953) 89.

[27]Isa 63:16, 65:13. See Hanson, *Dawn*, 134-208.

[28]See Tcherikover, *Hellenistic Civilization and the Jews*, 152-203; O. Plöger, *Theocracy and Eschatology* (Richmond, VA: John Knox Press, 1968) 1-9.

[29]Montgomery, *Daniel*, 458-59; N. Porteous, *Daniel* (London: SCM, 1965) 168.

[30]H. L. Ginsberg, "The Oldest Interpretation of the Suffering Servant," *VT* 3 (1953) 400-4. Ginsberg also notes the use of other biblical allusions in Daniel 11.

[31]See ibid., 403-4; Nickelsburg, *Resurrection*, 11-27.

[32]H. W. Wolff, *Hosea* (Hermeneia; Philadelphia: Fortress, 1974) 118-19.

[33]Ezek 37:11. See the comments of W. Zimmerli, *Ezechiel* (BKAT 12/2; Neukirchen-Vluyn: Erziehungsverein, 1969) 891-902.

[34]So C. Larcher, "La doctrine de la résurrection dans l'AT," *Vie et Lumière* (1952) 19. Surprisingly, Nickelsburg (*Resurrection*, 18), following R. Martin-Achard (*From Death to Life: A Study of the Development of the Doctrine of Resurrection in the Old Testament* [Edinburgh: Oliver and Boyd, 1960] 135), argues that the contrast with the overlords who do not rise "makes this interpretation untenable." On the contrary, the contrast can more easily be explained if the reference is to the restoration of Israel, while the power of the Assyrians is decisively broken.

[35]For the spectrum of possible interpretations of the extent of the resurrection, see B. Alfrink, "L'idée de résurrection d'après Dn XII,1,2," *Bib* 40 (1959) 358; Delcor, *Daniel*, 252-53.

[36]Isa 66:24: "and they shall go forth and look on the dead bodies of the men that have rebelled against me; for their worm shall not die and their fire shall not be quenched," does not imply that the bodies in question are in any sense raised or alive, and does not imply an afterlife for the just.

[37]See above, Chapter V.

[38]Cf. 1 Cor 15:51.

[39]See Russell, *Method*, 286-87.

[40]See Nickelsburg, *Resurrection*, 15-16; also R. J. Clifford, "History and Myth in Daniel 10-12," *BASOR* 220 (1975) 23-26.

[41]See further, J. Collins, "Apocalyptic Eschatology as the Transcendence of Death," 21-43.

[42]The OT prophets also get glimpses of the heavenly world by their visions of the divine council--Isaiah 6, 1 Kings 22, Jer 23:18, Ezekiel 1. However, the prophets relay threats and promises, on the basis of this experience. Daniel relays knowledge of heavenly mysteries. See above, Chapter III.

[43]For a full discussion of the heavenly world in inter-testamental Judaism, see H. Bietenhard, *Die himmlische Welt im Urchristentum und Spätjudentum* (Tübingen: Mohr, 1951).

[44]Only a few scholars claim to find a belief in resurrection at Qumran. For a review of scholarly opinions, see Nickelsburg, *Resurrection*, 144-45.

[45]On the peculiar blend of realized and imminent eschatology at Qumran, see Kuhn, *Enderwartung*, 176-88.

EXCURSUS ON THE PRAYER IN DANIEL 9

We have argued in Chapter I that the prayer in Daniel 9 does not come from the pen of the same author as the rest of chs. 7-12. This position is widely accepted,[1] although there are some spirited dissenters.[2]

Irrespective of its authorship, the prayer clearly belongs to a traditional type of which the basic elements are found in 1 Kings 8. It is essentially a prayer of confession. The prayer is made in time of crisis, and the crisis is interpreted as a punishment for sin. The confession is followed by a plea for mercy. There are several examples of this type of confession in the OT and intertestamental writings--e.g., Psalms 79, 106; Ezra 9:6-15; Neh 1:5-11, 9:5-37; Tob 3:1-6; The 'Words of the Luminaries' (4QDibHam) 1:8-7:2; 1QS 1:24b-2:1; CD 20:28-30; Bar 1:15-3:8; the prayer of Azariah; LXX prayer of Esther; 3 Macc 2:1-20.

These prayers span a time period which extends from the Babylonian exile to the fall of the second temple. They have been studied by O. H. Steck, who shows that there is little literary interdependence between the different prayers.[3] Rather, the similarity between them derives from a live ongoing homiletic tradition in which the Deuteronomic view of history was embodied. Steck argues that this tradition was kept alive in the post-exilic period by Levitical circles and had its *Sitz im Leben* in covenant-renewal ceremonies.[4] These may have been held at regular intervals but could also be held specially in times of crisis.

There is little evidence for either the Levitical circles or the covenant renewal ceremonies. We know that there was a covenant ceremony at Qumran. One of the confessional prayers, 1QS 1:24b-2:1, is explicitly set in the context of this ceremony. Outside of Qumran, we can only hypothesize. However, the frequency with which these confessional prayers occur in the literature, and the fact that they do not show literary interdependence, supports Steck's theory of a live tradition.

The essential feature of this tradition, and of the prayer in Daniel 9 in particular, is its Deuteronomistic theology of

history. The crisis in which the people find themselves is a
punishment for sin. They can hope to relieve the crisis by
confessing their sin and appealing to the mercy of God. Historical events are highly personalized. Crises are punishments
for sin. The course of history can be changed if the people
repent. This understanding of history contrasts sharply with
what we find in the rest of Daniel. There history is predetermined. The "time of the end" is set. There will be a fixed
period of 70 weeks of years from the end of the exile to the
time of the end. The persecution of Antiochus is not a punishment for the sin of the people. It is a consequence of the
king's own revolt against God. It may also be a test to
"purify" the *maskîlîm* but it is not a punishment. No repentance or prayer on the part of the people can alter the decreed
duration of the persecution. God does not alter the course of
history in response to prayer. The *maskîlîm* are those who
understand what is happening in history and adapt to it properly.

B. W. Jones has argued that the Deuteronomistic prayer is
deliberately inserted here by the author of Daniel to highlight
the novelty of the angel's interpretation.[5] The angel would
then directly contradict the expectations of the prayer:

> The prayer is needed to "set the stage" for Gabriel,
> and when the prayer is ignored we are being told, in
> effect, that the calamity was decreed and will end at
> the appointed time, quite apart from prayers and
> quite apart from previous ideas of retribution.[6]

This interpretation is compatible with the idea that the
author did not compose the prayer. He may have simply inserted
a traditional prayer at this point.[7] It is probably easier,
however, to suppose that the prayer was added by a redactor.
Nothing elsewhere in Daniel suggests that the visionary was
deliberately polemicizing against a Deuteronomistic view of
history. The contrast between the two views of history is not
noted by the angel. In fact his reply to Daniel had already
been sent forth "at the beginning of your supplications" (Dan
9:23). For this reason, some scholars see the prayer as simply
a device to provide flight time for the angel.[8] Such a device

was scarcely necessary, but at least the passage makes clear
that no importance is attached to the content of Daniel's
prayer. The fact that the prayer is so completely ignored,
plus the literary feature that the prayer's introduction (vs.
4a) and conclusion (vs. 20) needlessly repeat vss. 3 and 21,
argue that the prayer was inserted by a redactor rather than
the original author. The redactor was presumably someone who
believed in the Deuteronomic view of history and felt this
prayer was appropriate for Daniel. We may compare the insertion of the prayer of Azariah in the Greek translation of
Daniel and the prayer of Esther in LXX Esther. Neither of
those insertions could have had a literary motivation such as
Jones suggests for Daniel 9. They reflect a redactional practice of inserting prayers to bring the books in question into
line with orthodox piety, or simply to add to their power of
edification. Most probably the redactor was not even conscious
of the contrast between the two views of history.

As the text of Daniel now stands, the prayer in ch. 9
certainly contrasts sharply with the view of history in the
rest of the book. Whether this contrast was intended by either
the author or the redactor, it highlights the gulf which
separated the apocalyptic view of history from the traditional
Deuteronomic view found in the prayer.

NOTES

EXCURSUS

[1]Cf. Charles, *The Book of Daniel*, 226; Bentzen, *Daniel*, 75.

[2]Plöger, *Daniel*, 137-39; Gilbert, "La prière de Daniel," 284-310.

[3]O. H. Steck, *Israel und das gewaltsame Geschick der Propheten* (WMANT 23; Neukirchen-Vluyn: Erziehungsverein, 1967) 110-36. Literary dependence between Dan 9:4-19 and Bar 1:15-2:19 has been suggested but cannot be proved. See C. A. Moore, "Toward the Dating of the Book of Baruch," *CBQ* 36 (1974) 313-14.

[4]Steck, *Israel*, 133-36, followed by Reese, "Die Geschichte Israels," 65. Cf. also K. Baltzer, *The Covenant Formulary* (Philadelphia: Fortress, 1971) ch. 3.

[5]B. W. Jones, "The Prayer in Daniel IX," *VT* 18 (1968) 488-93.

[6]Ibid., 493.

[7]Moore ("Toward the Dating of the Book of Baruch," 316) argues that the prayer should be dated to the fourth or early third century B.C. on the basis of its language.

[8]So Barr, "Daniel," 599.

CHAPTER VII

DANIEL AS A POLITICAL MANIFESTO: THE FUNCTION OF THE VISIONS

The eschatological visions of Daniel are not meditations on timeless truths, nor detached discourses on universal history. Rather, they are interpretations of a very specific historical situation--the persecution of the Jews by Antiochus Epiphanes. The vision of the eschatological state is held in tension with the historical present in such a way as to provide guidance and strength. The maskîlîm have not withdrawn from the political arena. They are not only said to understand, they also "stand firm and take action" (Dan 11:32).

From the aspect of the function of the book, the interest in history reflects an interest in politics. The political concern is shown by the persistent references to kings and kingdoms. Insofar as the book expresses a judgment on the world-kingdoms, especially on the kingdom of Antiochus Epiphanes, and insofar as it commends the action of the maskîlîm who resist Antiochus, Daniel may be understood as a political manifesto.

The most obvious clue to the political stance of Daniel is the use of the schema of four kingdoms followed by the intervention of God. The four kingdoms are not only found in Daniel 2 and 7. They also constitute one of the major structuring elements of the book.[1] Chapters 1-6 refer in sequence to the three kingdoms of Babylon (chs. 1-5:29), Media (5:30-6:28) and Persia (6:28). A parallel sequence is found in chs. 7-12, which are dated to the kingdoms of Babylon (chs. 7, 8), Media (ch. 9) and Persia (ch. 10) with a detailed prophecy of the coming kingdom of Greece, which is not within the lifespan of Daniel (ch. 11). Since Babylon was not conquered by the Medes, the inclusion of Media in the sequence, in both halves of the book, must be derived from a traditional schema. The fact that this schema is used as a structuring principle in Daniel immediately relates the book to the anti-Hellenistic resistance literature of the Near East.

191

Anti-Hellenistic Resistance in the Near East

The schema of the four kingdoms is found not only in
Daniel but also in the Persian Zand-ī Vohūman Yasn, the Roman
writer Aemilius Sura, and an oracle from the Hellenistic period
embedded in *Sib. Or.* 4:49-101.[2] All of these passages were
probably written before the composition of Daniel.

The diversity of the sources in which the schema is found
argues that it was very widely known and used. J. W. Swain has
argued that it was associated with a series of revolts against
the Seleucids, beginning with the rise of the Parthians shortly
after 250 B.C.[3] In the reign of Antiochus III (223-187 B.C.),
we find revolts led by Greek generals who exploited native
unrest. Such were Molon in Media and Achaeus in Asia Minor.
Antiochus III himself was killed in battle with the people of
Elam in 187 B.C. when he was attacking the temple of Bel.
Diodorus Siculus says that he accused the temple priests of
declaring war against him.[4] In Aemilius Sura and in all the
Jewish sources, Media figures as the second world empire. This
may seem odd since the Medes never ruled over Babylon, Syria,
Palestine or any western area of the Near East. The oddity is
explained if we assume that the schema originated in Persia or
Media, or in some place where Media had ruled. The schema became popular in the western areas with the spread of the revolts. In all instances, the schema appears hostile to the
Greeks, who were the last empire and whose demise could therefore be expected soon. The function of this schema in Near
Eastern propaganda was to strengthen resistance to the Seleucids
by showing that the Greek kingdom was doomed to pass.

The Jews were not the only people in the ancient Near East
who had been deprived of their national monarchy by the Greeks
and who hoped for the restoration of a native king (or in Jewish
terms, a messiah). The messianic hopes of other Near Eastern
peoples in the Hellenistic age are reflected in legends about
the glorious monarchs of the past--Nektanebo, Nebuchadnezzar,
Semiramis--or in oracles which foretold the advent of an ideal
king in the future, such as the Egyptian Demotic chronicle and
Potter's Oracle, or the Persian oracle of Hystaspes. In each

case the hope was political and directed towards the restoration of an oriental monarchy. However, kingship in the Near East (and all over the ancient world) was essentially a religious concept. The rule of a native king was only the earthly counterpart of the rule of the national god.

Consequently, in each case the restoration of Near Eastern kingship was envisaged in religious terms. The Egyptian Potter's Oracle looked for a king "from the sun" who would be "sent by Isis."[5] The Hellenistic Persian oracle of Hystaspes expected that god would send a "great king from heaven."[6] The similarity between the expectations of the various states can be illustrated by Daniel 2. When Daniel tells Nebuchadnezzar that "the god of heaven will set up a kingdom which will never pass to another people," a Babylonian would most naturally assume that the reference was to Marduk and a Babylonian kingdom while a Jew could understand it as a reference to Yahweh and a Jewish messianic kingdom. We have argued in Chapter II that a Babylonian political oracle is used in Daniel 2 to illustrate the superior wisdom of Daniel and the power of his god. Usually nationalist propaganda concerned with the restoration of a native kingship drew more explicitly on its native tradition. So the Egyptians hoped for a king sent by Isis (Potter's Oracle) or that Nektanebo would return and defeat the Persians[7] and Jews hoped for the restoration of a Davidic monarchy (*Pss. Sol.* 17:23). Similarly in Daniel 7-12, where the visionary is concerned with the destruction of the fourth kingdom, rather than the wisdom of Daniel, he draws primarily on Israelite and Canaanite traditions.

In short, the resistance literature of the Hellenistic Near East shows parallel developments in the various nations. Some motifs such as the four kingdoms schema were international but each nation also cherished its native traditions.[8] These traditions were re-vitalized and provided the basis for nationalistic propaganda in the Hellenistic period. In this literature of resistance to Hellenism, politics and religion were inseparably fused.

The Maccabean Revolt

The Maccabean revolt in Judea must be seen in this broader context of Near Eastern resistance to Hellenism. Despite the frequent assertion in the older scholarship that the Jews were the only people who resisted Hellenization,[9] the crisis in Jerusalem is not without parallel. Other peoples also resisted when they felt that their national religion was threatened.[10] The people of Elam resisted when Antiochus III tried to raid the temple of Bel, and the king was killed in the battle. Precisely contemporary with the disturbances in Jerusalem, in 168 B.C., there was an incident in Babylon.[11] Several statues of Hellenized gods were made from gold taken from the E-sagila treasure and set up in the temple. Certain "thieves" then attacked the temple and stripped the statues. For this offence they were condemned to death and cast into fire. We are familiar from Josephus with the use of the term "thieves" (*lēstai*) to designate patriotic fighters.[12] There can be little doubt that the individuals in question were motivated by religio-nationalistic feelings, not by a desire for booty. The Maccabean revolt was much more extensive and successful than these other incidents, and it is true that Jewish monotheism was less tolerant than other Near Eastern religions of Antiochus' pretensions to divinity, but the fusion of religion and nationalism was typical of the Hellenistic Near East.

The immediate causes of the Maccabean revolt were primarily religious. The Jews had lived peacefully for more than three hundred years under Persian and Greek dominion. The reason was that there had been little interference in internal Jewish affairs. The Jews had a significant measure of self-government and were free to practice their traditional cult and observe their ancestral laws. Only in the time of Antiochus Epiphanes was the freedom of the Jewish people to live according to its traditions seriously endangered. In particular, the violation of the temple, and the prohibition of the law were the sparks which kindled the revolt.

However, we should not think that the revolt was concerned only with the restoration of the temple and the law. The

religious persecution which actually triggered the revolt was
only the outgrowth of the deeper problem which involved the
entire political order. The first principle of the revolt was
the rejection of the authority of Antiochus Epiphanes. This
was the common element which unified the Jewish resistance
movement. The question of rightful kingship was therefore at
issue, as was also the case in non-Jewish resistance to Hellenistic dominion. Within the Jewish movement, there was room
for a variety of viewpoints on the precise nature of the order
which should replace Antiochus, and on the methods which were
appropriate for the revolution. The temple and the law figured
with varying degrees of prominence in the various viewpoints,
but they were only part of a larger picture. The essential
element was the rejection of the kingship of Antiochus Epiphanes, and its replacement by an ideal religio-political
order, however conceived. Religion and politics were inex-
tricably fused.

Like all Near Eastern resistance, the Maccabean revolt
formulated its ideology in terms of old native traditions. Our
main sources for the ideology of the revolt are the first and
second book of Maccabees. First Maccabees was written about
100 B.C. and may be taken as the court history of the Hasmonean
dynasty.[13] The provenance of Second Maccabees is more complex
as it is essentially a summary of an earlier work by Jason of
Cyrene. In Second Maccabees the temple figures as the central
symbol of the Jewish people, and is much more prominent than in
1 Maccabees. Most probably Jason was in close contact with
priestly circles in Jerusalem.[14] While the original work was
much closer in time to the revolt than 1 Maccabees and Jason
may even have been a contemporary of the events he describes,[15]
the viewpoint of the Maccabees is more likely to be preserved
in the Hasmonean source than in the temple-oriented 2 Maccabees.

The Viewpoint of 1 Maccabees

Both books of Maccabees make clear that the revolt drew
heavily on old traditions of holy war. The battles of Judas
Maccabee echo the wars of the conquest and Judges. So before

the battle of Beth-horon, Judas' soldiers ask "How can we, few as we are, fight against so great and strong a multitude? And we are faint, for we have eaten nothing to-day." Judas replied, "It is easy for many to be hemmed in by a few, for in the sight of heaven there is no difference between saving by many or by few. It is not on the size of the army that victory in battle depends, but strength comes from Heaven" (1 Macc 3: 17-19). We are reminded of Gideon, who had to reduce his army "lest Israel vaunt themselves against me by saying 'my own hand has delivered me'" (Judg 7:2). Again, when we read that "terror fell on the Gentiles round about them" (1 Macc 3:25) we recognize a familiar motif of holy war.[16]

1 Maccabees presents a particular understanding of holy war which is based on the synergism of Yahweh with his heavenly army and the human forces of the Maccabees. Strength comes from heaven, the victory is achieved by God, but the role of the human forces is vitally important. God fights with the swords of the Maccabees. The importance of the human military action is expressed clearly in the words of Mattathias, after a group of pious Jews had been slaughtered on the sabbath:

> If we all do as our brethren have done and refuse
> to fight with the Gentiles for our lives and our
> ordinances, they will quickly destroy us from the
> earth. (1 Macc 2:40)

We find here echoes of the oldest strands of holy war. In Judges 5, the Song of Deborah, while the battle is clearly decided by the divine warrior, Yahweh, yet the inhabitants of Meroz are cursed "because they came not to the held of the Lord, to the help of the Lord against the mighty" (Judg 5:23). The human armies cannot be dispensed with; every tribe must pull its weight.

Consequently, 1 Maccabees attaches great value to the military action of the Maccabees. Their prototype is Phinehas, who proved his devotion with his spear in Num 25:6-15, by transfixing an Israelite and his Midianite concubine. So Mattathias and his sons "burned with zeal for the law as Phinehas did against Zimri the son of Salu" (1 Macc 2:26). We find in 1 Maccabees the essential values which inspired the

Zealot movement down to the time of the Jewish revolts against
Rome.[17] The heroes of the revolt are the mighty warriors. The
praises of Judas Maccabee in 1 Macc 3:3--"like a giant he put
on his breastplate; he girded on his armor of war and waged
battles, protecting his host by his sword"--echoe the description of Yahweh arming himself for battle in Isa 59:17. The
militant action of Judas is the means of salvation: "thus he
turned away wrath from Israel" (1 Macc 3:8).

The salvation wrought by the Maccabees is described in
the praises of Simon in 1 Macc 14:4, 11-15:

> The land had rest all the days of Simon.
> He sought the good of his nation,
> his rule was pleasing to them
> as was the honor shown him all his days...
> He established peace in the land
> and Israel rejoiced with great joy.
> Each man sat under his vine and his fig-tree,
> and there was none to make them afraid.
> No one was left in the land to fight them
> and the kings were crushed in those days.

The picture here is one of national restoration. The original
objectives of the revolt were to attain national and religious
independence in the face of the encroachments of Antiochus:

> Even if all the nations that live under the rule
> of the king obey him, and have chosen to do his
> commandments, departing each one from the religion
> of his fathers, yet I and my sons and my brothers
> will live by the covenant of our fathers. Far be
> it from us to desert the law and the ordinances.
>   (1 Macc 2:19-21)

The religious motivation here is simple adherence to national
tradition. This is supported by a holy war in which the
Maccabees fight for and with their god. The outcome is an era
of national restoration marked by ideal peace. The revolt of
the Maccabees blends nationalism and religion in a manner quite
possible for any Near Eastern state in revolt against the
Seleucids. Their revolt was more successful than others but
was not essentially different in kind.

The Viewpoint of 2 Maccabees

The Maccabean viewpoint as presented in 1 Maccabees was
not the only political stance related to the revolt. 2 Maccabees

presents the same events from a somewhat different perspective.
Again the traditional framework of Holy War is used. Judas and
his followers fight in synergism with Yahweh and the angelic
host. Judas could encourage his followers in the face of
greater numbers by telling them:

> They trust to arms and acts of daring...but we trust
> in the Almighty God who is able with a single nod
> to strike down those who are coming against us, and
> even the whole world. (2 Macc 8:18)

The heavenly host takes an active part in the battle:

> When the battle became fierce there appeared to the
> enemy from heaven five resplendent men on horses
> with golden bridles, and they were leading the
> Jews. Surrounding Maccabeus and protecting him
> with their own armor and weapons, they kept him from
> being wounded. And they showered arrows and thunder-
> bolts upon the enemy, so that, confused and blinded,
> they were thrown into disorder and cut to pieces.
> (2 Macc 10:29-31)

Various differences may be noted between the two books of
Maccabees. Where 1 Maccabees emphasizes the law, 2 Maccabees
emphasizes the temple, and the story culminates with the statement, "From that time the city has been in the possession of
the Hebrews. So I too will here end my story" (2 Macc 15:37).
2 Maccabees ignores Mattathias and credits Judas with the organization of the revolt. Most important for our purpose, however, is the fact that the human role in the holy war is not
confined to military action. 2 Maccabees dwells at great
length on the deaths of the martyrs, in chs. 6 and 7. When
Judas is beginning his campaign, he calls on God to "hearken to
the blood that cried out to him" (8:3). The success of Judas
is due not only to his valor but also to the fact that God
wreaks vengeance through him for his city and the martyrs. The
deaths of the martyrs are not the only factor which arouses the
vengeance of God, but it is at least clear that the zealot warriors are not the only ones who contribute to the victory.
They also serve who only stand and suffer.

The Viewpoint of the Testament of Moses

A third political stance from the time of the Maccabean
revolt is attested in the Testament of Moses. In its present

form, this work dates from the last years of the pre-Christian era, but there is considerable probability that the main body of the text dates from the persecution of Antiochus.[18] Even if the Testament did not originate in Maccabean times, it at least represents one possible type of reaction to persecution in ancient Judaism.

The Testament contains a description of persecution which is strikingly similar to that inflicted by Antiochus:

> He will stir up against them the king of the kings
> of the earth and one that ruleth with great power,
> who shall crucify those who confess to their circum-
> cision...their young sons shall be operated on by
> the physicians in order to bring forward their
> foreskin. And others amongst them shall be punished
> by tortures, fire and sword, and they shall be forced
> to bear in public their idols, polluted as they are
> like those who keep them. And they shall likewise
> be forced by those who torture them to enter their
> innermost sanctuary.... (TM 8:1-5)

This account is followed in 9:5-7 by the reaction of a certain Taxo of the tribe of Levi, who exhorts his seven sons:

> Ye know that this is our strength and thus we will
> do. Let us fast for the space of three days and on
> the fourth let us go into a cave which is in the
> field and let us die rather than transgress the
> commands of the Lord of Lords, the God of our
> fathers. For if we do this and die, our blood shall
> be avenged before the Lord.

The manner of the vengeance is illustrated in 10:1, 8-10:

> And then his kingdom shall appear throughout all
>   His creation
> And then Satan shall be no more...
> And then thou Israel shalt be happy...
> and he will cause thee to approach to the heaven
>   of the stars...
> and thou shalt look from on high and see thy enemies
>   in Gehenna.

The exaltation of Israel here is strikingly similar to Daniel 12. The kingdom of God does not consist of, or even involve, the establishment of a Maccabean kingdom on earth. No reference is made to the restoration of the temple. Instead, we have a separation of Israel, which is exalted to the stars, from its enemies, who go down to Gehenna. Since this state of affairs is brought about by the martyrdom of Taxo and his sons,

it is reasonable to assume that the exaltation to the stars
involves the resurrection of the martyrs as it does in Daniel
12.

The Testament of Moses and 2 Maccabees share an interest
in martyrdom as the human contribution to holy war. However,
in 2 Maccabees, martyrdom was only one factor among others. In
the Testament of Moses it is the only factor mentioned and it
triggers the advent of the kingdom directly.[19] In 2 Maccabees
the militant action of Judas is still the instrument of God's
vengeance. In the Testament of Moses the destruction is
wrought by an angel with no reference to human militants. Taxo
and his sons appear as thorough quietists, who attain their
ends by non-violent submission to martyrdom.

Taxo and his sons are often related to the story in 1
Maccabees of the "many who were seeking righteousness and justice" and "went down to the wilderness to dwell there" (1 Macc
2:29). They were attacked on the sabbath and since they refused to violate the day of rest by fighting, they were mas-
sacred. These were obviously pious people who were prepared
to die rather than break the law. It does not follow that they
were quietistic. Even active militants sometimes refused to
fight on the sabbath.[20] Also, there is nothing to suggest that
this group was deliberately looking for martyrdom, as is explicitly the case with Taxo. However, it is not impossible
that Taxo is modelled on a member of this group. It is striking that these martyrs call on heaven and earth to bear witness
to their death, in a manner which recalls Taxo's confidence
that he will be avenged by the Lord.

The Testament of Moses, which has been described as a rewriting of Deuteronomy 31-34,[21] is drawing on a paradigm for
holy war which is different from that used by the Hasmoneans.
This paradigm is supplied by Deut 32:35-43:

> Vengeance is mine and recompense...
> for he avenges the blood of his servants
> and takes vengeance on his adversaries.

This passage suggests the attitude to holy war which we find in
the Testament--the human role is to provoke the vengeance of
God by letting the blood of his servants be spilled. Significantly, the martyrs in 2 Macc 7:6 refer explicitly to Deut

32:36: "And he will have compassion on his servants." In
short, whatever differences there may be between them, 2 Maccabees, the martyrs in 1 Maccabees 2 and the Testament of
Moses, all share an attitude to martyrdom which is based on the
expectation of divine vengeance.

The Hasidim

In 1 Maccabees 2, shortly after the martyrdoms in the
cave, we are told that Judas was joined by "a company of
Hasideans, mighty warriors of Israel, everyone who offered himself willingly for the law." Because of the juxtaposition in
1 Maccabees 2, the Hasideans are very widely believed to be the
party to which the martyrs in the cave belonged. Both the
martyrs in the cave (1 Macc 2:29) and the Hasidim (1 Macc 7:12)
are characterized by the pursuit of justice. At most, the
martyrs may have been one group of Hasidim. The identification
is by no means conclusive, but it is compatible with what we
otherwise know of the Hasidim.

The party of the Hasideans has grown in recent scholarship
from an extremely poorly attested entity to the great Jewish
alternative to the Maccabees at the time of the revolt. There
has been no corresponding growth in the evidence. There are
three references to the Hasidim in the books of Maccabees. In
1 Macc 2:42, they are "mighty warriors of Israel." In 1 Macc
7:12-13, they seem to be identified with the group of scribes
who sought peace with Alcimus:

> Then a group of scribes appeared in a body before
> Alcimus and Bacchides to ask for just terms. The
> Hasideans were the first among the sons of Israel
> to seek peace from them, for they said: 'A priest
> of the line of Aaron has come with the army, he
> will not harm us.'

Their confidence was ill-founded, and sixty of them were
seized and put to death. In 2 Macc 14:6, they are mentioned
by Alcimus, before this latter incident, in his report to
Demetrius on the intentions of the Jews:

> Those of the Jews who are called Hasideans, whose
> leader is Judas Maccabeus, are keeping up war and
> stirring up sedition and will not let the kingdom
> attain tranquility.

These three passages seem to refer to the Hasidim as an
organized party in Judaism. Other allusions to *ḥasîdîm* as
"pious ones" in psalmody cannot be taken as references to this
party. While earlier commentators, such as Duhm, saw an explicit reference to the Hasidic party of Maccabean times in the
"assembly of the pious" (*qᵉhal ḥasîdîm*) of Ps 149:1, recent
scholars have rejected this identification.[22] The references
to the "assembly of the *ḥasîdîm*" (11Qps[a] 154) and "Israel, your
ḥasîdîm" (11Qps[a] 155) in the Qumran psalms scroll[23] echo the
phraseology of the biblical psalms and cannot be taken as references to the Maccabean political party. Our only evidence
for an organized party in Maccabean times lies in the three
references in 1 and 2 Maccabees.

Despite the paucity of evidence, recent scholars have attributed to these Hasidim the collection and canonization of
the prophetic books,[24] the roots of both the Essene and the
Pharisaic movements, and the authorship of a wide range of
apocalyptic writings, including Daniel.[25] While the Hasidim
may in fact have been responsible for some of these developments, the resulting picture is certainly an oversimplification.
The Jewish resistance movement is presented as consisting of
two coherent and organized parties, the militant Maccabees, and
the Hasidim, who joined the revolt only reluctantly after the
slaughter of their companions and were eager to lay down arms
at the restoration of a high-priest of the legitimate line,
such as Alcimus.

This picture of the Hasidim has been forcefully challenged by Tcherikover.[26] He accepts the usual identification
of those who were killed on the sabbath as Hasidim but argues
that they were not "harmless and peaceful people, deliberate
conscientious pacifists." Rather their flight to the desert
represented "the first organization of the forces of national
resistance." On Tcherikover's reconstruction, the Hasidim were
the scribal leaders of the people, a thesis supported by 1 Macc
7:12-13. They had in fact begun the rebellion by ousting Jason
from Jerusalem. This disturbance led to the intervention of
Antiochus IV Epiphanes who saw it as a rebellion against himself. This was what caused the persecution.[27] The flight of

the Hasidim to the wilderness was a preparation for militant resistance.[28] Even after the Maccabees came to the fore, the Hasidim were still a very significant bloc in the resistance movement, as can be seen from 2 Macc 14:6: "Those of the Jews who are called Hasideans, whose leader is Judas Maccabeus."

Tcherikōver's reconstruction of the Hasidim is persuasive because it incorporates all the data we are given in 1 and 2 Maccabees. The Hasidim were a party of scribes (1 Macc 7:12-13) whose motivation was trict fidelity to the law (1 Macc 2:42). They were prepared to fight for the law, when necessary and when permitted by the law itself. They could not initially break the law by fighting on the sabbath, even to save their lives. They were prepared to lay down arms at the prospect of a legitimate high-priest who would remove the religious abuses of the Hellenizers.

We must emphasize that the Hasidim found the Maccabees acceptable and allied themselves with them for most of the revolt. There is no evidence that they had any qualms about the methods of Judas. Their objectives were different, insofar as they were primarily interested in restoring acceptable religious conditions, especially a legitimate priesthood. When they believed they had found such a priest in Alcimus, they were apparently ready to break with the Maccabees. Many scholars believe that they broke decisively with the Maccabees at a later point when Jonathan (152 B.C.) assumed the high priesthood, or, more definitely in 142 B.C., when Simon was proclaimed "high priest forever, until a faithful prophet should arise" (1 Macc 14:41-47). At this point, it was clear that a non-Zadokite priestly dynasty was being established. Frank Cross has argued that this was the occasion for a definite break between the Maccabees and at least some elements of the Hasidim, who then proceeded to found the community at Qumran.[29] While the evidence for this break is not conclusive, Cross's hypothesis has provided a coherent explanation of the origins of the Qumran community which is widely accepted. It is highly compatible with what we have seen of the Hasidim. We should note that if Cross was correct, the alliance between the Maccabees and the Hasidim broke down, not because of their different political ideologies, but because of the claims of rival houses to the High Priesthood.

The relations between the Hasidim and the Maccabees may well be reflected in the differences between 1 and 2 Maccabees. 2 Maccabees enthusiastically admires Judas Maccabee and has no reservations about his methods. It differs from 1 Maccabees in the greater prominence it gives to the temple, and to the role of the martyrs in the holy war. Since the calendar used in 2 Maccabees is that which was used in the temple in Jerusalem, it is likely that Jason of Cyrene, whose history is abridged in 2 Maccabees, was in close contact with priestly circles.[30] If Cross is right, the Hasidim also had a strong priestly component. While 2 Maccabees, as we have it, cannot be taken simply as a product of the Hasidim, it very probably preserves much of their viewpoint. This viewpoint differs in motivation from the Maccabean stance presented in 1 Maccabees, but it could still wholeheartedly endorse the career of Judas.

Neither 1 nor 2 Maccabees can be described as apocalyptic. They are histories which chronicle a revolt which had attained its goal. They do not look for a greater eschatological fulfillment in any form. However, the supporters of the Maccabees could express their ideology in apocalyptic form. This is shown by the so-called Animal Apocalypse of *1 Enoch* 83-90. This is an allegorical review of history from creation to the resurrection. A human figure is used for the archangel Michael (90:14, 17, 22) and the rulers of the nations (possibly angelic rulers) are described as shepherds. The other characters in the drama are referred to as animals--bulls, sheep, etc. In the Hellenistic period, the Jews were exposed to persecution: "the sheep cried out because their flesh was being devoured by the birds" (90:3). Then "lambs were borne by those white sheep and they began to open their eyes and to see and to cry to the sheep" (90:6). However, no attention was paid to them so they resorted to more forceful methods: "horns grew upon those lambs" and "a great horn on one of those sheep" (90:9) and they did battle with their oppressors. Eventually "a great sword was given to the sheep" until "the Lord of the sheep came unto them in wrath" (90:19, 15). Then follows an apocalyptic judgment in which the stars and the shepherds are condemned and cast into a fiery abyss. A new temple is built and "all that had been destroyed and dispersed" assembled there. Then all the beasts are transformed into "white bulls" --the description used for Adam at the beginning of the vision.

Because of the allegorical nature of the imagery, we do not get a fully clear picture of the ideology of this work. However, a few points are evident. The violent revolution of the Maccabees is wholeheartedly endorsed, and Charles is surely correct when he identifies the sheep with the great horn as Judas Maccabee.[31] The eschatological tableau which envisages a paradisiac condition around a new temple, and apparently involves resurrection, seems closer to 2 Maccabees than to 1 Maccabees. Charles has suggested that the lambs of 90:6-9 who initiate the revolt are the Hasidim, and this is extremely plausible. In any case, the document shows how an apocalyptic vision could be used to endorse and arouse support for the militant policies of the Maccabees. Since there is no reference to the historical restoration or the death of Judas, the apocalypse was probably written during the revolt.

The Spectrum of Viewpoints

Either 2 Maccabees or the Animal Apocalypse might be considered at least compatible with the viewpoint of the Hasidim, and might reflect shades of opinion within that party. The Testament of Moses stands in contrast to these works. Taxo does not appear as a "mighty warrior" who is forced to submit to martyrdom because of the requirements of the sabbath observance.[32] He deliberately chooses martyrdom as the means of inducing the vengeance of God, therefore as his contribution to the holy war. Also the kingdom promised by the Testament of Moses cannot be conceived as the restoration of an acceptable condition on earth such as might be brought about by a legitimate high priest. (The highly allegorical Animal Apocalypse is ambiguous on this point.) The kingdom in the Testament is a transcendent one where Israel is elevated to the stars. It is, of course, conceivable that the Testament of Moses was

produced by a quietist prior to the massacre in the wilderness
and that its author revised his strategy when the Hasidim
joined the Maccabees (1 Macc 2:42). However, the document as
we have it has no place for human militance. It represents one
possible reaction to the crisis which is very different from
that of the Maccabees or from what we know of the Hasidim.
Taxo's synergism with God's holy war takes the form of self-
purification and martyrdom. His commitment is bolstered by the
expectation of a transcendent kingdom of God in which he and
his fellow-countrymen will mingle with the stars.

We find then a significant range of different attitudes
within the Jewish resistance to Antiochus Epiphanes. The nationalist militancy of the Maccabees, best represented by 1
Maccabees, occupies one extreme of the spectrum. The Hasidim
were motivated by different concerns, but found the methods
and leadership of Judas Maccabee acceptable. There may have
been different shades of opinion within this movement. The
Animal Apocalypse envisages an apocalyptic judgment and the
restoration of a paradisiac state as the outcome of the revolt.
2 Maccabees, written after the events had unfolded, speaks more
clearly of the restoration of the temple in earthly terms. On
the other end of the spectrum, the Testament of Moses does not
endorse militant resistance at all. The role of the faithful
Jew is to purify himself and undergo martyrdom. In that way
he can hasten the transcendent kingdom of God.

We must emphasize that all of these stances fall within
the range of political resistance to Antiochus. All are political, insofar as they demand a stand over against the political
powers of the day. All operate within a religious framework,
specifically the Israelite traditions of holy war. The type of
response to the political situation demanded by each is different, but all are cast within the political context. None of
them is concerned with a purely private spirituality.

The Stance of Daniel

The documents we have discussed do not necessarily exhaust
the possible nuances in the Jewish resistance movement, but

they give a good indication of the range of viewpoints. The use of the four kingdoms schema shows that Daniel belongs somewhere in the domain of resistance literature. Can we specify its position more exactly?

Like each of the other documents we have considered, Daniel works within the traditions of holy war. The political situation, as he sees it, involves not only the conflict of human powers, but also the patron angels of the nations. The real conflict takes place on the mythical level in the confrontation of the beasts and the rider of the clouds and in the battle of Michael against the "prince" of Greece. The role of the faithful Jews in this conflict is discussed only in ch. 11. There we read of the onslaught of Antiochus against "the holy covenant" (Dan 11:30). Various groups within the Jewish people react differently. "Those who violate the covenant" are won over by the king, but "those who know their God" stand firm and take action. The *maskîlîm*, the "wise instructors of the people," must be either identified with the latter group or regarded as a subdivision of it. Two other groups are barely mentioned. The *rabbîm* or "many" seem to be the neutral multitude, undifferentiated at the outbreak of the revolt. The "little help," often understood as the Maccabees, more probably refers to those of the *rabbîm* who respond to instruction and join the efforts of the *maskîlîm*.

The action of these *maskîlîm* is twofold. They suffer persecution "to refine and to cleanse them and to make them white." Endurance of sufferings was common to all shades of political resistance. The emphasis on purification here is particularly similiar to the Testament of Moses. The second form of action is not attested in any contemporary document. The *maskîlîm* will "make many understand" (11:33) and thereby turn them to righteousness (12:3).

We have already discussed the nature of the wisdom of the *maskîlîm* and concluded that it is primarily the wisdom manifested in the visions themselves. It is, then, the eschatological interpretation of visions and scriptures. The wisdom is relevant to the *maskîl* in his time of crisis, because it enables him to choose the right side in the conflict. More important,

it gives him the strength to undergo suffering and even death
in the present because he is assured of a glorious afterlife.

The mythical symbolism of the visions of Daniel is designed to inspire active but non-militant resistance. The
maskîlîm are not said to fight. The warfare is left to Michael
and to God. The *maskîlîm* play their part by their suffering
and teaching. In ch. 7 the entire conflict is resolved by a
judgment. The symbolism of the visions does not encourage
zealotry. Rather, it provides a framework within which the
wise man does not need to fight, but can express his resistance
to the power of the king by non-compliance with his orders, and
endurance of whatever suffering results. The mythic patterns
assure the wise man that there is a meaning in life even in the
darkest crisis. Specifically, the symbolism of the angelic
world assures him that there is another dimension of reality
which is more important than the empirical reality of everyday
life. The symbolism of resurrection and exaltation assures him
that he can attain that higher dimension of life, therefore
that he can afford to lose his physical life if necessary. He
can transcend any sufferings imposed on him, even death itself.
The conviction of the *maskîl* that there are transcendent
values and transcendent meaning in life, which are not destroyed by death, is expressed in symbolic form. Neither the
kingdom of the "one like a son of man" nor the assimilation to
the stars can be read as simply literal descriptions. Rather,
they are the imaginative expressions of a hope that goes beyond
the bounds of the empirical world and could inspire the *maskîlîm* to reject the kingdom of Antiochus and remain faithful to
their religion in the face of death.

We may note a certain measure of similarity here between
the *maskîlîm* in Daniel and the martyrs in 2 Maccabees 7. When
confronted with gruesome tortures and death, the martyrs could
defy the king:

> You accursed wretch, you dismiss us from this present
> life, but the King of the universe will raise us up
> to an everlasting renewal of life, because we have
> died for his laws (2 Macc 7:9)

for "one cannot but choose to die at the hands of men and to cherish the hope that God gives of being raised again by him" (7:14). For the martyrs of 2 Maccabees, salvation is two-fold. The individual martyrs hope for bodily resurrection, while there is no indication as to when or where this will take place. But there is also the restoration of the nation. This is brought about by the sword of Judas, and the purification of the temple.

While Daniel doesn't exclude a national restoration on the earthly level, he expresses no interest in it. His interest lies rather in the *maskîlîm*. Their salvation consists of "shining like the stars," of being transformed to an angelic state. This is the destiny not only of individuals but of all the *maskîlîm*, whether they have undergone martyrdom or not. It is clear that this transformation cannot be brought about by militant action. Unlike the Maccabees, even the martyrs of 2 Maccabees 7, the *maskîlîm* envisage no goal which can be attained by violent revolution. For them, the kingdom is the heavenly angelic kingdom. The victory then must be completely the work of God and/or the heavenly host. The *maskîlîm* play their part in that victory by preparing themselves and others for transformation: themselves by the sufferings which purify them and make them white, others by instruction in the eschatological mysteries.

It is clear that Daniel stands much closer to the Testament of Moses than it does to either 1 or 2 Maccabees. In both books, the eschatological tableau is used to motivate faithful Jews in a crisis which demands martyrdom. Both promise a salvation which transcends death, in the form of assimilation to the stars or angelic host. This is not envisaged as a private salvation in either book. Elevation to the stars does not imply the ascent of the soul by ascetic holiness. Rather, it is part of a transformed world order, which includes *inter alia* the political order. So the transformed *maskîlîm* in Daniel, and Israel in the Testament of Moses, can be said to participate in a *kingdom*, of the holy ones in Daniel, of God in the Testament. It is clear that the symbolism of personal resurrection gives some place for personal mysticism, but this has to be integrated in a sense of the political order. The transformation of the *maskîlîm* can only fully take place when the beast has been slain and the hostile kingdom of Antiochus overthrown.

The Wisdom of the *Maskîlîm*

The main difference between the Testament of Moses and Daniel is the great insistence on wisdom in Daniel, which finds no echo in the Testament. This wisdom provides an element of present fulfillment in Daniel which is lacking in the Testament. The resistance of the *maskîlîm* is not based only on future expectation but also on the present experience of wisdom. This wisdom enables them to withstand persecution and to transcend suffering and death. It gives them immediate, if only partial, access to a higher world which must wait for its full political manifestation until the time of the end. This does not mean that they opt out of the political situation. Rather, their wisdom enables them to withstand the kingdom of the beasts in the name of heaven which will ultimately destroy all human kingdoms.

The wisdom of the *maskîlîm*, which enables them to transcend persecution and death, inevitably reminds us of another Jewish work from the turn of the era, the Wisdom of Solomon. There the wicked are said to have "reasoned unsoundly, saying to themselves, 'short and sorrowful is our life...and no one has been known to return from Hades'" (Wis 2:1). Therefore they resolve to "let our might be our law of right, for what is weak proves itself to be useless" (2:11). In particular, they are determined to get rid of the righteous man "because he is inconvenient to us and opposes our actions" (2:12). So they condemn him to a shameful death. But their schemes are in vain for "they did not know the secret purposes of God" (2:22). The wise man is not destroyed by their violence for "the souls of the righteous are in the hand of God and no torment shall ever touch them. In the eyes of the wicked, they seem to have died...but they are at peace" (3:3).

The account of the righteous man in Wisdom has a number of striking parallels to Daniel. He professes to have knowledge

of God (2:13). In Daniel, the maskîlîm are "the people who
know their God" (Dan 11:32). The sufferings of the righteous
are a test "like gold in the furnace he tried them" (Wis 3:6).
In Dan 11:35, "some of those who are wise shall fall, to refine
and to cleanse them." The verb *to refine* (ṣrp) is used of re-
fining precious metals in the OT.[33] The vindication of the
righteous is expressed in terms reminiscent of Dan 12:3: "in
the time of their visitation they will shine forth, and will
run like sparks among the stubble" (Wis 3:7). The enigmatic
sparks have suggested to some that astral immortality is implied here.[34] Even if this suggestion is not accepted, the
"shining" is clearly reminiscent of Daniel 12. Further, in
Wis 5:5, the righteous are explicitly associated with the angels: "Why has he been numbered among the sons of God? And why
is his lot among the saints?" Finally this exaltation after
death can be expressed as a *kingdom*: "They will govern nations
and rule over peoples" (3:8) and "they will receive a glorious
crown and a beautiful diadem from the hand of the Lord" (5:16).[35]

The eschatological rule of the righteous is the only reference in Wisdom 1-5 which admits of a political connotation.
Unlike Daniel, the situation which gives rise to the persecution is not a political crisis but the random violence of individuals. It is very probable that these passages in Wisdom
are drawing on an older apocalyptic source.[36] In its present
context in Wisdom, the testing of the righteous has lost its
political dimension. Also the nature of his reaction is al-
tered by the introduction of a body-soul dichotomy which is
foreign to Jewish apocalyptic.[37] Yet the continuity between
Wisdom and Daniel is striking. In both books, the righteous
man is able to withstand persecution because he understands the
eschatological mysteries. By wisdom he is able to transcend
death and share in a heavenly kingdom.

In the political context of Daniel, then, the resistance
of the maskîlîm is not inspired by the desire to restore a
national kingship, but by allegiance to a heavenly kingdom.
The heavenly kingdom is such that it does not demand militant
cooperation from the faithful, but rather purity and wisdom.
There is a stronger element of mysticism in Daniel than any of

the other political ideologies we have considered. Yet it is
not a private individual mysticism. Daniel is vitally concerned with the political order. This is the point of depar-
ture for all his visions. The salvation he envisages is not a
purely individual salvation, but involves a community, the
"people of the holy ones" or the *maskîlîm*.

Learned Wisdom and Popular Politics

The similarities between Daniel and the Wisdom of Solomon
are most likely due to apocalyptic influence on Wisdom. They
do not argue that Daniel depends on the Jewish wisdom tradition. As we have seen earlier, the importance of wisdom for
the *maskîlîm* derives primarily from the example of Daniel in
the court-tales. Daniel, the ideal figure in whose name the
apocalyptic visions are presented, was himself a wise man
skilled in the interpretation of dreams and signs. In each of
the tales (chs. 2, 4 and 5), his interpretations have political
import. In at least one case, Daniel 2, his dream interpretation is a political oracle with an eschatological conclusion.

It is of importance for the social function of the book of
Daniel that its hero is a learned man who produces his political statements by the use of his professional skills. The visions attributed to Daniel must also be considered as learned
compositions.[38] One prophecy is an explicit interpretation of
a scriptural text. The others are presented as interpretations
of enigmatic visions. The imagery of the visions is highly
complex and laced with allusions to earlier biblical writings
and ancient myths. We should not think of these visions as
folk-literature arising anonymously from the popular resistance
movement, but as the product of a wise author who was a learned
man after the manner of Daniel.[39] The apocalyptic visions
should not be understood as spontaneous formulations of the
dreams of the people, but as a learned phenomenon.

This interpretation is supported by the explicit statements about the *maskîlîm* in Daniel 11. They are not a widespread popular movement, but rather an elite few, distinguished
from others by their knowledge. The author of Daniel almost
certainly belonged to this group.

However, the visions of Daniel are not esoteric messages to the author's own elite circle. Despite the injunction in Daniel to "seal the book," it is clear that the time of the end has now come and the mysteries must be revealed. The *maskîlîm* themselves have as their task to "make many understand" by conveying to them a proper understanding of their political situation and inspiring them to the proper reaction. The visions of Daniel must also be directed to that purpose. Accordingly, they are indeed a political manifesto, produced by one section of the intelligentsia but designed to affect the populace. Daniel was not addressed to only one social class. In view of the learned circles in which it originated and circulated, we cannot accept the theory of Norman Cohn that Jewish apocalyptic was "directed to the lowest strata of the Jewish population."[40]

The manifesto which we find in Daniel is one of resistance. The reader is challenged to make a choice in the holy war between Michael and his angels and the armies of Antiochus. This is not an internal spiritual battle. Antiochus and his armies are very real factors in the political world. The reader of Daniel is challenged to resist Antiochus, and the apocalyptic visions of the outcome of the battle provide the basis for this decision. However, the resistance evoked is not military action, but the non-violent assertion of their religious loyalty and submission to martyrdom if necessary. The righteous co-operate with the angelic host, not by the sword, but by wisdom and purification, which prepare them for their final transformation. The military victory is the work of Michael. In Daniel 7, even Michael doesn't fight. The conflict is resolved by the judgment of the Ancient of Days.

The visions of Daniel are designed to promote this response to the political situation. They constitute a political manifesto because they demand a specific reaction to the existing political state. However, they differ sharply from other contemporary political oracles insofar as their alternative to the current kingdom is not a restored national kingship, even an idealized one depicted in religious terms. Rather, it is a transcendent kingdom where the *maskîlîm* share the eternal angelic life. The political claims of Antiochus are therefore confronted not only with the claims of another national kingdom, but with the invisible kingdom symbolized by the angelic world.

The apocalyptic perspective of Daniel cannot be adequately explained by the social and political circumstances in which the book was composed. It is a well-known fact that millenarian expectations and apocalyptic visions flourish in times of acute crisis when the conditions of the present are intolerable. However, the persecution of Antiochus was no more severe on the *maskîlîm* of Daniel than it was on the Maccabees. Yet the Maccabees did not turn to an apocalyptic eschatology but to the more practical expedient of armed rebellion. In short, an acute crisis did not inevitably produce apocalyptic visions, even among those who drew on essentially the same traditions of holy war. There was another factor involved, which was more peculiar to the visionary and his circle. This was a difference in theological attitude, and perhaps also in temperament. The author of Daniel was a learned wise man. His vision of the way God works and of his understanding of revelation determined his reaction to the crisis of persecution. Consequently, his vision was quite different from that of the Maccabees, who were informed by a different theology.

There is a widespread consensus among modern scholars that Daniel was composed by one of the Hasidim.[41] The extent of our knowledge of the Hasidim scarcely warrants such a consensus. One of the few clear points about them is that they joined the militant movement of Judas Maccabee. There is nothing in Daniel to suggest that such a course of action would be acceptable to its author.[42] It is possible, of course, that Daniel represents an early stage, or a divergent strand of the Hasidic movement, but this is pure possibility, unsupported by evidence. We have seen that the Jewish resistance movement incorporated a wide spectrum of attitudes and motivations, all of which had something in common, but which were not necessarily representative of clearly defined parties. Daniel differs from what we know of the Hasidim in the methods of resistance which it advocates.

The Tradition of Non-violent Resistance

How far the maskîlîm of Daniel succeeded in winning adherents to their ideology we do not know. Certainly the revolt was dominated by the militant Maccabees. Later, after the advent of Pompey, Jewish resistance to the Romans is associated primarily with the violence of the Zealots, who consciously continued the tradition of the Maccabees.[43]

Yet there was also a strand of non-violent resistance.[44] The Testament of Moses was updated and re-edited about the turn of the era. Its message contrasted sharply with the program of Judas of Galilee and other insurrectionist movements of the time.[45] In the first century A.D., we find a number of instances of non-violent resistance in action. When Pontius Pilate threatened to slaughter a crowd of Jews who had gathered at Caesarea to request the removal of the Roman standards from Jerusalem, they lay on the ground and bared their necks to the sword, rather than break their law. Pilate had the standards removed.[46] There was a similar confrontation between Petronius and the Jews when Caligula wanted to place a statue in the Jerusalem temple. In this case, a massacre was averted by the death of the emperor.[47] While messianic prophecies played a part in arousing the Jews to revolt against Rome in 66 A.D., such predictions were not always used as an incitement to militancy. Some of the prophets active in the years before the revolt evidently believed the kingdom would be ushered in by the direct action of God. Josephus is unsympathetic to these people. After describing the sicarii, or dagger-men, in JW 2.13.3 (254-48), he goes on:

> In addition to these there was formed another group of scoundrels, in act less criminal but in intention more evil, who did as much damage as the murderers to the well-being of the city. Cheats and deceivers, claiming inspiration, they schemed to bring about revolutionary changes by inducing the mob to act as if possessed, and by leading them out into the wild country on the pretence that there God would show them signs of approaching freedom. Thereupon Felix, regarding this as the first stage of revolt, sent cavalry and heavy infantry who cut the mob to pieces.
> (JW 2.13.4(258-60) Cf. Ant., 20.8.6(167-68)

We are inevitably reminded of the massacre in the cave in
1 Maccabees 2 and of Taxo and his sons in the Testament of
Moses. On Josephus' own admission, these "scoundrels" did not
intend to initiate a militant revolt but expected God to manifest himself as divine warrior and overthrow the Romans. Their
role, like that of the Qumran community, was to "prepare in the
desert a highway for our God,"[48] to make ready to receive the
theophany by fulfilling prophecy.

The community of Qumran also adopted a non-violent attitude to its enemies, at least for the present:

> To no man will I render the reward of evil,
> with goodness will I pursue each one,
> for judgment of all the living is with God.
> (1QS 10:17-18)

The non-violence of the sectarians was a temporary measure. They looked forward to executing God's judgment when the
time came:

> As for the multitude of the men of the Pit
> I will not lay hands on them till the Day of Vengeance.
> (1QS 10:19)

The War Scroll describes in detail how they would participate
in the final battle on that day. Even here, however, the sectarians saw that the battle was in the hands of God and his
angels. Their own role was subordinate. They could not bring
about the kingdom of God by initiating an armed rebellion.
They could only co-operate with the action of God.

In any of these cases where Jews adopted a non-violent
form of resistance, they were not motivated by love of their
enemies. Rather, they aspired to a perfection of hatred. In
the words of Krister Stendahl:

> Non-retaliation is grounded in the eschatological
> intensity of the "eternal hatred towards the men
> of perdition" (1QS ix,21f)....With the Day of
> Vengeance at hand the proper and reasonable atti-
> tude is to forego one's own vengeance and to leave
> the vengeance to God. Why walk around with a little
> shotgun when the atomic blast is imminent?[49]

We find the same motivation in early Christian texts.
Paul exhorts the Romans:

Beloved, never avenge yourselves, but leave it to
the wrath of God; for it is written, "vengeance is
mine, I will repay, says the Lord." No, "if your
enemy is hungry feed him; if he is thirsty give him
drink; for by so doing you will heap burning coals
upon his head." (Rom 12:19-20)

The human instinct for vengeance is deferred in anticipa-
tion of the more effective vengeance of God. Similarly, the
Apocalypse of John calls primarily for endurance of suffering
and warns that "if anyone kills by the sword, by the sword must
he be slain" (Rev 13:10). The passive attitude is adopted in
view of the eschatological manifestation of Christ, equipped
with a sharp sword to smite the gentiles (Rev 19:15).

The Apocalypse of John continues the tradition of Daniel
by interpreting Holy War in such a way that violence is left to
God, and humans play their part by self-purification and understanding the eschatological mysteries. How far the tradition
of non-violent resistance was directly influenced by the book
of Daniel is not within the scope of this study. We need only
think of the phrase "Son of Man" to realize that the book enjoyed widespread influence. Even apart from the question of
literary influence, Daniel is clearly of great importance for
understanding the development of early Christianity. When
Jesus came preaching that the kingdom of God is at hand, he
inevitably suggested that his message had a political dimension. There can be little doubt that the Romans who executed
him saw him as another messianic pretender and feared that his
preaching was the beginning of a revolt. Despite the arguments
of Brandon and others, it is clear that the Romans were mis-
taken. Jesus was not a zealot in the Maccabean tradition.[50]
The kingdom he preached was not the restoration of a national
Davidic or Hasmonean kingship.

However, Jesus was not the first Jew who envisaged a kingdom of God other than the national Jewish state, and not the
last either. His conception of the kingdom insofar as we can
reconstruct it from the parables has its own distinctive features, and the very medium of parables should warn us that he
was not strictly an apocalypticist.[51] Yet he shared with
Daniel a basic concern for the political order, which led him

to use the term "kingdom," and a view of salvation which
transcended time and space. The manner of transcendence envisaged by the parables is different, but it can only be understood in the context of the apocalyptic perspective on politics
of which Daniel is a major example.

NOTES

CHAPTER VII

[1] See above, Chapter I.

[2] See above, Chapter II. The sequence Assyria, Media, Persia is also attested in Tob 14:4-7. Since the passage does not mention Macedonia, it may well be dated to the Persian period. See J. Lebram, "Die Weltreiche in der jüdischen Apokalyptik," *ZAW* 76 (1964) 328-31.

[3] Swain, "Four Monarchies," 8-9.

[4] Diodorus Siculus 28.3.1; 29.15.1. Cf. Strabo 16.1.18; Justin 32.2. See Eddy, *The King is Dead*, 133.

[5] See J. Collins, *The Sibylline Oracles*, 41.

[6] Lactantius, *Institutiones* 7.17.11; Hinnells, "The Zoroastrian Doctrine of Salvation," 132.

[7] Pseudo-Callisthenes (C. Müller, ed.; Paris, 1856) 3. See J. Collins, *The Sibylline Oracles*, 133 n. 106.

[8] See especially J. Z. Smith, "Native Cults in the Hellenistic Period," *HR* 11 (1971) 236-49; J. J. Collins, "Jewish Apocalyptic against its Hellenistic Near Eastern Environment," *BASOR* 220 (1975) 27-36.

[9] See Tcherikover (*Hellenistic Civilization and the Jews*, 178) for a critique of the older understanding of the reasons for the revolt.

[10] On the following see further Eddy, *The King is Dead*, 133-35.

[11] See Pinches, *The Old Testament*, 480, 561; A. T. Olmstead, "Intertestamental Studies," *JAOS* 56 (1936) 247.

[12] See M. Hengel, *Die Zeloten* (AGSU 1; Leiden: Brill, 1961) 25-46. A striking parallel to this incident is recorded in Josephus *Ant.*, 17.6.2-3(149-63); *JW* 1.33.2-4(651-54). Shortly before his death, Herod erected a golden eagle over the entry to the temple in Jerusalem. A group of Jews, led by two "doctors of the law," pulled it down and suffered martyrdom as a result.

[13] So Tcherikover, *Hellenistic Civilization*, 190.

[14] See J. Starcky, *Les Livres des Maccabées* (Paris: Cerf, 1961) 35-43; D. Arenhoevel, *Die Theokratie nach den 1 und 2 Makkabäerbuch* (Mainz: Matthias-Gruenewald, 1967) 118-22.

[15]See especially Tcherikover, *Hellenistic Civilization*, Appendix I, 381-90. Tcherikover argues that Jason wrote before 152 B.C.

[16]Cf. Ex 15:15-16, 23:27-28; Josh 2:9; Deut 2:25, 11:25. See Miller, *The Divine Warrior*, 116.

[17]See especially W. R. Farmer, *Maccabees, Zealots and Josephus* (New York: Columbia University, 1956).

[18]See the discussion between J. J. Collins and G. W. Nickelsburg in *Studies on the Testament of Moses* (G. W. Nickelsburg, ed.; Cambridge: SBL, 1973) 15-43.

[19]See especially the study of J. Licht, "Taxo, or the Apocalyptic Doctrine of Vengeance," *JJS* 12 (1961) 95-103.

[20]Cf. Josephus *JW* 2.16.4(392); *Ant.*, 14.4.2(63). See R. North, "The Maccabean Sabbatical Years," *Bib* 34 (1953) 501-15; Yadin, *The Scroll of the War*, 5, 20 n. 1.

[21]So D. J. Harrington, "Interpreting Israel's History: The Testament of Moses as a Rewriting of Deut 31-34," in Nickelsburg, ed., *Studies on the Testament of Moses*, 59-68.

[22]See H.-J. Kraus, *Psalmen* (BKAT; Neukirchen: Erziehungsverein, 1959) 2. 966.

[23]J. A. Sanders, *The Psalms Scroll of Qumran Cave 11* (DJD 4; Oxford: Clarendon, 1965) 64-66, 71; Hengel, *Judaism and Hellenism*, 1. 176-77. On the "first Hasidim" (*haḥasîdîm hārîšônîm*) in the rabbinic tradition, see S. Safrai, "Teaching of Pietists in Mishnaic Literature," *JJS* 16 (1965) 15-33.

[24]O. Plöger, *Theocracy and Eschatology* (Richmond, VA: John Knox Press, 1968) 23.

[25]See Hengel, *Judaism and Hellenism*, 1. 175-80; M. Delcor, "Le milieu d'origine et le développement de l'apocalyptique juive," *La Littérature Juive entre Tenach et Mischna* (W. C. van Unnik, ed.; Leiden: Brill, 1974) 101-17.

[26]Tcherikover, *Hellenistic Civilization*, 198.

[27]Ibid., 175-203. Tcherikover's reconstruction is based on his interpretation of 2 Maccabees.

[28]For flight to the wilderness as a recurring motif in the history of the Zealots, see Hengel, *Die Zeloten*, 255-61.

[29]See Cross, *Ancient Library*, 129-47.

[30]See Starcky, *Les Livres des Maccabées*, 35-43.

[31]Charles, *APOT*, 2. 257.

[32]It is possible that Taxo and his seven sons were deliberately conceived as an anti-type to Mattathias and his five. See J. Collins, "The Date and Provenance of the Testament of Moses," in Nickelsburg, ed., *Studies in the Testament of Moses*, 28.

[33]E.g., Ps 66:10, Zech 13:9.

[34]So A. Dupont-Sommer, "De l'immortalité astrale dans la 'Sagesse de Salomon' (3:7)," *REG* 62 (1949) 80-86.

[35]We may add that both works have apparently been influenced by the suffering servant in Isaiah. For Daniel, see Ginsberg, "The Oldest Interpretation," 400-4. For Wisdom, see D. Georgi, "Der vorpaulinische Hymnus, Phil. 2:6-11," *Zeit und Geschichte* (E. Dinkler, ed.; Tübingen: Mohr, 1964) 263-93.

[36]This has been argued at length by L. Ruppert, *Der leidende Gerechte* (Forschung zur Bibel 5; Würzburg: Echter, 1972) 70-105; also Nickelsburg, *Resurrection*, 58-62.

[37]Cf. especially Wis 9:15, "for a perishable body weighs down the soul." The reference to the "souls of the righteous" in 3:1 must be seen in the light of this dichotomy.

[38]On the learned character of Jewish apocalyptic, see the Excursus in Chapter IV on the availability of ancient myths.

[39]Gunkel (*Schöpfung und Chaos*, 208) insists that apocalyptic writings were not composed by individuals but were accumulations of traditional material. However, Gunkel's insight into the traditional nature of religious imagery is quite compatible with composition by a learned individual.

[40]N. Cohn, *The Pursuit of the Millenium* (New York: Oxford University, 1970) 20.

[41]So Tcherikover, Hengel, Plöger, Delcor, Heaton.

[42]Sahlin ("Antiochus IV Epiphanes und Judas Mackabäus," 41-68) identifies the "Son of Man" as Judas because he naively assumes that "one like a son of man" must refer to an individual human.

[43]See Farmer, *Maccabees, Zealots and Josephus*, 47-158, and "Judas, Simon and Athronges," *NTS* 4 (1958) 147-55.

[44]See G. W. Buchanan, *The Consequences of the Covenant* (NovTSup 20; Leiden: Brill, 1970) 31-41; K. Stendahl, "Hate, Non-Retaliation and Love," *HTR* 55 (1962) 343-56.

[45]See J. Collins, "Some Remaining Traditio-Historical Problems in the Testament of Moses," in Nickelsburg, ed., *Studies in the Testament of Moses*, 38-39.

[46]Josephus, *JW* 2.9.1-3(169-74); *Ant.*, 18.3.1(55-59).

[47]*JW* 2.10.4(195-98); *Ant.*, 18.8.3(269-72).

[48]Isa 40:3, 1QS 8:14.

[49]Stendahl, "Hate, Non-Retaliation and Love," 343-45.

[50]Contra S. G. F. Brandon, *Jesus and the Zealots* (New York: Scribners, 1967). See the critiques by O. Cullmann, *Jesus and the Revolutionaries* (New York: Harper and Row, 1970) and M. Hengel, *Victory over Violence, Jesus and the Revolutionists* (Philadelphia: Fortress, 1973).

[51]See especially J. D. Crossan, *In Parables* (New York: Harper, 1973).

CONCLUSION

The book of Daniel is a literary structure in which traditional motifs and patterns are remoulded to form a new vision of life and reality. This vision is firmly rooted in a particular historical situation, the persecution of Antiochus Epiphanes. However, its use of mythic language ensures that its relevance is not confined to that situation. The persecution is presented as one crystallization of the perennial conflict of cosmos and chaos, or of human revolts against the kingdom of God.

Two features of the vision of Daniel seem especially distinctive. The first is polarization--the sharp antithesis of heaven and earth, the end-time and the present, the kingdom of the "Son of Man" and that of the beasts. The second is the emphasis on wisdom--the elect are defined as "wise teachers"-- which entails a measure of incipient mysticism. The visionary not only hopes for a future salvation but transcends the limitations of the present by his wisdom and his heavenly visions. This does not involve a withdrawal from the world. The visionary continues to act in the political arena. His interest in and allegiance to the heavenly world serves to sharpen his confrontation with the kingdoms of the earth.

Daniel's vision of life was evoked by a situation of crisis. It is not a philosophy for all seasons. Its relevance is greatest in times of change and uncertainty when the beasts of chaos seem again to rise from the sea. Such a vision, however, is often relevant in our century. Ever since Yeats heralded a "Second Coming" and announced that "things fall apart; the centre cannot hold, mere anarchy is loosed upon the world," modern poetry has been troubled with images of impending chaos. The poets' views have been confirmed by political crises, both in the major wars of the century and in an endless succession of violent revolutions all over the globe. Even theology has been roused from its contemplation of dogmas and creeds to speak to the political present in terms of hope, revolution and liberation.

There has, in fact, been a revival of interest in Jewish apocalyptic, usually focused on the book of Daniel, among modern theologians. However, little attention has been paid to the distinctive features of Daniel's vision--the polarization and the importance of wisdom. Yet these features seem especially relevant to modern thinking on revolution and liberation. Hope for the future cannot be based on a naive expectation that things will always improve by a process of evolution underwritten by biblical eschatology. Rather, we must recognize with Ernst Bloch that contradiction is the root of all movement and vitality. Any utopian vision must of necessity involve a critique of the present order. The sharpness of that critique may vary from one situation to another. The book of Daniel speaks most eloquently to situations where a radical change is required.

Modern revolutionaries and theologians of liberation repeatedly stress the importance of "psychological revolution," or of "consciousness raising." The *maskîlîm* of Daniel prepared for their revolution by *instructing* the masses. No doubt the content of their instruction was extremely different from modern ideas of revolutionary consciousness. The significant point, however, is Daniel's insistence that the Kingdom of God is not simply a change of external circumstances or social structures, but requires the conversion of individuals too.

Finally, we should emphasize the essential bond between the wisdom of the visionary and his political stance. The book of Daniel is attributed to a learned wise man whose main skill is taken up with heavenly visions and their explanation by an angel. Yet these visions are focused on the political situation and determine the visionary's reactions to the powers of his time. Wisdom or mysticism are not posed as alternatives to politics, but provide criteria by which the political situation can be assessed. The visions enable the wise teachers to be "in the world but not of it," to act in their society without accepting it as the source of their values. Such a stance, which combines participation in the political order with a critical independence of it, can serve as a model not only for Christian theologians, but for any reflective persons concerned with the society in which they live.

Alexander, P. J. "Medieval Apocalypses as Historical Sources,"
    AHR 73 (1968) 997-1018.

Alfrink, B. J. "L'idée de résurrection d'après Dn XII,1,2,"
    Bib 40 (1959) 355-71.

Anklesaria, B. T. *Zand-ī Vohūman Yasn and Two Pahlevi Frag-
    ments*. Bombay: published privately, 1957.

Arenhoevel, Diego. *Die Theokratie nach den 1 und 2 Makkabäer-
    buch*. Mainz: Gruenewald, 1967.

Baltzer, Klaus. *The Covenant Formulary*. Philadelphia: For-
    tress, 1971.

Barr, James. "Daniel," *PCB*. Matthew Black and H. H. Rowley,
    eds.; London: Nelson, 1962.

_____. *Biblical Words for Time*. SBT 33; Naperville:
    Allenson, 1962.

_____. "Philo of Byblos and his Phoenician History," *BJRL*
    57 (1974) 17-68.

Baumgartner, Walter. "Ein Vierteljahrhundert Danielforschung,"
    TRu 11 (1939) 59-83, 125-44, 201-28.

Bentzen, Aage. *Daniel*. HAT 19; Tübingen: Mohr, 1952.

_____. "Daniel 6: Ein Versuch zur Vorgeschichte der
    Märtyrerlegende," *Festschrift Alfred Bertholet*. Tübingen:
    Mohr, 1950. 58-64.

Betz, Otto. *Offenbarung und Schriftforschung in der Qumran-
    sekte*. WUNT 6; Tübingen: Mohr, 1960.

Bietenhard, Hans. *Die himmlische Welt im Urchristentum und
    Spätjudentum*. Tübingen: Mohr, 1951.

Bishop, E. F. "Qumran and the Preserved Tablets," *RevQ* 5
    (1964/65) 253-56.

Blenkinsopp, Joseph. "Prophecy and Priesthood in Josephus,"
    JJS 25 (1974) 239-62.

Bloch, Joshua. *On the Apocalyptic in Judaism*. Philadelphia:
    Dropsie College, 1952.

Boll, Franz. *Aus der Offenbarung Johannis*. Berlin: Teubner,
    1914.

Boman, Thorlief. *Hebrew Thought Compared with Greek*. London:
    SCM, 1960.

Brandon, S. G. F. *Jesus and the Zealots*. New York: Scribners, 1967.

Braun, Martin. *History and Romance*. Oxford: Blackwell, 1938.

Breech, Earl. "These Fragments I have Shored against my Ruins: the Form and Function of 4 Ezra," *JBL* 92 (1973) 267-74.

Brekelmans, C. W. "The Saints of the Most High and their Kingdom," *OTS* 14 (1965) 305-29.

Bright, John. *The Kingdom of God*. Nashville: Abingdon, 1953.

Brown, R. E. *The Semitic Background of the Term "Mystery" in the New Testament*. Facet Books, Biblical Series 21; Philadelphia: Fortress, 1968.

Bruce, F. F. *Biblical Exegesis in the Qumran Texts*. Grand Rapids: Eerdmans, 1959.

Buber, Martin. *Kampf um Israel: Reden und Schriften*. Berlin: Schocken, 1933.

_____. *Pointing the Way*. New York: Harper, 1957.

Buchanan, G. W. *The Consequences of the Covenant*. NovTSup 20; Leiden: Brill, 1970.

Bultmann, Rudolf. *History and Eschatology*. New York: Harper, 1957.

Burgmann, Hans. "Die vier Endzeittermine im Danielbuch," *ZAW* 86 (1974) 543-50.

Caquot, André. "Sur les Quatre Bêtes de Daniel VII," *Semitica* 5 (1955) 5-13.

Charles, R. H. *The Book of Daniel*. Oxford: Clarendon, 1929.

Clapham, L. R. *Sanchuniathon: The First Two Cycles*. Unpublished dissertation; Cambridge: Harvard, 1969.

Clifford, R. J. "History and Myth in Daniel 10-12," *BASOR* 220 (1975) 23-26.

Cohn, Norman. *The Pursuit of the Millenium*. New York: Oxford University, 1970.

Collins, A. Yarbro. *The Combat Myth in the Book of Revelation*. HDR 9; Missoula: Scholars Press, 1976.

Collins, J. J. *The Sibylline Oracles of Egyptian Judaism*. SBLDS 13; Missoula: Scholars Press, 1974.

_____. "Jewish Apocalyptic as the Transcendence of Death," *CBQ* 36 (1974) 21-43.

Collins, J. J. "The Son of Man and the Saints of the Most High in the Book of Daniel," *JBL* 93 (1974) 50-66.

_____. "History and Tradition in Amos," *ITQ* 41 (1974) 120-33.

_____. "The Place of the Fourth Sibyl in the Development of the Jewish Sibyllina," *JJS* 25 (1974) 365-80.

_____. "The Symbolism of Transcendence in Jewish Apocalyptic," *BR* 19 (1974) 5-22.

_____. "The Date and Provenance of the Testament of Moses," *Studies in the Testament of Moses*. G. W. Nickelsburg, ed.; Cambridge: SBL, 1973. 15-32.

_____. "Some Remaining Traditio-Historical Problems in the Testament of Moses," ibid., 38-39.

_____. "The Court-Tales in Daniel and the Development of Apocalyptic," *JBL* 94 (1975) 218-34.

_____. "Jewish Apocalyptic against its Hellenistic Near Eastern Environment," *BASOR* 220 (1975) 27-36.

Colpe, Carsten. "Ho Huios tou Anthrōpou," *TDNT* 8 (1972) 408-20.

Coppens, Joseph. "La vision daniélique du Fils d'Homme," *VT* 19 (1969) 171-82.

_____ and Dequeker, Luc. *Le Fils de l'homme et les Saints du Très-Haut en Daniel VII*. Louvain: Publications universitaires, 1961.

Cowley, A. E. *Aramaic Papyri from the Fifth Century B.C.* Oxford: Clarendon, 1923.

Cross, F. M. "Le travail d'édition des fragments manuscrits de Qumrân," *RB* 63 (1956) 56-58.

_____. *The Ancient Library of Qumran*. Garden City: Doubleday, 1961.

_____. "New Directions in the Study of Apocalyptic," *Apocalypticism*. R. W. Funk, ed.; *JTC* 6 (1969) 157-65.

_____. *Canaanite Myth and Hebrew Epic*. Cambridge: Harvard, 1973.

Crossan, J. D. *In Parables*. New York: Harper, 1973.

Cullmann, Oscar. *Jesus and the Revolutionaries*. New York: Harper, 1970.

Cumont, Franz. "La plus ancienne géographie astrologique," *Klio* 9 (1909) 263-73.

Cumont, Franz. *Astrology and Religion Among the Greeks and Romans*. New York: Dover, 1960; reprint of 1912 edition by G. P. Putnam's Sons.

_____. *Lux Perpetua*. Paris: Geuthner, 1949.

Danielou, Jean. *The Theology of Jewish Christianity*. London: Darton, Longman and Todd, 1964.

Daumas, F. "Littérature prophétique et exégétique égyptienne et commentaires esséniens," *A la Rencontre de Dieu*. Memorial A. Gelin; Paris: Le Puy, 1961. 203-11.

Delcor, Mathias. *Le Livre de Daniel*. SB; Paris: Gabalda, 1971.

_____. "Le milieu d'origine et le développement de l'apocalyptique juive," *La Littérature Juive entre Tenach et Mischna*. W. C. van Unnik, ed.; Leiden: Brill, 1974. 101-17.

Denis, Albert-Marie. *Introduction aux Pseudépigraphes Grecs d'Ancien Testament*. Leiden: Brill, 1970.

Dequeker, Luc. "Dan VII et les Saints du Très-Haut," *ETL* 36 (1960) 353-92.

_____. "Les Qedôšîm du Ps LXXXIX à la lumière des croyances sémitiques," *ETL* 39 (1963) 469-84.

_____. "The 'Saints of the Most High' in Qumran and Daniel," *OTS* 18 (1973) 133-62.

Dodds, E. R. *The Greeks and the Irrational*. Berkeley and Los Angeles: University of California, 1966.

Dommershausen, Werner. *Nabonid im Buche Daniel*. Mainz: Gruenewald, 1964.

Dougherty, R. P. *Nabonidus and Belshazzar*. Yale Oriental Series 15; New Haven: Yale, 1929.

Driver, G. R. *Semitic Writing*. London: British Academy, 1948.

Dupont-Sommer, André. "De l'immortalité astrale dans la 'Sagesse de Salomon' (3:7)," *REG* 62 (1949) 80-86.

Eddy, S. K. *The King is Dead*. Lincoln: University of Nebraska, 1961.

Ehrlich, E. L. *Der Traum im Alten Testament*. BZAW 73; Berlin: de Gruyter, 1953.

Elliger, Karl. *Studien zum Habbakuk-Kommentar vom Toten Meer*. BHT 15; Tübingen: Mohr, 1953.

Eissfeldt, Otto. "Die Menetekel-Inschrift und ihre Deutung," *ZAW* 63 (1951) 105-14.

_____. "Daniels und seiner 3 Gefährten Laufbahn im babylon-ischen und persischen Dienst," *ZAW* 72 (1960) 134-48.

_____. *The Old Testament: An Introduction*. New York: Harper, 1965.

_____. "El and Yahweh," *JSS* 1 (1956) 25-37.

Eliade, Mircea. *The Myth of the Eternal Return*. New York: Pantheon, 1954.

Emerton, J. A. "The Origin of the Son of Man Imagery," *JTS* 9 (1958) 225-42.

Farmer, W. R. *Maccabees, Zealots and Josephus*. New York: Columbia University, 1956.

_____. "Judas, Simon and Athronges," *NTS* 4 (1958) 147-55.

Farrer, Austin. *A Rebirth of Images: The Making of St. John's Apocalypse*. London: Dacre, 1949.

Festinger, Leon. *When Prophecy Fails*. New York: Harper, 1964.

Festugière, A. M. J. *La Révélation d'Hermès Trismégiste* 1. *L'Astrologie et les Sciences Occultes*. Paris: Gabalda, 1950.

Finkel, Asher. "The pesher of dreams and scriptures," *RevQ* 4 (1963) 357-70.

Fitzmyer, J. A. "Further Light on Melchizedek from Qumran Cave 11," *JBL* 86 (1967) 22-41.

Flusser, David. "The four empires in the Fourth Sibyl and in the Book of Daniel," *Israel Oriental Studies* 2 (1972) 148-75.

Freedman, D. N. "The Prayer of Nabonidus," *BASOR* 145 (1957) 31-32.

Frye, Northrop. *Anatomy of Criticism*. Princeton: Princeton University, 1957.

Gadd, C. J. "The Harran Inscriptions of Nabonidus," *Anatolian Studies* 8 (1958) 35-92.

Gammie, J. G. "Spatial and Ethical Dualism in Jewish Wisdom and Apocalyptic Literature," *JBL* 93 (1974) 356-85.

_____. "The Classification, Stages of Growth and Changing Intentions in the Book of Daniel," *JBL* 95 (1976) 191-204.

Georgi, Dieter. "Der vorpaulinische Hymnus, Phil. 2:6-11,"
    Zeit und Geschichte. E. Dinkler, ed.; Tübingen: Mohr,
    1964. 263-93.

Gilbert, M. "La prière de Daniel," *RTL* 3 (1972) 284-310.

Ginsberg, H. L. *Studies in Daniel*. New York: The Jewish
    Theological Seminary of America, 1948.

_____. "The Oldest Interpretation of the Suffering Servant,"
    VT 3 (1953) 400-4.

Glanville, S. R. K. *The Instructions of 'Onksheshonqy*. Cata-
    logue of Demotic Papyri in the British Museum 2; London:
    British Museum, 1955.

Grayson, A. and Lambert, W. G. "Akkadian Prophecies," *JCS* 18
    (1964) 7-30.

Gunkel, Hermann. *Schöpfung und Chaos*. Göttingen: Vandenhoeck
    und Ruprecht, 1895.

Haag, Ernst. *Studien zum Buche Iudith*. Trier: Paulinus, 1963.

Hammer, Raymond. *The Book of Daniel*. Cambridge Bible Commen-
    tary; Cambridge: Cambridge University, 1976.

Hanhart, Robert. "Die Heiligen des Höchsten," *Hebräische Wort-
    forschung*. Festschrift for W. Baumgartner, VTSup 16;
    Leiden: Brill, 1967. 90-101.

_____. "Kriterien Geschichtlicher Wahrheit in der Makka-
    bäerzeit," *Drei Studien zum Judentum*. Theologische Exis-
    tenz Heute 140; München: Kaiser, 1967. 7-22.

Hanson, P. D. "Jewish Apocalyptic against its Near Eastern
    Environment," *RB* 78 (1971) 31-58.

_____. "Zechariah 9 and the Recapitulation of an Ancient
    Ritual Pattern," *JBL* 92 (1973) 37-59.

_____. *The Dawn of Apocalyptic*. Philadelphia: Fortress,
    1975.

Harrington, D. J. "Interpreting Israel's History: The Testa-
    ment of Moses as a Rewriting of Deut 31-34," *Studies on
    the Testament of Moses*. G. W. Nickelsburg, ed.; Cambridge:
    SBL, 1973. 59-68.

Hartman, Lars. *Prophecy Interpreted*. Lund: Gleerup, 1966.

_____. "The Functions of Some So-Called Apocalyptic Time-
    tables," *NTS* 22 (1976) 1-14.

Hartman, L. F. "The Great Tree and Nebuchodonosor's Madness,"
    The Bible in Current Catholic Thought. J. L. McKenzie,
    ed.; New York: Herder, 1962. 75-82.

Hasel, G. F. "The Identity of the 'Saints of the Most High' in Daniel 7," *Bib* 56 (1975) 173-92.

Heaton, E. W. *The Book of Daniel*. London: SCM, 1956.

Heidel, Alexander. *The Babylonian Genesis*. Chicago: University of Chicago, 1951, reprinted 1972.

Hengel, Martin. *Die Zeloten*. AGSU 1; Leiden: Brill, 1961.

_____. *Victory over Violence. Jesus and the Revolutionaries*. Philadelphia: Fortress, 1973.

_____. *Judaism and Hellenism*. Philadelphia: Fortress, 1974. 2 vols.

Hinnells, J. R. "The Zoroastrian doctrine of salvation in the Roman world," *Man and His Salvation: Studies in Memory of S. G. F. Brandon*. E. J. Sharpe and J. R. Hinnells, eds.; Manchester: Manchester University, 1973. 125-48.

Holm-Nielsen, Svend. *Hodayot*. Aarhus: Universitetsforlaget, 1960.

Honig, Edwin. *Dark Conceit*. Evanston: Northwestern University, 1959.

Humphreys, W. Lee. "A Life-Style for the Diaspora: A Study of the Tales of Esther and Daniel," *JBL* 92 (1973) 211-23.

Jacoby, Felix. *Die Fragmente der Griechischen Historiker*, 3.C. Leiden: Brill, 1958.

Jansen, H. Ludin. *Die Henochgestalt*. Skrifter utgitt av Det Norske Videnskaps-Akademi i Oslo II. Hist. Filos. Klasse. 1; Oslo: Dybwad, 1939.

Janssen, Enno. *Das Gottesvolk und seine Geschichte*. Neukirchen-Vluyn: Erziehungsverein, 1971.

Jaubert, Annie. *La Notion d'Alliance dans le Judaisme*. Patristica Sorbonensia 6; Paris: Seuil, 1963.

Jeremias, Gert. *Der Lehrer der Gerechtigkeit*. SUNT 2; Göttingen: Vandenhoeck und Ruprecht, 1963.

Jones, B. W. *Ideas of History in the Book of Daniel*. Unpublished Dissertation; Berkeley: Graduate Theological Union, 1972.

_____. "The Prayer in Daniel IX," *VT* 18 (1968) 488-93.

Jonge, M. de and Woude, A. S. van der. "11Q Melchizedek and the New Testament," *NTS* 12 (1966) 301-26.

Kapelrud, A. S. "Temple-building, a Task for Gods and Kings," *Orientalia* 32 (1963) 56-62.

232

Koch, Klaus. "Die Weltreiche im Danielbuch," *TLZ* 85 (1960) 829-32.

_____. "Spätisraelitisches Geschichtsdenken am Beispiel des Buches Daniel," *Historische Zeitschrift* 193 (1961) 1-32.

_____. *The Rediscovery of Apocalyptic*. SBT 2/22; Naperville: Allenson, 1972.

Koenen, Ludwig. "Die Prophezeiungen des 'Töpfers,'" *Zeitschrift für Papyrologie und Epigraphik* 2 (1968) 178-209.

_____. "The Prophecies of a Potter: A Prophecy of World Renewal becomes an Apocalypse," *Proceedings of the Twelfth International Congress of Papyrology*. D. H. Samuel, ed.; Toronto: Hakkert, 1970.

Kraus, H.-J. *Psalmen*. BKAT; Neukirchen: Erziehungsverein, 1959.

Kroll, Wilhelm. "Nechepso," *PW* 16 (1935) 2160-67.

Kruse, H. "Compositio libri Danielis et idea filii hominis," *VD* 37 (1959) 147-61.

Kuhl, Curt. *Die Drei Männer im Feuer*. BZAW 55; Giessen: Töpelmann, 1930.

Kuhn, Heinz-Wolfgang. *Enderwartung und Gegenwärtiges Heil*. SUNT 4; Göttingen: Vandenhoeck und Ruprecht, 1965.

Lacocque, André. *Le Livre de Daniel*. CAT 15b; Neuchâtel: Delachaux et Niestlé, 1976.

Lamberigts, S. "Le sens de *qdwšym* dans les textes de Qumrân," *ETL* 46 (1970) 24-39.

Larcher, C. "La doctrine de la résurrection dans l'AT," *Vie et Lumière* (1952) 11-34.

Leach, Edmund. "Genesis as Myth," *Myth and Cosmos*. John Middleton, ed.; Garden City: Natural History Press, 1967. 1-13.

Lebram, J. C. H. "Apokalyptik und Hellenismus im Buche Daniel," *VT* 20 (1970) 516-22.

_____. "Perspektiven der gegenwärtigen Danielforschung," *JSJ* 5 (1974) 1-33.

_____. "König Antiochus im Buch Daniel," *VT* 25 (1975) 737-72.

Lella, A. A. di. "The One in Human Likeness and the Holy Ones of the Most High in Daniel 7," *CBQ* 39 (1977) 1-19.

233

Lenglet, A. "La structure littéraire de Daniel 2-7," *Bib* 53 (1972) 169-90.

Lévi-Strauss, Claude. *The Savage Mind*. Chicago: University of Chicago, 1966.

Licht, Jacob. "Taxo, or the Apocalyptic Doctrine of Vengeance," *JJS* 12 (1961) 95-103.

Lindblom, Johannes. *Prophecy in Ancient Israel*. Oxford: Blackwell, 1962.

Luckenbill, D. D. (ed.). *The Annals of Sennacherib*. Chicago: University of Chicago, 1924.

Macler, F. "Les Apocalypses Apocryphes de Daniel," *RHR* 33 (1896) 37-53, 163-76, 288-319.

Martin-Achard, Robert. *From Death to Life: A Study of the Development of the Doctrine of Resurrection in the Old Testament*. Edinburgh: Oliver and Boyd, 1960.

May, H. G. "Some Cosmic Connotations of *Mayim Rabbim*, 'Many Waters'," *JBL* 74 (1955) 9-21.

McCown, C. C. "Hebrew and Egyptian Apocalyptic Literature," *HTR* 18 (1925) 357-411.

Meeks, Wayne. "The Man from Heaven in Johannine Sectarianism," *JBL* 91 (1972) 44-72.

Mertens, Alfred. *Das Buch Daniel im Lichte der Texte vom Toten Meer*. SBM 12; Würzburg: Echter, 1971.

Metzger, B. M. "Literary Forgeries and Canonical Pseudepigrapha," *JBL* 91 (1972) 3-24.

Meyer, Rudolf. *Das Gebet des Nabonid*. Sitzungsberichte der sächsischen Akademie der Wissenschaften zu Leipzig, Phil.-hist. Kl. Bd. 107, Heft 3; Berlin: Akademie Verlag, 1962.

_____. "Prophecy and Prophets in the Judaism of the Hellenistic-Roman Period," *TDNT* 6 (1968) 812-28.

Milik, J.-T. "'Prière de Nabonide' et autres écrits d'un cycle de Daniel," *RB* 63 (1956) 407-15.

_____. *Ten Years of Discovery in the Wilderness of Judaea*. London: SCM, 1959.

Miller, P. D. "Animal Names as Designations in Ugaritic and Hebrew," *UF* 2 (1971) 177-86.

_____. *The Divine Warrior in Early Israel*. HSM 5; Cambridge: Harvard, 1973.

234

Montgomery, J. A. *The Book of Daniel*. ICC 19; New York: Scribners, 1927.

Moore, C. A. "Towards the Dating of the Book of Baruch," *CBQ* 36 (1974) 312-20.

Moore, G. F. *Judaism*. 2 vols.; New York: Schocken, 1971, reprint of 1927-1930 edition by Harvard University.

Morgenstern, Julian. "The King-god among the Western Semites and the meaning of Epiphanes," *VT* 10 (1960) 138-97.

_____. "The 'Son of Man' in Dan 7,13f," *JBL* 80 (1961) 65-77.

Mowinckel, Sigmund. *He That Cometh*. Nashville: Abingdon, 1959.

Müller, H.-P. "Magisch-mantische Weisheit und die Gestalt Daniels," *UF* 1 (1969) 79-94.

_____. "Mantische Weisheit und Apokalyptik," *Congress Volume, Uppsala*. VTSup 22; Leiden: Brill, 1972. 268-93.

_____. "Märchen, Legende und Enderwartung," *VT* 26 (1976) 338-50.

Müller, Ulrich. *Messias und Menschensohn in jüdischen Apokalypsen und in der Offenbarung Johannes*. Gütersloh: Mohn, 1972.

Nickelsburg, G. W. *Resurrection, Immortality and Eternal Life*. HTS 26; Cambridge: Harvard, 1972.

_____, ed. *Studies on the Testament of Moses*. Cambridge: SBL, 1973.

Nock, A. D. "Oracles Théologiques," *Revue des études anciennes* 30 (1928) 280-90.

_____. "Religious Attitudes of the Ancient Greeks," *Proceedings of the American Philosophical Society* 85 (1942) 472-82

North, Robert. "The Maccabean Sabbatical Years," *Bib* 34 (1953) 501-15.

_____. "Prophecy to Apocalyptic via Zechariah," VTSup 22 (1972) 47-71.

Noth, Martin. "Noah, Daniel und Hiob in Ez 14," *VT* 1 (1951) 251-60.

_____. "The Understanding of History in Old Testament Apocalyptic," *The Laws in the Pentateuch and Other Essays*. Philadelphia: Fortress, 1967. 194-214.

_____. "The Holy Ones of the Most High," ibid., 215-28.

Nötscher, Friedrich. "Himmlische Bücher und Schicksalglaube in Qumran," *RevQ* 1 (1958/59) 405-11.

Olmstead, A. T. "Intertestamental Studies," *JAOS* 56 (1936) 242-56.

Osswald, Eva. "Zum Problem der vaticinia ex eventu," *ZAW* 75 (1963) 27-44.

Osten-Sacken, Peter von der. *Die Apokalyptik in ihrem Verhältnis zu Prophetie und Weisheit*. Theologische Existenz Heute 157; München: Kaiser, 1969.

_____. *Gott und Belial*. SUNT 6; Göttingen: Vandenhoeck und Ruprecht, 1969.

Oppenheim, A. Leo. "The Interpretation of Dreams in the Ancient Near East," *Transactions of the American Philosophical Society* 46 (1956) 179-255.

Perrin, Norman. "Wisdom and Apocalyptic in the Message of Jesus," *Proceedings of the Society of Biblical Literature* (1972) 543-72.

_____. "Eschatology and Hermeneutics: Reflections on Method in the Interpretation of the New Testament," *JBL* 93 (1974) 3-14.

_____. *A Modern Pilgrimage in New Testament Christology*. Philadelphia: Fortress, 1974.

Peters, F. E. *The Harvest of Hellenism*. New York: Simon and Schuster, 1970.

Pinches, T. G. *The Old Testament in the Light of Historical Records and Legends of Assyria and Babylonia*. London: SPCK, 1908.

Plöger, Otto. *Das Buch Daniel*. KAT 18; Gütersloh: Mohn, 1965.

_____. *Theocracy and Eschatology*. Richmond, VA: John Knox Press, 1968.

Pope, Marvin H. *Job*. AB 15, 3rd ed.; Garden City: Doubleday, 1973.

_____. *El in the Ugaritic Texts*. VTSup 2; Leiden: Brill, 1955.

_____. "Attar," *Wörterbuch der Mythologie* 1. *Götter und Mythen im vorderen Orient*. H. W. Haussig, ed.; Stuttgart: Klett, 1965. 249-50.

Porteous, Norman. *Daniel*. London: SCM, 1965.

Pothyress, V. S. "The Holy Ones of the Most High in Daniel VII," *VT* 26 (1976) 208-13.

236

Procksch, Otto. "Der Menschensohn als Gottessohn," *Christentum und Wissenschaft* 3 (1927) 425-43.

Rad, Gerhard von. *Theologie des Alten Testaments*. Vol. 2. 4th ed.; München: Kaiser, 1965.

Redford, D. B. *A Study of the Biblical Story of Joseph*. VTSup 20; Leiden: Brill, 1970.

Reese, Günther. *Die Geschichte Israels in der Auffassung des frühen Judentums*. Unpublished Dissertation; Heidelberg: Heidelberg University, 1967.

Reiling, Joseph. "The Use of Pseudoprophētēs in the LXX, Philo and Josephus," *NovT* 13 (1971) 147-56.

Resch, Andreas. *Der Traum im Heilsplan Gottes*. Freiburg: Herder, 1964.

Ricoeur, Paul. *The Symbolism of Evil*. Boston: Beacon, 1969.

Riess, Ernestus. "Nechepsonis et Petosiridis fragmenta magica," *Philologus Supplementband* 6 (1892-93) 329-88.

Robinson, H. Wheeler. *Corporate Personality in Ancient Israel*. Facet Books, Biblical Series 11; Philadelphia: Fortress, 1964.

Rogerson, J. W. "The Hebrew Conception of Corporate Personality: A Re-examination," *JTS* 21 (1970) 1-16.

Rosenthal, L. A. "Die Josephgeschichte mit den Büchern Ester und Daniel verglichen," *ZAW* 15 (1895) 278-85.

Rössler, Dietrich. *Gesetz und Geschichte*. WMANT 3; Neukirchen: Erziehungsverein, 1960.

Rouse, W. H. D. *Nonnos: Dionysiaca*. LCL; Cambridge: Harvard, 1940. 3 vols.

Rowley, H. H. *Darius the Mede and the Four World Empires*. Cardiff: University of Wales, 1935.

_____. "The Unity of the Book of Daniel," *The Servant of the Lord and Other Essays on the Old Testament*. London: Lutterworth, 1952. 237-68.

_____. *The Relevance of Apocalyptic*. New York: Association, 1964.

Ruppert, Lothar. *Der leidende Gerechte*. Forschung zur Bibel 5; Würzburg: Echter, 1972.

Russell, D. S. *The Method and Message of Jewish Apocalyptic*. Philadelphia: Westminster, 1964.

237

Sachs, A. J. and Wiseman, D. J. "A Babylonian King List of the Hellenistic Period," *Iraq* 16 (1954) 202-12.

Sachau, Eduard. *Aramäische Papyrus und Ostraka aus einer jüdische Militär-Kolonie zu Elephantine*. Berlin: König-liche Museen, 1911.

Safrai, Samuel. "Teaching of Pietists in Mishnaic Literature," *JJS* 16 (1965) 15-33.

Sahlin, H. "Antiochus IV Epiphanes und Judas Mackabäus," *ST* 23 (1969) 41-68.

Sanders, J. A. *The Psalms Scroll of Qumran, Cave 11*. DJD 4; Oxford: Clarendon, 1965.

Schmid, Herbert. "Daniel, der Menschensohn," *Judaica* 27 (1971) 192-221.

Schmidt, Nathaniel. "The Son of Man in the Book of Daniel," *JBL* 19 (1900) 22-28.

Schmidt, W. H. *Königtum Gottes in Ugarit und Israel*. BZAW 80; Berlin: Töpelmann, 1966.

Schnabel, Paul. *Berossos und die babylonisch-hellenistische Literatur*. Leipzig: Teubner, 1923.

Siegman, E. F. "The Stone Hewn from the Mountain (Daniel 2)," *CBQ* 18 (1956) 364-79.

Skehan, P. W. "A fragment of the 'Song of Moses' (Deut 32) from Qumran," *BASOR* 136 (1954) 12-15.

Smith, J. Z. "Wisdom and Apocalyptic," *Religious Syncretism in Antiquity*. B. Pearson, ed.; Missoula: Scholars Press, 1975. 131-56.

_____. "Native Cults in the Hellenistic Period," *HR* 11 (1971) 236-49.

Soden, W. von. "Eine babylonische Volksüberlieferung vom Nabonid in der Danielerzählungen," *ZAW* 53 (1935) 81-89.

Starcky, Jean. *Les Livres des Maccabées*. Paris: Cerf, 1961.

Stauffer, Ethelbert. "Das theologische Weltbild der Apokalyp-tik," *ZST* 8 (1931) 203-15.

Steck, O. H. *Israel und das gewaltsame Geschick der Propheten*. WMANT 23; Neukirchen-Vluyn: Erziehungsverein, 1967.

Stendahl, Krister. "Hate, Non-Retaliation and Love," *HTR* 55 (1962) 343-56.

Stone, M. E. "Apocalyptic Literature," *Compendia Rerum Judai-carum ad Novum Testamentum* 2b. Philadelphia: Fortress, forthcoming.

Swain, J. W. "The Theory of the Four Monarchies: Opposition History under the Roman Empire," *Classical Philology* 35 (1940) 1-21.

Szörenyi, A. "Das Buch Daniel, ein kanonisierter pescher?" VTSup 15; Leiden: Brill, 1966. 278-94.

Talmon, Shemaryahu. "'Wisdom' in the Book of Esther," *VT* 13 (1963) 419-55.

Tcherikover, Viktor. *Hellenistic Civilization and the Jews*. New York: Atheneum, 1970, reprint of 1959 edition by the Jewish Publication Society.

Todorov, Tzvetan. *The Fantastic*. Cleveland: Case Western Reserve, 1973.

Towner, W. S. "The Poetic Passages of Daniel 1-6," *CBQ* 31 (1969) 317-26.

Trever, J. C. "Completion of the Publication of some Fragments from Qumran Cave 1," *RevQ* 5 (1964/65) 323-44.

_____. "1Q Dan^a, the latest of the Qumran Manuscripts," *RevQ* 7 (1969/70) 277-86.

Vermes, Geza. "The Use of Bar-Nāsh/Bar-nāshā in Jewish Aramaic," *An Aramaic Approach to the Gospels and Acts*. Matthew Black, ed.; 3rd ed.; Oxford: Clarendon, 1967. 310-30.

Wakeman, Mary K. *God's Battle with the Monster*. Leiden: Brill, 1973.

Wellhausen, Julius. "Zur apokalyptischen Literatur," *Skizzen und Vorarbeiten* 6 (1899) 225-34.

Wernberg-Moeller, P. "A Reconsideration of the Two Spirits in the Rule of the Community (1Q Serek III,13-IV,26)," *RevQ* 3 (1961) 413-41.

Wheelwright, Philip. *Metaphor and Reality*. Bloomington: Indiana University, 1962.

Windisch, Hans. *Die Orakel des Hystaspes*. Verhandelingen der Koninklijke Akademie van Wetenschappen te Amsterdam, Afdeeling Letterkunde, Nieuwe Reeks, Deel 28/3; Amsterdam: Koninklijke Akademie van Wetenschappen, 1929.

Wiseman, D. J. et al. *Notes on some Problems in the Book of Daniel*. London: Tyndale Fellowship, 1965.

Wolff, H. W. *Hosea*. Hermeneia; Philadelphia: Fortress, 1974.

Woude, A. S. van der. "Melchizedek als himmlische Erlösergestalt in den neugefundenen eschatologischen Midraschim aus Qumran, Höhle XI," *OTS* 14 (1965) 354-73.

Yadin, Yigael. *The Scroll of the War of the Sons of Light against the Sons of Darkness*. Oxford: Oxford University, 1962.

Young, E. J. *The Prophecy of Daniel*. Grand Rapids: Eerdmans, 1953.

Zevit, Ziony. "The Structure and Individual Elements of Daniel VII," *ZAW* 80 (1968) 385-96.

Zimmerli, Walther. *Ezechiel*. BKAT 12/2; Neukirchen-Vluyn: Erziehungsverein, 1969.

Zimmermann, F. "Hebrew Translation in Daniel," *JQR* 51 (1960/61) 109-208.